BAND *of* GOLD

A Memoir

FREDA PAYNE

TULSA

ISBN: 918-1-954095-81-6 (Paperback)
    978-1-954095-82-3 (Hardcover)

Band of Gold: A Memoir

Back Cover and Author Photo of Freda: Alan Mercer
Author Photo of Mark: Sergio Kardenas

Yorkshire Publishing
1425 E 41st Pl
Tulsa, OK 74105
www.YorkshirePublishing.com
918.394.2665

Published in the USA

BAND *of* GOLD

A Memoir

FREDA PAYNE

WITH INTRODUCTION BY MARY WILSON OF THE SUPREMES

MARK BEGO

CONTENTS

"When I was recently asked to sing on a track with Freda, I was over the moon! I had always thought of her as an absolute knockout who was primarily an excellent pop singer. Little did I know that she is also a very accomplished jazz singer along with being a charming and wonderful human being. While my time spent working with Freda may have been very brief, it was nevertheless a wonderful experience and I became an instant fan. She also has an excellent story to tell!"

—Johnny Mathis

"Where do I begin when it comes to my sweet 'baby-lady' Freda Payne? We first met at Danny Simms' club in NY when she was 18 years old, and from that time to the present she has never ceased to amaze or surprise me. From touring the 'chitlin' circuit' to traveling around the world, I have treasured every moment we have spent together just living, laughing and loving. She is as beautiful a person, inside and out, as will ever walk the planet."

—Quincy Jones

"Freda I like you. You're a really good singer, and you are a lady!"
—Frank Sinatra

"Freda Payne, who I hoped would become my first big female star!"

—Berry Gordy Jr.

"Freda Payne…a singer of remarkable tone and range as well as an actress and dancer, she eventually established a long and productive stage, television, and film career. In recent years, she's returned more actively to her jazz roots."

—Lee Mergner, *JazzTimes*

"Class! Elegence! Beauty! Talent! Just four words to describe my friend Freda Payne. A voice and style so smooth and distinct, it can cool down a volcano."

—Donald Welch, Playwright

"A song comes to life when it has heart, soul and believable energy. Freda Payne delivers all in every performance. Her new book *Band of Gold* has captured this remarkable talent and her rise to stardom. The words seem to flow naturally—a really comfortable journey."

—Cousin Bruce Morrow, WABC Radio, NYC

DEDICATION

I would like to dedicate this book to: My mother, Mrs. Charcle Farley; my stepfather, Samuel G. Farley; my grandmother, Mrs. Ada Lee Brack; my grandfather, Clarence Brack; Uncle Johnny Hickman, my mother's only sibling; my sister, Scherrie Payne; my son, Gregory Abbott Jr.; and my niece, Shoshana Payne Phillips.

ACKNOWLEDGEMENTS

In my life and career I have been so blessed to have met, worked with, and / or been inspired by several singing and acting stars who have in one way or another encouraged me in my career. They include: Sammy Davis Jr., Duke Ellington, Lionel Hampton, Lena Horne, Dinah Washington, Jerry Lewis, and Frank Sinatra. I would also like to thank performer and Detroit columnist Ziggy Johnson who predicted that I would one day become a star, and he was right!

I would like to thank the following people who have given me help and encouragement along the way. Some of them are friends, some of them are mentors, but all of them have added in one way or another to this adventure I call "my life." They include: Quincy Jones, Eddie Holland, Lamont Dozier, Brian Holland, Berry Gordy Jr., Allen Early Jr., Mercer Ellington, Ruth Ann Johnson my piano teacher, Don Large from WJR's *Make Way For Youth*, Mrs. Beatrice Summers, Taboo, Ike Sutton of *Jet* magazine for always photographing me, Mack Ferguson one of my first mentors—he taught me a lot, Sidney Bernstein my first agent at GAC in NYC, Joe Scandore my first manager, Mel Shayne and Randy Irwin former managers, Larry Steel & His Smart Affairs who gave me the opportunity to work in Las Vegas and Atlantic City in the 1960s, choreographer and friend Lon Fontaine, a special thank you to David Baumgarten who was a mentor and President of APA, Jay Leno, Don Rickles, Walter Winchell, Jeffrey Patterson my first European promoter in the 1960s, my dear friend Mary Wilson, Sandra McPherson my roommate and talented dancer who talked me into auditioning for *Hallelujah Baby!* as understudy to Leslie Uggams, Billy D. Williams, Tony Camillo who is responsible for the original arrangement of "Band of Gold," Mr. Lenny Bleecher and his wife—Baba Baldwin Bleecher—who became like a surrogate mother to me after my mother passed away in 1977, Otis Smith vice president of Invictus Records while I was signed to them, Sydney Miller a promotion man for Capitol Records and founder of Black Radio Exclusive magazine who is one of my dear friends to this day, John V. Tunney, Maureen O'Hara who was a wonderful wonderful person, my dear friend and spiritual advisor and road manager—Bobby Lucas, Chicago TV host Irv Kupcinet, many thanks and appreciation to Michael Viner, Larkin Arnold who signed me to Capitol Records, Frank Wilson who produced my first album on Capitol who later became an ordained minister, thank you Maurice Hines for bringing Ella Fitzgerald into my life who I portray on-stage with great joy, Martha Reeves, Belinda Carlisle and her manager Ron Stone, a special thank you to David Gest who was my best friend for 38 years up until his death, Michael McDonald, Phil Jones, record producer Preston Glass who I love working with, Michael Feinstein who I always love working with, Darlene Love, Bikram Choudhury who introduced me to Hatha Yoga some 47 years ago, Herb Alpert, Sir Cliff Richard who I dueted with—"Saving a Life"—I will never forget touring with him as it was like being in Heaven, Johnny Mathis who I've always loved from the '60s up until now and I am so happy to have recently done a duet with him, Donald B. Welch who is an excellent screenplay writer and director and producer and dear friend, Obba Babatundé who I have worked with several times through the years, Aretha Franklin who I admired for her spirituality and the soulfulness of her song stylings, Ronald Dunbar who worked with me at Invictus Records, Reggie Dozier sound engineer, and last but not least—my spiritual advisors who are no longer with us: the Rev. Ronald McGrew and Betty Comes.

—Freda

Mark Bego would like to thank: Bob & Mary Bego, Jim Bahanna, Tom Cuddy, Jack Cunningham, Michael Goetz, Gary Graff, Sergio Kardenas, Kent Kotal, Joe Marchese, Dave Marken, Scott Mendel, Markos Papadatos, David Salidor, Andy Skurow, Steve Walter, Adam White, and Dan Zelinski, as well as Samantha Ryan, Roger Chasteen, and T. Kent and Laura Denmark of Yorkshire Publishing.

"I would like to dedicate my work on this book to the memory of my best and dearest friend, Mary Wilson."

—Mark

INTRODUCTION

by Mary Wilson

Freda Payne is an amazingly talented performer and singer, and she has been one of my closest and dearest friends for decades. Both being from Detroit, our paths crossed when we were teens, but the first time I remember meeting her and really getting to know her was in England in 1965. We, The Supremes, were among the stars of *The Motortown Revue* who were performing in Europe, and Freda was there at the same time to perform her jazz act in nightclubs.

I recall her coming to the theater in Manchester, England where we were appearing, and that she knew Motown Records president Berry Gordy Jr. from back in Detroit. We were all really happy to see Freda in the U.K., because she was from our hometown.

After meeting her in England I found out all of the impressive things she was doing. I discovered that Freda was a very accomplished jazz singer.

There are a lot of misconceptions about Freda and her singing talent. First of all, most people know her from her hit records, and her singing, which is impressive on its own. But in reality, she has always been more of a jazz and cabaret singer, and not so much a rock & roll singer. People who only know her from "Band of Gold" have no idea how talented she really is, and they don't realize she is a truly amazing jazz singer, and throughout the years she has worked with all of the great jazz people.

Since Freda and I have known each other from the beginnings of our careers, there has always been a bond between us. Then the two of us became even closer friends in the 1970s. We both lived in Los Angeles by then and we really got to know each other well. We became best friends, and we hung out together all of the time.

Freda and I have so much in common. We are both stylish girls, and we love dressing up and being out on the town. We share that same kind of upbeat energy to this day. The two of us just love being out there and having fun. From the first time we met, Freda and I hit it off instantly, and we are dear friends right up to today.

Freda, you have been promising to write your life story for years, and you have finally done it. What an incredible journey you have had! This book is as much fun as you are. Honey, you took score, and you named names. Well done!

—Mary Wilson

PROLOGUE

"Band of Gold"

I t was late 1969, and it was a cold fall day in Detroit. It felt good to be back in my old hometown to catch up with friends, and stay with my mom and dad. But my main reason to be here, and not in New York City where I lived at the time, was this new music business opportunity that had just fallen into my lap.

This was the one time I simply said, "Yes, I'll sign the contract" with absolutely no hesitation. At the age of 28 I had already been offered a contract with Duke Ellington's band, and a contract with Motown Records, and both fell apart in the negotiations. I had always wondered what would have happened if I had signed either one of those deals. I couldn't find myself in this position again, where I was left to wonder if I had made a mistake or not.

From the minute this new offer was made, I knew it was something I should not miss. Hell, even a gypsy fortune teller had foretold me of this particular deal that was going to fall into my path. No negotiating this time. I simply signed the contract and said, "When do we start?"

This career move was going to be something new and different for me. Although I was still so young I had already appeared in the lead role of a Broadway show, become a favorite guest of *The Tonight Show* with Johnny Carson, and headlined at nightclubs throughout

Europe and America. In addition to that, I had already been through three recording deals with three albums to my name, and not a hit record between them.

At this point I was already well known in the business as a jazz singer. Could I make the leap into becoming a pop / R&B / soul singer? I figured, "Why not accept this new recording contract with Invictus Records?" So, back to my hometown of Detroit I went.

This particular offer was different. It wasn't just any record deal, it was the opportunity to be produced in the studio by Eddie Holland, Lamont Dozier, and Brian Holland. As the songwriting and producing team of Holland-Dozier-Holland, they became the hit-making trio whose music put Martha Reeves & The Vandellas, The Supremes, and The Four Tops at the top of the charts. They were one of the driving forces behind the success of Motown Records, and now they were going to focus their time, their energy, and their musical magic on my career. *Voila!*

Since Holland-Dozier-Holland had recently left Motown Records to establish their own label, Invictus Records, they had been looking for a solo female star to sign. It made perfect sense to be signed to a company founded by people I had grown up with and trusted. Lamont went to school with me. And I had known Eddie since he was brought over to my house by Berry Gordy Jr. to sing in our family living room when I was 14 years old. As Eddie once quoted to me, "Freda, we wanted to sign you, because Berry wanted you bad."

Since then, Holland-Dozier-Holland had become world famous as hit-makers in the music business. In certain circles they were simply referred to as "H-D-H."

Once I was back in Detroit, we already had a routine by this particular week. Invictus songwriter Ron Dunbar would pick me up at my parents' house on Monte Vista Street, and he would take me over to Eddie Holland's apartment. When we got settled there, he would play the demo track of a song for me, and then we would go through the lyrics of it over-and-over again, so I could learn it and get the feel of the song. After I had learned the lyrics, and understood the mood and message of the song, we would record it.

On this particular cold Detroit day, I dressed comfortably for our recording session. I was wearing a smart pair of slacks, and a sweater. I was also wearing a stylish pair of boots, and my mink coat. I had to stay warm to protect my voice.

The song we were working on today was one that was called "Band of Gold." In reality, it was written by Holland-Dozier-Holland. However, since they were embroiled in a lawsuit with Motown Records and Berry Gordy Jr., they could not write any new songs under their name until the suit had been settled. To get around this, the songwriting credit was attributed to Ron Dunbar and Edythe Wayne. In actuality there was no Edythe Wayne, it was simply a name that was given to the woman who was Eddie's girlfriend at the time, and her real name was Vernelle Craighead.

Ron and I sat in Eddie's apartment that day because it was a private place to rehearse. Ron played the musical track for me, and I sang the lyrics. The original version of the song was to be over three and a half minutes long. The song had a plot to it, which was about a woman lamenting that her new husband was unable to make love to her on their wedding night. It also had a very upbeat and unique musical track.

There were two "takes" to the plot of this song. One opinion of this song's lyrics is that the girl was frigid, and had turned her new husband away, and now is regretting it. The other "take" is that the guy was either gay or impotent. Either way it was controversial. The listener could decide.

We went through the song a couple of times and I said to Ron, "What kind of lyric is this? What kinda girl would turn away her husband on her wedding night?"

"Don't worry about it," he said. "Consider it a mystery, and just get into the girl's heartbreak."

"'That night on our honeymoon…separate rooms…,' isn't it a little teenybopperish? This is the kind of song a 15- or 16-year-old girl would sing, not a 28-year-old woman," I complained.

"Freda," Ron smiled and said, "you don't have to like it, just sing it."

"Okay, Ron, that is what I'll do."

I thought to myself, "I am going to look at this song as an acting assignment. And for nearly four minutes I am going to be that young girl whose heart is broken."

I sang the song a few more times, and finally Ron said, "You've got it! You're ready. Let's record it."

I put on my mink coat and we stepped out into the cold outdoor air, and got back in Ron's car. Our destination was located on East Grand River Boulevard at Myers. That was where the studio was located that H-D-H was recording in. It was a building that had originally been The Town Theater. Once H-D-H bought it, they debated whether they should tear it down or not, but instead they decided to renovate it.

When we entered the building, we had to walk past several rows of theater seating, which were still bolted down to the floor. We walked down what used to be the theater's aisle until we got to the back of the building where the stage had been. Once there we went through a doorway and entered a nicely appointed and fully modern state-of-the-art recording studio.

As we started the recording session, I was standing in the sound booth. I had taken off my boots and was now wearing some comfortable flat shoes. The booth had a rug in it so that my feet didn't make any noise. I got comfortable, and I was ready to sing. I put my headphones on and began to listen to the musical track of "Band of Gold."

Eddie, Lamont, and Brian were in the control room behind the glass. With them was the sound engineer Lawrence Horn. When they played the track for me the first time in the studio, I had to admit that I was very impressed with the sound on the big speakers.

The instrumental track for "Band of Gold" was truly top notch. Tony Camillo came up with some of the musical licks, and he also did the song's arrangement. At Invictus Records H-D-H hired members of the house band from The 20 Grand nightclub, and several other musicians they had worked with at Motown as well. They also augmented it with some additional star musicians. For "Band of Gold," guitar man Dennis Coffey is heard on the sitar, and a young kid by the name of Ray Parker Jr. played the distinctive lead guitar, which made the intro so memorable. The background vocals had not yet been added to the track, so it was still somewhat a "work in progress" when I was recording it.

I was in the sound booth with headphones on, and the microphone and the lyrics were in front of me. I would sing one "take" of the song, and occasionally Eddie would stop me and give me directions on how he wanted me to phrase the vocals, or to tell me what emotion I should have for each line of the lyrics. Lamont would chime in from time-to-time as well. Singing pop music is different than singing the jazz standards I was used to, but I was willing to go along with whatever they said. I had decided to sing the song the way they wanted me to, because I wanted a hit.

Finally H-D-H got the exact sound they were looking for, and we left the studio and we began work on the next song for my album. It wasn't until after I returned to New York City that they added the background vocals to the recordings I did in Detroit. There were six background singers on "Band of Gold." They include my sister, Scherrie Payne, along with Joyce Vincent Wilson and Telma Hopkins. Joyce and Telma later joined Tony Orlando to form the singing group Dawn. Telma Hopkins then became an actress, and was featured in several TV sitcoms including *Family Matters*. Also singing on the track were Joyce's sister Pam Vincent, as well as Rock Wilson and Eric Grays. Scherrie was later to tell me, "Lamont wanted a really big sound." Well, they certainly achieved it!

My visit to Detroit went quickly, and in a very short period of time I had recorded all of the songs for my first album on Invictus Records. In a matter of weeks I was already back in Manhattan, not knowing for sure what was going to happen in my career after it was released. When I heard a test pressing of the album I was indeed impressed with the sound that H-D-H had created for me. Would it be a hit, or would it be another disappointment for me? The first single released from the album was a song called "Unhooked Generation." I really liked it, but it didn't seem to make much noise on the record charts. Little did I know at the time, but it was the next single, "Band of Gold," that was not only going to become a Number One record, it was the song that was to become the pivot point for my entire career. Once it became a hit, my life would never be quite the same.

CHAPTER ONE

"Detroit, Where It All Began"

I have both good and bad memories about Detroit. You could say growing up in the Motor City might have been hard, but back during those years—many decades ago, it was pleasant, fun, and oh so full of love. That's when I remember all the relatives who are no longer with us, including my grandmother Ada Lee, uncles, cousins, grandfather Clarence Brack, and so many dear friends.

I was a child in the 1940s, and that is something I will never forget. When I was born, America was still at war. It was World War II, and it didn't end until 1945. I was born on September 19, 1942.

My baby sister, Scherrie, was born November 4, 1944. Although I barely remember her as a baby, I do have some recollection of us together riding in my dad's car, and Mama was holding Scherrie in a blanket. I remember us as little girls playing, and—at times—getting into trouble.

By the time I was three-and-a-half years old, my mother, Charcle Lee, had divorced our father, Fred Payne. My mother was a very attractive, beautiful woman. She had long dark brown hair and lovely brown almond-shaped eyes. She was born in Birmingham, Alabama, but her mother had moved the family up to Detroit when she was only three years old.

Her mother, my grandmother, was a very strong woman. Her

husband, my grandfather, passed away from tuberculosis (TB), a disease that was running rampant back then. We are talking about 1920. A cure for that disease was not found until the late 1940s to the early 1950s, and even then, my Uncle Johnny, who was Mama's brother, died from TB at the young age of 32. I was nine years old at the time.

Mother was born Charcle Lee Hickman. Mama never got to see her father, James Hickman. He had died when she was six months old. Mama was married to Fredrick Payne, at Bethel A.M.E. Church on December 7, 1941, by the Rev. Peck. The Gordy family also attended that church.

My parents had the largest wedding the church had known at that time. Little did they know, but at the same time the wedding was going on, Pearl Harbor, in Honolulu, Hawaii was being bombed. That was the beginning of World War II with Japan. The United States was already fighting in Europe against the Germans. I was born almost a year later, followed by Scherrie, two years after me. I remember Mama telling me how she had cried that afternoon in the basement of the African Methodist Episcopal church before the wedding ceremony had taken place. I have sometimes wondered, did she have a premonition that this marriage was not going to work out?

Personally, I like to think that it was the good Lord's will that she married Fred Payne. If she hadn't, I don't think I would have been blessed with the gifts of a singing voice. As it turned out, I have been a professional singer since I was 17 years old. And, my sister, Scherrie, is a successful singer as well, and a songwriter, and playwright. In the 1970s she became a member of The Supremes. In other words, the singing voices we were born with have been a blessing.

Life is funny. Scherrie didn't start singing professionally until she was in her mid-20s. We certainly didn't get our singing talent from Mama's side of the family, the Hickman's, that is for sure. It was the Payne's who were the vocalists.

My dad, Fred Payne, was born and raised in Asheville, North Carolina on December 7, 1917. He was one of nine children: they were a family of six girls and three boys. It was my Aunt Monzella who had a pretty terrific voice. She never sang professionally, but she and a couple of her sisters had a singing group who sang in church. Back then, people who were professional performers were considered risqué and sinful. I had a lot of uncles who were preachers, so it was something of an old fashioned family back there in the South.

Back in those days, it was unheard of to go around singing in clubs or places where alcohol was being served. Only women of questionable virtue would even be seen in a drinking establishment. The reason was that, back in those days, folks were strict Christians, and church-going people. My father's mother, my paternal grandmother, was an Evangelist Pentecostal preacher. Her maiden name was Julia Logan. Her father was William Logan, of Asheville, North Carolina. He was the original owner of the land that the Biltmore estate is built upon. It was George Vanderbilt who negotiated with him to switch land locations with him, so that he could build where his now-mansion, Biltmore Estate, is located. It has become a tourist attraction, and has been famous for several decades now.

My great-grandfather, William Logan, was George Vanderbilt's butler, and some of my great aunts also worked for the Vanderbilt's. They were paid employees, never slaves. The original Paynes migrated from England, to escape religious persecution. They were Caucasian Europeans, and they intermarried with black people.

William Logan became George Vanderbilt's butler in the early 1900s. Another Payne was George Washington Henry Payne. He had a long name, which I have since seen in documentation. He was the blacksmith for the Vanderbilt estate. Another sister of my father's had been a brown-capped nun. I never got to meet her. She was my Aunt Lillian, but she dedicated her life to the church to become a Catholic nun. None of my aunts on my father's side of the family are still living. In fact, none of my aunts or uncles on either side of the family are still alive.

My maternal grandmother, Ada Lee, was originally married to James Hickman—who had died, and then she was married to Clarence Brack. Grandma Ada Lee Brack was the "rock" and the anchor to the family. At least that is how I saw it. The women in my family have always been the ones to "hold down the fort," so to speak. The men were of great support as well, especially in financial matters—going to work and paying the bills. But, it was the women who were the "glue," and they provided the spiritual support the family needed.

My step-grandfather, Clarence Brack was a proud gun owner. One time when I was about seven years old, he and my grandmother had a big argument, and my grandfather threatened her with a gun. She came running over to our house for refuge, and then ended up staying with a friend for a week, until things "cooled down" with Grandpa. In other words, he wasn't taking "any shit" from my grandmother!

Grandma Ada Lee bought a house at 101 Horton Street, right off the corner of John R Street, and a block from Woodward Avenue—which is the main street running down the middle of Detroit. The house had seven bedrooms. There were two stories, and then on a smaller third floor there was a little apartment. In recent years, because of the decline of Detroit in the twenty-first century, there is only one of those buildings still standing on that whole block. Miraculously, the drugstore building on the corner remains there. Over the years it has been several things, and it is now a liquor store—but it is still standing.

Grandma took in roomers at her house, and their rent helped to pay for the mortgage on the house. On the second floor was where three different roomers resided, and on the third floor / attic there was another bedroom she rented out. My grandmother and granddad had the entire first floor of the building to themselves. They had a living room that was small in the front, a sitting room next to that, as well as a dining room, kitchen, pantry, and one bedroom. When I visualize it by today's standards, the bedrooms were very small.

There was also a large backyard. When my mother divorced my father, she bought an apartment building right around the corner from my grandmother's house. You could look over to my grandmother's fenced-in backyard from our back porch. We lived that close to her house. Since she had a backyard, and we didn't, they set up a swing set for us to play in, with a seesaw, a teeter-totter, a sandbox, and a slide. Scherrie and I played there, and the kids from the neighborhood would come there and play with us.

You could look out of my grandmother's bedroom, and you could see an alleyway where there were several Mayflower trucks parked in the alley. There was a Mayflower garage there too. I remember those trucks, because they were painted yellow and green with the word "Mayflower" on them. We are talking about the 1940s, and those Mayflower moving trucks are still painted those same distinctive shades of yellow and green to this day.

My mother was dating my stepfather, back when I was six years old. The day she married him, I will always remember. Actually she never did give us a clue that she was going to marry him, until they were husband and wife.

That day she said, "Freda! Scherrie! Come here into the living room, I have something I want to tell both of you."

She was standing there with Sam G. Farley. Everybody just called him "Sam."

Mom announced to us, "Sam and I got married. He's now your new daddy."

At that point, Scherrie ran up to him and jumped in his arms. And I just stood there. I felt mixed emotions. I also felt some sort of resentment at first. The first thing that I thought was, "Wow. Mama married him?"

He was nice, but I didn't quite know how to take this. But, I have to say, Sam turned out to be a great father. He was a really good and devoted dad to us from the time he married Mom, until the time he passed away in 2001.

Although I was partially happy for Mom, I also felt that Sam's presence would also represent time that Mom wouldn't have for me. I used to like to crawl into her bed at night, and sleep with her. It dawned on me, "I can't do that anymore! She's got a husband now, and there is not enough room for the three of us!"

I can relate to this with my son Gregory. From the time he was very, very young, in the middle of the night he would come running into my bedroom, and get in bed with me. He would drag his little security blanket with him. I remember that blanket, it was a yellow blanket that was a baby shower gift.

Sam Farley wasn't a Detroiter. He was originally from Winfield, Louisiana. At one point he had joined the army, and he served in World War II. When the war ended in 1945, he did not return to Louisiana. He came straight to Detroit seeking new job opportunities instead.

The first job he landed was at *The Detroit News*. Then he started training to be a Deputy Sheriff for the Police Department of Wayne County. Eventually, Sam and my mother put their money together, and whatever they had in savings, and they purchased a bar in Detroit. It was called The Collingwood Bar & Lounge.

They bought the bar in 1953. At that point, Sam's main occupation was to run the bar. He also became the president of the Liquor Association in Detroit. He was quite a guy. At the time he wasn't allowed—as a Deputy Sheriff—to hold a liquor license, so the liquor license was in my mother's name, and she was listed as the owner of the bar.

Sam loved to follow baseball. Whenever there was a World

Series, I don't care where it took place, he would always go to those games.

Every holiday he would give Scherrie and me presents. There was a holiday that seems to have disappeared, called Sweetest Day. It is in October, and it is a romantic holiday like Valentine's Day, where candy or sweets were presented to a loved one. On Sweetest Day, Sam would give us candy, as well as on Valentine's Day when we would get candy and a card. And of course our birthdays and Christmas were especially celebrated, and we always got presents from my mother and Sam. We always got whatever we asked Santa Claus for.

Sam Farley was a wonderful dad. He took that role very seriously. He would even take us freshwater fishing over in Canada. That was where I first experienced the joys of fishing. At the time, we had a dog by the name of Butch. He was part boxer and part bulldog. On one occasion we tried to take Butch with us into Canada on our fishing trip, but we were not allowed to take a dog across the border into Canada, so we had to turn around at Customs and come back! We dropped Butch off at home, and we continued on our fishing trip.

Sam took us to Tiger Stadium to see baseball games. We would be sitting way up in the rafters, way up high. He would always attend any events that had anything to do with me and Scherrie. If we had a piano recital or anything like that, he and Mom would always be there to see us perform.

When I became a professional entertainer, even when I appeared in different cities, Sam would come see my shows in Las Vegas or in Canada. When I appeared on Broadway in *Hallelujah Baby!*, he and my mother and Scherrie drove all the way to New York City to see me in it.

We moved from John R Street when I was seven years old. Our new home was on the west side of Detroit, where we lived at 1699 Atkinson Street. It was a three story flat. My mother purchased the building and we lived on the second floor. The neighborhood had previously been all Jewish, but it changed when African American folks started moving into the area.

I remember there was a white family who lived next door to us. The man was a police officer who worked nights. I remember playing hopscotch on the sidewalk in front of the house. The police officer's daughter would yell out to us from her porch, "Would you kids be quiet! You are making too much noise, my dad is trying to sleep!"

I started going to a school in the neighborhood called Crosman Elementary School. After that I attended Hutchins Junior High School. Some of my homeroom classmates were Lamont Dozier, Tyrone Hunter, and Margaret Norton. Margaret became Mrs. Berry Gordy Jr. many years later. Aretha Franklin attended Hutchins Junior High at that time as well.

My granddaddy Clarence had a daughter. Her name was Moselle. She had a daughter whose name was Barbara Jean, who was about five years older than me. A lot of times Barbara Jean would be left to baby-sit me. I have vague memories of her taking me on the Woodward Avenue streetcar to The Paradise Theater to see Billy Eckstine. The Paradise Theater was not as far south as Grand Circus Park—which is right downtown—but it was located in that direction.

My mother would tell this story about how I was just two years old when Barbara Jean took me downtown to The Paradise Theater. I remember Billy Eckstine singing, and there was a duo doing an Adagio dance routine. It was a man and a woman dancing, and I specifically remember that. In addition to the Adagio dance team, there was also a comedian, but I don't remember his name.

Back then, in the 1940s, Billy Eckstine was a true superstar crooner on the jazz circuit. Needless to say, I was mesmerized by his singing. It never occurred to me at the time, that one day this would be my calling, since I was only two years old. Years later I was in New York City, performing at The Apollo Theater singing on the same stage with Billy Eckstine!

No one would believe me at the time, but my cousin Barbara Jean was quite abusive to me. I didn't know whether she liked me or not. Sometimes she would just haul off and sock me in the arm, and it really did hurt. Then she would suddenly hit me in the stomach for no reason at all. When she hit me in the stomach, I literally doubled over in pain, because it would knock the wind out of me. I would tell my mother, but she didn't seem to believe me, or believe that Barbara Jean would do anything to purposely harm me. So, nothing changed in Barbara Jean's behavior, until later on. At first my mother just played it off, like it was typical childhood behavior which was exaggerated by me. It was later that my mother finally realized the truth, that both Barbara Jean and her mother, Moselle, were not properly taking care of me.

Moselle was my mother's step-sister, so she suspected no possible wrongdoing. Later she realized that Moselle and Barbara Jean were bad people. Moselle was very immoral, and my mother would later talk to me about her. Clearly Moselle was very jealous of my mother, and I think that Barbara Jean was in turn very jealous of me too, and I never really knew what the reason for this was. It wasn't that I was a pretty little girl with attractively wavy hair. I was very fair, and my hair was nappy, and my mother wasn't good at braiding it.

When I think back on this era, it is evident to me that Barbara Jean was not just mean to me, she was downright abusive. On occasion she would take me around her friends, and I would witness her grinding herself against the neighborhood boys. I was standing right there, and she had no business exposing me to that kind of behavior. But those were common things that went on when I was around Barbara Jean.

By the time we had moved to Atkinson Street, my mother came to the realization that Moselle was very "loose" and that her daughter Barbara Jean was just as bad. So, Mother decided to put an end to associating with them, and keeping us away from them. She also kept us away from several of our closer blood relatives she considered to be undesirable.

"Oh, they are 'fast' girls. I don't want you hanging out with them," she would say about several of our relatives. By the time I was about ten years old, my mother suddenly cut off any close relationship with Moselle and Barbara Jean, and kept them at "arms length."

Barbara Jean and Moselle were obviously "cut from a different cloth" than my mother. They were not blood related to us at all, as Moselle was my mother's half stepsister. She later told me that Moselle was very jealous of her. My mother was modest, polite, beautiful and a lady in every sense of the word. Moselle was an attractive woman, but she was anything but modest, nor was she a lady. Looking back on this time, she and Barbara Jean were very promiscuous women to say the least.

I recall one of those cold Detroit mornings back when we still lived on John R Street, and Mama came into the bedroom where my sister and I slept, waking us up hastily.

"You girls better wake up! It's time for school," she commanded.

Not wanting to crawl out of those toasty warm sheets and blankets, I took my time, partly pretending not to hear her. Dreading the cold room that awaited us, Scherrie and I finally scurried out of bed. We carefully brushed our teeth and washed our little faces to get ready for school.

Our apartment was cold that morning, as it was the dead of winter. Some mornings the heat was very late coming up into our apartment. We had those old steam radiators that you could hear making knocking sounds as they heated up. There we were, huddled in our kitchen. Mama had turned the gas oven on, she opened the door, and then she proceeded to lay out our underwear and socks on the oven racks to warm them up. To this day, I still hate cold weather, and especially getting out of bed when the room is chilly.

The phone would ring right on schedule. It would be our grandmother calling to tell Mama to tell us to come by her house after school. Scherrie was in nursery school, and I was in the first grade at the time. My elementary school was located about two blocks away. It was called Palmer Elementary School.

Since it was right in the neighborhood, I walked to and from school all by myself. Although I was only five years old and in Kindergarten, I knew the way by myself.

While all of this was going on, there were several influences at play, which led me to my interest in music. Grandma always listened to gospel music, and I think it was her idea to talk my mother into me starting to take piano lessons. So, Mom did just that. My piano lessons began when I was six years old, and continued for years.

I remember my mother telling me to get dressed, and we'd get in the car and drive to The Detroit Conservatory of Musical Arts, right over by Wayne State University. I took lessons there for several months, long enough to play in my very first piano recital.

In 1947 we were the first family in the neighborhood to get a television set. It was at my grandmother and grandfather's house. It was a box, and the screen was round and about 10 or 12 inches in diameter. TV was very new back then, and some of the neighbors would come over to sit in our living room and watch it with us. I remember watching *Your Show of Shows* with Sid Caesar and Imogene Coca, and Jackie Gleason's show, and George Burns & Gracie Allen. At the time, I never suspected that years later I would perform at Caesar's Palace in Las Vegas with George Burns!

I have to give credit to my Uncle Johnny for being the first one to expose me to jazz and classical music. Uncle Johnny was a true music fan, and he had a huge collection of records. He would have all sorts of valuable recordings. Back then records were much more breakable than later vinyl LP's. These were the kind which could easily become chipped or broken. They had to be handled very gingerly with care. Uncle Johnny had everything in his collection from Duke

Ellington, to Mozart, to Tchaikovsky, to Rachmaninoff, to Lionel Hampton, to B.B. King.

In addition, Uncle Johnny was a wonderfully talented tap dancer. He wasn't a professional tap dancer, as he worked for Ford Motor Company, but on the weekends he would go to the clubs at night and he would dance. People would throw money at him in appreciation. He would bring his money home, and he would share it with my mother.

My mother said he would come home from the nightclubs, throw the money he had made from dancing on the bed and say, "Here Charcle, take what you want."

Not only did Uncle Johnny work at Ford Motor Company, but most of the men in my family did as well, including my father, Frederick; and my grandfather, Clarence; who was the only grandfather I ever knew. It seemed that everyone else we knew back then either worked for Ford Motor Company or General Motors in some capacity as well.

Uncle Johnny would help me practice on the piano. One particular Sunday he made me practice, and I seemed to hit some of the wrong notes. When I did so, he would hit my hand with a ruler. Not hard, but just hard enough to let me know he was not pleased. I remember I was doing well, and then finally I hit some obviously wrong notes. I didn't do it on purpose; I just couldn't help it.

He punished me by not letting me go to the movies with my little sister Scherrie, and some of our neighborhood friends. I was devastated and so hurt that day. Sunday was the one day of the week we set aside as "movie day." Of course, church and Sunday school were a "must" on our weekly agenda. The rule was that if you didn't attend either Sunday school or church, there was no movie.

From that day on I felt differently about Uncle Johnny. He didn't have to escalate my punishment to that extreme a degree! I cried and cried that day. I remember looking out the window and seeing my sister and our friends walking down the street to the movies.

I thought it was just plain "mean" of him at the time. But, as I look back on it in retrospect, I do have to thank him for planting some good seeds in my brain, to appreciate jazz and classical music.

When I was nine years old, my Uncle Johnny died. The really sad thing is that he never got to see me perform or sing in public at all. He would have been so proud watching my career unfold.

Uncle Johnny's passing was the first time I had experienced a death in the family. Then a year later, my beloved grandmother passed away when I was ten years old. She suffered a cerebral hemorrhage, which is another term for a stroke. My whole world seemed to fall apart after that. You see, I really loved my grandmother even more than I loved my own mother. I always thought that my grandmother understood me better than anyone else. My world seemed to crumble.

After Uncle Johnny's death I would think to myself: "Maybe he is looking over me from the spirit world, giving me inspiration." I would continue to take piano lessons. Scherrie was also taking piano lessons at the same time as well, but not at The Detroit Conservatory.

My mother found a woman by the name of Ruth Anne Johnson, who would come over every Tuesday afternoon, and she would give us our piano lessons. We would get half an hour apiece.

However, by the time I turned 12 years old, I had lost a great deal of interest in playing the piano. Here is the reason why. This is the period in my journey of life that changed everything I ever thought I wanted to be in life. Up until that point, I wasn't quite sure what I wanted to do when I grew up. At one point I wanted to be a doctor, but my grades weren't strong enough. Then I set my sights on becoming a nurse.

Here is what my mother did. She enrolled us in ballet school. I was 12, and Scherrie was 10. If you would have seen me at the age of 12, you would have thought I was a 16- or 18-year-old girl. I had a full bra size of 34C, which I have to this day. I was fully grown in height at five feet, five and a half inches tall. I was so well-developed that those dirty boys were always after me at school. And, I had to fight sometimes to get away.

I was quite feisty at the age of 12. In fact, around this same time I turned the tables on abusive cousin Barbara Jean. She was about five years older than I was, and when we were kids she was always bragging how she could outrun me physically. As I got older, it got to the point where I could outrun her, and more. Finally the day of revenge came, when I was 12 years old. We got into an argument, and I beat her up! Not only did I even the score, I literally beat her up. Boy, was she ever surprised!

Scherrie and I got along pretty well together most of the time. But, as sisters often do, we fought and argued as well. Sometimes the fights were over something as trivial as a bobby pin. It is hard to believe, but it is true. At the end of the day, we never stayed angry at each other, and that is a really good thing.

Our mother was a strict disciplinarian. She never cursed, and she taught us to always be ladies. Of course, I have sometimes veered off that course, in an effort to be my own person.

We had an Aunt Myrtle who lived in Romulus, Michigan on a farm. Aunt Myrtle had married my mother's father's brother. She would grow soy beans on her farm. She used to say, "Your mother raised you girls to be ladies. Well, maybe she should have raised you to be bitches!"

Her opinion was that Scherrie and I were too nice—to a fault. And maybe that was the reason people tried to take advantage of us, for being so nice. But I believe that your reputation has a direct line to the life you end up with, and that "You reap what you sow."

Life was pretty good back then in Detroit. Ford and General Motors Corporation were thriving. Black men and women—and the rest of the population, too—had jobs, and the city was buzzing with activity. This was in the late 1940s and the early 1950s.

Back then they called people of color "colored" or "Negro." In the 1950s and 1960s, if you used the term "black people" that was an insult, and not taken very well. Those were "fighting words." It didn't become fashionable until the late 1960s when the "black is beautiful" movement was underway. Now the context has changed and the term "black" can be used, or—more appropriately—"African American."

Nowadays a lot of people are having their DNA tested, and people are finding that they are not just "black" or "white." The majority of people on the planet today seem to be a mixture of several backgrounds. Black people in America today are mixed with European blood, and Spanish blood, and Indian blood, and African blood.

I did one of those DNA tests, and I now know that I am 58% from the African continent, and the rest of me is almost all European, including: Irish, English, Scandinavian, and a small percentage of Asian as well.

There was an amusement park in Detroit back then called Eastwood Park. It was there where I went on my first roller coaster ride. I was ten years old at the time. Before I actually got on the roller coaster, it looked like so much fun to ride. I never had a clue how much I would hate it. As we flew up, and down, and around through the air, I cried out, "Oh Lord, please save me, Jesus!" I have never been on another roller coaster ride since then. After that frightening experience I just could not force myself to ever take it again! I can ride a Ferris wheel. No problem there. But when it comes to roller coasters, I am a big sissy!

Around about this time, my mother had purchased a small cottage in Northern Michigan. Idlewild, Michigan was a resort town that was very popular in the 1950s and 1960s with black families. It was an all-black resort, located about 250 miles outside of Detroit. It is as far north as Ludington, Michigan, near Baldwin.

Idlewild has a beautiful freshwater lake that is there naturally. The best part was that there was a skating rink, located right at the beach! That is where our parents would drop us off to go nightclubbing. There were two nightclubs up there in Idlewild that catered to black people. One was called The Flamingo, and the other one was called The Paradise which contained a performance room called The Fiesta.

The first time we went up there I was nine years old, and we stayed at a lodge. My grandmother was with us, and we had a lovely time. It was perfect for us kids. Especially when the grown ups would go to the nightclubs and drop us off at the skating rink. Then they would come back and pick us up just before the rink was closing. Scherrie and I had some really good times at The Polk Skating Rink.

On the adult side of things, the nightclub scene was also very hot at that time. The Flamingo—was located right across the street from the skating rink—and The Paradise was just a few minutes' drive away. The Paradise would have these great matinee shows, and sometimes Scherrie and I would be treated to the matinee performances, where kids were allowed to attend. We were allowed in the clubs, only if we were accompanied by our parents. Those were some of the best times. We saw all kinds of top notch entertainers there. The headliners were people like Della Reese, or Jackie Wilson. We even saw The Four Tops, who were not yet headliners, but they were the opening act. This was long before their Motown days. We would see The Five Stairsteps, Slappy White, Timmy Rogers, Nipsey Russell, George Kirby, Etta James, Al Hibbler, Roy Hamilton, and even Cab Calloway.

Idlewild was recognized as the premiere black resort town in the U.S. There were lots of black families from Detroit, Cleveland, and Chicago who would go to Idlewild during the summer. Detroit hotel owner Arthur Braggs owned The Paradise Club. It was very well-known, and *The Arthur Braggs Idlewild Revue* played there from

1954 to 1964.

At The Paradise Club they had dancers and chorus girls, and even strippers. They weren't billed as "strippers," they were called "shake dancers" back then.

Nowadays we see on TV videos of beautiful female singers, performing their multi-Platinum songs, dancing around and performing with other dancers who, in-a-fashion, qualify as being modern day "shake dancers."

I was brought up as a singer in the '60s, where it was not acceptable for a stand-up singer—a "chanteuse"—to bump-and-grind like a stripper. These movements were considered to be the actions of someone selling sex only.

You would never see The Supremes—Mary Wilson, Florence Ballard, and Diana Ross—ever perform like that. We were taught to be proper ladies on-stage. And you certainly would never see Lena Horne, or Diahann Carroll, or Barbara McNair perform like that. But in today's world, there has been a social change, and an unfortunate movement to turn women into pure sex objects. There is no mystery, and no charm to that. We were not expected to be bumping and grinding in a nightclub. And there were no added dancers gyrating and dancing around you back then. The spotlight was just fixed on the singer, and it was magical.

What is accepted today as mainstream show business attire and behavior, is far more over-the-top than what was done back in the 1950s and 1960s. The dancers today are much more athletic than when I came along. Sure, there was that occasional dancer who could do a flip or a back flip, or something acrobatic. But those were mostly people who practiced gymnastics.

Someone who embodies all of the modern attributes of the body, the voice, the talent, *and* the suggestive dance moves, is Beyoncé. She seems to have it all—she can move and gyrate suggestively on-stage, and being married to Jay Z has only enhanced her draw and her appeal even more. Beyoncé has that "it" factor that draws crowds and creates fans. She has also demonstrated talent in acting as well, and her unmistakable beauty—inside and out—cannot be denied.

When a really good singer comes along, they stand head and shoulders above the rest. I believe that sometimes too much production takes away from, rather than enhances an artist's performance. It's like "less is more," but it ends up "more is more!"

I see a lot of this on some of today's music awards shows. Well, I guess that is what keeps the ratings up. People love to see production numbers and some flash.

One of the well-known "shake dancers" back in the '50s billed herself as: "Lottie the Body." She was so famous, she became known as "the black Gypsy Rose Lee." "Lottie the Body" was from Detroit, and I remember her dating one of The Harlem Globetrotters. His name was Goose Tatum.

When I think about it, it seemed pretty exciting to me to have been exposed to these early nightclub entertainers while I was just 12. Scherrie was only ten at the time. We heard comedians who told dirty jokes, we saw really good tap dancers, and heard some truly great singers as well. I recall that this was the beginning of me visualizing my becoming a professional singer. What I saw up on-stage was truly inspiring.

At that time I was especially impressed by the singing of Della Reese. The Paradise used to have showgirls and chorus girls. There was this very beautiful showgirl whose name was Ricki Ford. She had to be at least six-feet two-inches tall, with short red hair. She was very fair-skinned. If she was around today, I am certain she would be a very successful model.

When I saw Della Reese, the featured singing group who was on the show were The Four Tops, and they were just in their late teens at that time. Clineice, who married their lead singer, Levi Stubbs, was in the chorus line in Idlewild. And Obie Benson, who was also one of the The Four Tops, met his first wife Val there. She was performing as a chorus girl in Idlewild as well. Obie's marriage to Val only lasted a few years, but they had a beautiful daughter. My mom used to baby-sit for their daughter. To my knowledge both Val and their daughter are still living in Detroit to this day.

The Four Tops performed mostly standards back then. They didn't do any R&B at all. Levi Stubbs had to be 19 years old, as were the other members of the group: Duke Fakir, Lawrence Payton, and Obie Benson. They were like the funky version of The Four Freshmen. Of all the four "Tops," it was Obie who was always "the life of the party." He always had a smile on his face. He was the baritone in the group. Obie was always in a good mood, and he was constantly telling jokes. But underneath that, he was also very observant.

My history with The Four Tops goes way back, starting in the early '60s. Although we no longer have the full group of The Four Tops—Levi, Lawrence and Obie are gone—we still have Duke Fakir left with us. The group continues to work and tour to this day, with Duke and three new members. That way their music lives on.

When I was a child, I would have these fainting spells when I would start feeling weak. I had one when I was six, another at the age of eight, and again when I was 12. It was just a feeling of weakness, then the room seemed to turn pink. I would faint, and when I came out of it, I would get sick to my stomach and throw up.

There was one occasion when this happened—I was at a rehearsal for a choir recital. I was up on the third riser off the floor, and I could feel myself getting weak, and feeling dizzy. I remember trying to get off the riser, and the next thing I knew, I was waking up in a chair. The choir master had caught me as I passed out. I was 12 when that happened.

Every time this occurred my mother took me to a doctor at Children's Hospital in Detroit, to see what was going on with these sudden fainting spells. But the doctors found absolutely nothing wrong. In time this passed, and it never happened to me as an adult.

I didn't blossom until I was 12. I was something of a tomboy up until this point. It was my mother who pulled me out of myself, and put Scherrie and me in ballet class. My mother could see something in me that I couldn't see in myself. She could see that I worked hard at everything I did, and showed signs of talent in singing and dancing. She saw something special in me, and she wanted to make certain that others saw it, too. Before my mother recognized my talent, it was my grandmother who had seen it first. She used to say to my mother, "Don't worry about Freda. She is going to fool everybody!"

I remember one day my mother said, "Freda, come here. Come into the bathroom with me." She was holding in her hand a box of Clairol "Reddish Auburn" hair dye. "I want to dye your hair this color. Your hair is a mousey brown, and I think this will make you look more attractive."

She made certain that my hair was always nice and straight instead of keeping it frizzy or nappy. She always used a hot comb on my hair. That was back in the day before chemical hair relaxers came onto the market. Back then the fashion was to wear your hair straightened. Mom was right! Adding color to it gave my hair an extra dimension.

My mother would go to the beauty shop where she would get her hair done. She had long dark brown hair, she would get it straightened with a hot comb, and then they would add some curl to it. She would take Scherrie and me with her, and we'd get our hair done as well. Although my mother's hair was naturally curly, and not kinky curly, she would have it attractively styled.

Personally, I didn't feel that I was pretty at all. I didn't think I looked pretty because I was pale.

Nowadays, in my 70's, I look in the mirror and say to myself, "Girl, you look just fine!" But I feel better when I put make-up on! My family members all tell me I look good without make-up. And my son says that to me, too. But I am critical until I put my make-up on and then I can look in the mirror and say, "Girl, you sure look good!"

As a young girl, in my eyes I was something of "an ugly duckling" waiting to blossom. A lot of young girls suffer from self-esteem issues. You read all the time about frustrated teenage girls who turn to "cutting" themselves with knives or razors, literally maiming themselves. This is, of course, a sign of an emotional cry for help. I have to confess, there was one time when I was in such emotional pain, that I did some of that to eclipse the pain I felt inside. I wouldn't cut myself, but I had long fingernails, and I would scratch myself until I bled. But I got through that stage, and I survived. It kind of reminds me of Gloria Gaynor's "I Will Survive!"

I remember the first time when I felt that I was really pretty. At the time I was 11 years old, and I was in Idlewild, Michigan. We had our own little summer cottage up there at this point. This is why I never went to summer camp, because the whole family went to Idlewild for the summer. That particular night our parents had dropped Scherrie and me off at the roller skating rink, while they went out "clubbing."

I was standing there watching people at The Polk Roller Rink, and there was this one boy who went skating by. He was the cutest boy in the whole place. Every time he would skate by me, he would turn his head and look at me. I thought to myself, "Is he looking at me? He can't be looking at me."

I was on the sidelines watching all of the skaters go by. Finally, he skated past me again, and this time he stopped and he started talking to me. We sat down and he took off his roller skates. Then he invited me to take a walk with him outside on the beach. There was a nice freshwater lake there, so we decided to go out for a walk on the sand, and it was getting dark. When we sat down on the sand, we kissed. That was my first kiss. Nothing other than that happened: no petting, no fooling around, or anything like that. Just a kiss.

His name was Tony and he was from Cleveland, Ohio. Then he said to me, "We better get back to the rink before your parents get back."

When we returned, I didn't realize that I had some sand on the back of my head, in my hair. When my mother picked me up, she instantly saw the sand, and she demanded to know, "Where have you been young lady? How did you get that sand in your hair?"

I said, "I was just on the beach with this boy. We weren't doing anything, Mom."

She said to me, "*With a boy!* What did you do?"

And I said, "Nothing!"

Then she took me to the Ladies Room, and really began to grill me. She immediately assumed the worst case scenario, when in reality nothing had happened. It really hurt me to have her suspect that I had done something bad.

She acted like I was guilty, and I hadn't even done anything. "I hope you didn't let him feel your breasts, that would lead to you getting pregnant." Back then there were no birth control pills. The worst and most taboo thing that could happen to a young girl was that she would become pregnant. At this point I was on my way to becoming fully developed. I was already wearing a "B" sized bra.

That night I thought to myself, "How did this happen? I must be pretty!" I was becoming a woman, but I still had the mentality of a child.

By the way, I got my period shortly after my 11th birthday. This is why my mother was so freaked out.

To this day, when someone tells me, "You are beautiful," and I know that I don't have the right make-up on, there is a part of me that makes me think, "I know you are lying! You are just saying that to play up to me."

When we got back to Detroit, as fate would have it, our piano teacher, Mrs. Ruth Anne Johnson, was in the process of preparing for a forthcoming piano recital. She was kept busy auditioning all of her piano students to see if they were good enough to sing in an ensemble group. In the meantime, she already knew that Scherrie was a pretty good singer. Even as a child Scherrie was gregarious and outgoing. She was the kind of kid who, when company would come over, she would ask them, "You wanna hear me sing?!"

I was the exact opposite. In fact I was painfully shy as a child. So, Mrs. Johnson had never heard me sing, and I wasn't about to volunteer. I would never think of singing in front of anyone, unless I was standing behind a door or something else to hide behind. But all of this was about to change.

"I want you to sing for me," Mrs. Johnson said, and so I did. I stood there and sang the Nat King Cole song "Too Young to Go Steady." It was a big surprise to her when she heard my voice for the first time. In fact, she was amazed!

When I finished singing she said to me, "Why Freda! You have a lovely voice. I want you to sing a solo in the upcoming recital." The song she gave me to sing was, "Stars Are the Windows of Heaven." It was a solo, and the ensemble piece she put me in was a song entitled, "June Is Bustin' Out All Over," which I sang with a group of six people.

After the program was finished, all of my mother's friends were flabbergasted to hear this strong voice come out of me. They came up to her and said, "That was so surprising!" They all wanted to know why I would never sing for them until now.

Before then, it was always Scherrie who did the entertaining, while I stood in the background. After that night everything turned around. I began to enter talent contests. My mom's friends would invite me to sing at various functions, and I was officially coming out of my shell.

By the time I was around the age of 13, I was looked upon as something of a child prodigy around Detroit. I began to win singing competitions. Then I was on a TV talent show. But it was more than a talent show. It was called *The Ed McKenzie Dance Hour*. It came on every Saturday, at 2:00 in the afternoon. It was like Detroit's local version of Dick Clark's *American Bandstand*. This would have been around 1956 or 1957.

Every time I competed on the show I won, I would win a trophy and a record player. It wasn't long before I had a collection of record players and trophies! Every week they would have a guest artist on the program. It would usually be a celebrity who was headlining at one of the top Detroit supper clubs, like The Flame Show Bar, The Roostertail, or The Elmwood Casino—across the river in Windsor, Canada. The first time I was on the show and won, Sammy Davis Jr. was the guest star. Afterwards we took a photo together, and I still have the 8" x 10" black & white print.

Ed McKenzie's show was broadcast on the local NBC-TV affiliate station in Detroit, so this was a big deal at that time. The following week, when I went back to school I found that the kids and the teachers had seen it. Well, that certainly made me popular in school!

It was after I had won my second appearance on *The Ed McKenzie Dance Hour*, that Berry Gordy Jr. came into the picture. It was 1957, and I was 14 years old at the time. Berry had heard about me because I was singing around town. At the time Berry was writing songs for Jackie Wilson. Two of the hits he wrote for Jackie were the songs "Reet Petite" and "To Be Loved." This was before Berry founded Motown Records. Songwriting turned out to be a stepping stone towards his establishing his musical empire.

At the time Scherrie and I were taking ballet classes from a Russian ballet dancer who had a studio on Woodward Boulevard. His name was Nicholas Sukolas. He was a little short man.

At the ballet class I could hear one of the mothers saying that I looked older than the rest of the girls in the class. I was tall and well-developed for my age. I was only 12 when I started ballet, but I appeared to be 16. I looked like a full-grown woman, but I was just a child.

After a couple years of ballet, I started taking Afro-Cuban dance lessons from a man by the name of Taboo. Taboo had formerly danced with Katherine Dunham. He was hired by this lady whose name was Beatrice Summers. She was an African American woman, but she was into the arts and she put on a recital called *Seven Shades of Blue*. She mentored dancers and singers, and in a sense, she mentored me. She gave me vocal lessons, as well as dance lessons. Beatrice was a large woman who didn't dance herself, but she hired professionals, like Taboo, to conduct the dance classes.

The classes that I attended were held in the basement of her house. Back then in Detroit, people had recreation rooms in their basements. In our house we had a recreation room that had a bar and bar stools for entertaining.

Well, Berry Gordy Jr. used to come to Mrs. Summer's house to watch me dance. He would just stand there and watch me. I was still a junior high school student. I had no idea how closely he was paying attention to me, nor did I have a clue how much my Afro-Cuban dancing left an impression. Not only was Berry impressed with my dancing at that stage of my budding career, but he was impressed with my singing as well.

Berry closely watched me dance in those Afro-Cuban classes, and then he started writing songs for me. He wrote four songs especially for me to sing, and he recorded them. This was still years before Berry started Motown Records. One of the songs I recorded for Berry was called "Father Dear." Then there was one called "Applications For Love." The third one was entitled "The Moon Rock." The fourth song he composed with me in mind was called "Save Me a Star." That song was later recorded by Florence Ballard of The Supremes, and appeared on one of their compilation albums. He wrote that song especially for me, because he hadn't even met The Supremes, as there were no "Supremes" yet. Also, Claudette Robinson of The Miracles later recorded "Save Me a Star."

We went to the recording studio on West Grand Boulevard called United Sound, and I recorded all four of them. According to my friend George Solomon, who works with Motown Records, these recordings still exist in Motown's vaults. I have a copy of "Father Dear." Back then, United Sound was the premiere recording place in Detroit, located not far from The General Motors Building, The Fisher Theater, and what later became Motown / Hitsville.

I remember recording all of those songs, and I even recall some of the musicians who played on those songs. One of them was "Beans" Bowles on trombone, and Berry's sidekick, Robert Bateman, was there, too. I used to wonder, when Motown became so big, what happened to Berry's friendship with Robert Bateman? He was a key player at Motown, but Robert seemed to have been passed by in Motown's heyday.

At the time, around 1956-1957, Raynoma Gordy was Berry's very devoted wife. Raynoma had a son, Cliff, who was about two years old at the time. I remember that Cliff was a precocious little brat who used to kick me.

It was kind of sad, when I read Raynoma's memoir, how Berry talked her into getting out of the picture when Motown became an enormous success. Rightfully, she should have been part of the whole thing. Raynoma was certainly there with Berry when he was struggling to establish Motown. She was there at the label, but he convinced her to take her name off the legal papers listing her as one of the founders of the company.

What happened was that Berry now had these four demo recordings that he wrote, and I recorded, and he said, "I want to take these to New York, and see if I can get a deal with Roulette Records. I am going to have a meeting with Morris Levy." Morris was infamously known in the business for creating hit records, but rarely did he ever pay his artists the royalties that were due to them.

At the time Berry had a relationship with a guy named George Kelly, who was African American, and a nightclub owner. George had a girlfriend by the name of Francis Burnette. Francis was a singer as well, and a pretty good singer at that.

George had a brand-new white Cadillac with white leather interior, and he said, "I'll drive you, Berry, and Freda and her mother to New York City so that you can do this pitch to Morris Levy." It was my belief that George also helped to financially subsidize Berry. He would give him cash and help him along, and he was one of Berry's friends and business partners.

Driving on the freeway to New York, there were several rest stops that had Howard Johnson's restaurants in them. On one stop everyone wanted to go into the restaurant to use the bathroom and get something to eat. However, George didn't want to go in, and claimed, "I don't want to be seen with Berry wearing a 'do-rag' on his head!" Scherrie didn't want to go inside either, and she sat in the car.

We drove directly to New York City. It was me, Scherrie, and Mama, along with Berry and George. Instead of going to a hotel first, we drove straight to The Apollo Theater in Harlem where Little Willie John was performing, in fact he was headlining. We didn't go inside to see the show, we went to where the stage door was located and parked the car. Berry got out and walked up to the stage door, and Willie John came out to meet him. I remember he had a smoking jacket on, and his hair was "conked"—or greased back, just like Berry's.

George Kelly kept complaining to Berry, "Don't you get that hair grease on my white leather seats." During the trip he made Berry wear a black cloth on his head so that he didn't mess up the seats. They called them "do-rags," which were scarves meant to protect your hair.

Anyway, Berry and Little Willie John talked for a bit, and then Berry came back to the car. Little Willie John was the brother of Mabel John, and—like me—Mabel was another one of the first singers that Berry recorded. Little Willie John had become a star with big hit songs like the original version of "Fever" and "All Around The World"—with the chorus line "grits ain't groceries." Flashing forward, Little Willie John eventually got on the wrong side of the law, was sent to prison, and later got knifed and died behind bars. But that is a whole other story. His sister—who had several singles of her own including "Your Good Thing Is About To End"—is now known as Dr. Mabel John, and she is a Doctor of Theology.

So, after Berry met with Little Willie John, we went and checked into our hotel. It wasn't a "flea bag" of a hotel, but it was a decent hotel. Francis Burnette was there too. We ended up just staying one night—me, my mother and Scherrie. Berry had a meeting set up with Morris Levy, and he announced to us, "I'm going to stay over. I have more business to take care of, so I will fly back on my own." We ended up driving back to Detroit with George and Francis Burnette.

Then, a couple of days later, Berry was back in Detroit, and he wanted to have a meeting with Mama. Back then we lived on Glenn Court. It was a two-story house located on the corner of Glenn Court and 14th Street.

They had the meeting, and I was sitting on the staircase. The living room was on my right, and the dining room was to my left, so I could hear them talking. They were going back-and-forth about the terms of the proposed contract that would make me a teenage recording artist.

My mother said, "Well Berry, you said you want to 'manage' Freda. And, you say you want 20 percent of the money she makes?"

And then Berry said, "Yes."

"Well then, how much does the agent get?"

He said, "He gets 10 percent."

So then Mama said, "O.K., that's 10 percent more. So, that is 30 percent. Then who pays for my daughter's gowns, and airfares, and hotels?"

"Your daughter," Berry replied.

And then my mother said, "Well Berry, what does that leave for Freda?"

They kept going back-and-forth, back-and-forth. Then Berry brought up the fact that Elvis Presley's manager, Colonel Tom Parker, gets 50 percent of Elvis' earnings. Still, my mother was not convinced. He would never relent on his terms, nor would Mama. So, in the end it was like a gigantic stalemate. So, nothing happened. Neither of them would budge from their position. So, Berry left without a signed contract.

A few months went by, and meanwhile Berry had discovered another young teenage singer: Mary Wells. She was an aspiring singer and songwriter at the time. I remember performing at a "sock hop" at a local all-white high school. Since I was studying to be a dancer, I was dancing on the show, doing a modern dance. And Mary Wells sang one of the very first recordings she had done with Berry—"Bye Bye Baby"—or one of those very first songs she had recorded. She and I were around the same age.

Berry had also begun working with Marv Johnson. Marv was his first male artist on Berry's Tamla record label, which later became part of Motown Records. I remember Berry taking me to a house that was located on Gladstone Street in Detroit. That was when I first met Smokey Robinson and his wife Claudette, and the other three members of Smokey's group, The Miracles. Brian Holland was also there, and his brother Eddie. Back then it was a big deal just to have $500.00. So we looked up to Berry as though he was wealthy.

On another occasion, I remember that Berry came by our house, and he brought Eddie Holland along with him. At the time, Eddie was only 17 years old, and I was 14. Berry asked Eddie to get up in front of us and sing the song "Merry Go Round," for me and my mother, because he was a singer back then.

Since my mother and Berry could not come to an agreement on how he was going to manage my career, we had to walk away from what he was offering. He was not willing to adjust or compromise, and neither was my mother. As far as Berry was concerned, it was a "take it or leave it" kind of situation. And this was before there was any Tamla or Motown Records. Mama thought his demands were unfair for me, so that was the end of that.

Mama was very protective of me, and Berry already had a reputation for being promiscuous with women. Later on Berry developed into a real "starmaker" with his initial roster of singers at Motown Records, but I was not to be one of them. That was the end of "Round One" of my Motown story.

At the age of 14 I auditioned for a local radio show. It was called *Don Large's Make Way For Youth*, and he had a youth choir comprised of local girls and boys. Some of the members were in their early 20s, predominantly Caucasian, with the exception of two African American girls. One of them was Ursula Walker, and the other was Carmen Mathis. When I auditioned for Don Large, I was cast, giving the choir a third non-white female face. There were also two African American males in the chorus.

It was an unpaid choir, but it was a nationally broadcast program on the NBC affiliated station, and potentially thousands of people were listening to us. For me, this was a "big deal." The choir had about 16 or 18 members. We had rehearsals twice a week, it was Tuesdays and Thursdays in the evening. My mother would have to drive me to the studio for rehearsals, then we did the radio show "live" on-the-air on Saturdays. It was broadcast on Detroit radio station WJR, which is still in existence. The studio was located in the penthouse of The Fisher Building. On the first floor are several shops and The Fisher Theater.

Originally, the theater was constructed as an amazing movie theater, and the motif was of Aztec inspired design. It had a gorgeous lobby, and when you went to the second floor of the theater you could really see the Aztec design. There was an elaborate lobby with a fountain there, and it was very lush. They later renovated the theater, and with that most of the Aztec designs were gone, and it had a more modern look to it. It is currently used as a legitimate theater for plays and concerts. As I recall, it was much prettier as a movie theater, as it had a lot more character.

The Fisher Theater, as far back as the late 1940s and 1950s, was a movie theater I often attended. It would be me and Scherrie and some of our neighborhood friends and an adult: Mom, or an aunt, or an uncle. It was walking distance from where we lived on John R.

In 1985 I headlined a touring company of Duke Ellington's *Sophisticated Ladies*, and we appeared at The Fisher Theater for a two-week run. This was one of many *déjà vu* moments that have occurred in my life.

I was a member of *Make Way For Youth* for three years. While I was part of it I was exposed to a lot of music, and I learned a lot of great songs. You had to be a sight-reader of music. You couldn't say, "I'm a great singer, but I can't sight-read music." Fortunately, I had been taught to do that in school. That was back when "music" was regularly taught in public school. It has long since been discontinued, and I think it should be brought back.

One of the guys I went to school with was James Frazier Jr. We went out a couple of times. He was very nice, but he was someone who can best be described as being a "nerd." James excelled at classical music training and was a classically accomplished pianist.

I remember that he took me out to a classical symphony concert at Meadowbrook, an outdoor band shell venue in suburban Detroit, where you would sit out on the lawn and hear the classics. It is still a beautiful, classy venue to hear performers.

James was a really nice guy, and what I remember the most is that he didn't even try to kiss me that evening, although I was 16 years old at the time. After that, I labeled him as being "a total nerd!" Actually, I didn't care, I just wanted to go out and hear the music.

Then he took me out to a Big Boy drive-in restaurant.

"What do you want?" he asked me as he passed me the menu.

"A hamburger, onion rings, french fries, and a Coke," I replied. "What are you going to have?"

He looked a little miffed and said, "I'll just have a Coke, I guess." Apparently, when I ordered "the works," it totally drained what little money he had in his wallet.

After high school James had gone to University of Michigan, where he studied medicine. He could have been a doctor, but he decided to go into music instead. Then he became a classical conductor, and at one point was the assistant to highly revered conductor Eugene Ormandy. Eugene was famous for having been the conductor of The Philadelphia Philharmonic Orchestra. There are so many people who have come from Detroit and become big successes in show business. James Frazier was one of them. He had risen to become one of the first African American conductors for The Philadelphia Philharmonic Orchestra. Unfortunately, James died in his 40s of a massive heart attack. I was so shocked and saddened to read of his passing in the newspaper.

Because of my training in high school, I was taught a lot about music. That's when I learned how to sight-read, so that enabled me to get into the *Make Way For Youth* choir. Up to that point, Don Large was always picking Ursula Walker to do solos. Ursula was the premiere member of the choir, and she appeared on television a lot. She was a couple of years older than me, and she received an awful lot of local TV exposure. Ursula was a very good singer. I was aspiring to become as good a singer as Ursula. Although Ursula never left Detroit, she continued to sing. Eventually, she got married and had three children.

At first it was Ursula who got the lion's share of the solo spots in the broadcast. When I arrived and joined the choir, Don started giving me solos periodically. Then, he also said, "I want Freda, Ursula, and Carmen Mathis to perform as a trio, and I'm going to call you girls 'The Three Debs.'" So, from that point forward, whenever we did appearances, the three of us would perform with the choir, and then we would come out front as a trio. One of the songs that we did as The Three Debs was called "I Want To Love You" and another one was "Mississippi Mud."

Then, when I was 16 and still attending Central High School, that's when I auditioned for the nationally telecast *Ted Mack & The Amateur Hour* talent show which was broadcast from New York City. There was a talent scout who had come to Detroit, like they do these days with *American Idol, America's Got Talent*, and *The Voice*. I went down and auditioned, and they picked me to fly to New York City to do the show. So they made arrangements to fly my mother and me to New York: First Class! This was a big deal.

When people ask me what it was like to fly back then, I explain to them what First Class was like during that era. It was really "First Class!" They served appetizers during the flight, and one of the appetizers was made with caviar. But it wasn't quite "first" First Class. The caviar they served was that black lumpfish caviar. I remember tasting it for the first time in my life, and thinking, "This is caviar? It is fish eggs? This tastes more like fish shit!" Years later I was introduced to Beluga and Sevruga caviar from Russia, and also from the Caspian Sea, and there is some great Iranian caviar out there too. Instead of being black in color, the premier caviar is a shade of dark gray. Once you taste really good caviar, there is no going back!

We arrived in New York City, and they put us up at The Sheraton Hotel. It was a big deal as well. It was thrilling! When it came time for the show, I was really nervous, but I got myself together. I gave myself a little pep talk: "Girl, it's 'make-it-or-break-it' time. Get yourself pulled together." Well, it obviously worked, and I performed great on the show. There are still clips of me on the *Amateur Hour* that occasionally show up on YouTube from that show. That was in 1959. I came in second place on the show. The winner was an Italian tenor who had been on the show before, and he obviously had a lot of friends and relatives. This was his third time on the show, and he had built up a momentum of followers.

Viewers would vote by either calling in, or sending a post card. Although the tenor ended up winning, I still felt great about it, and my appearance on the program was an invaluable experience for me.

When I was 16 years old, I officially came out as a Cotillion debutante. My parents were members of The Cotillion Social Club, and The Cotillion Debutante Ball took place at The Latin Quarter in Detroit, which was located on West Grand Boulevard just off Woodward. It was a beautiful banquet room where this event was held, and Jimmy Wilkins had a 17-piece orchestra that played there. They were hired for special events which were held at The Latin Quarter. Jimmy Wilkins' band was the Detroit version of The Count Basie Orchestra, and they were hugely revered as being a great jazz band.

On a couple of occasions, Jimmy Wilkins would hire me to perform as one of the featured female vocalists at gigs with the band. I would sing maybe two or three songs during the show. He would pay me $45.00 for the evening, which was great for me! When he was only nine years old, "Little" Stevie Wonder performed there on one occasion.

That night at the Cotillion Debutante Ball, a girl by the name of Gabby Bradley won at the Coronation Ball, and I was one of the Ladies-In-Waiting. We were all wearing tiaras. Taking my step-father's last name, I was using the name Freda Payne Farley at the time. I still have a newspaper clipping from *The Michigan Chronicle* that reads:

"Miss Farley won Second Prize and Miss White, Third." Gabby and I attended the same high school: Central High.

That was the start of me appearing in the local Detroit newspapers. Then it blossomed into me being featured in national publications. At the time, Ike Sutton was the top photographer for *Jet* magazine. It was Robert Johnson, the executive editor of *Jet*, who became a champion for me and my career. In time, actress Jayne Kennedy and I frequently appeared in *Jet*. People would ask me, "How is it that you get in *Jet* so much?"

I would say, "Well, those people kind of adopted me." I was actively doing things, my career was thriving, and they just liked me! My first time in *Jet* was when I won "Second Prize" on *Ted Mack's Amateur Hour* when I was 16 years old. They wrote a two page article on me, with accompanying pictures. The second time I was in *Jet*, I was a bathing suit model, at the age of 16 as well.

Of all of the publications, the one that was the most loyal to me—at several phases of my career—was without a doubt *Jet* magazine. It was an all-black magazine that came out weekly from Johnson Publications located in Chicago. They were also the publishers of *Ebony* magazine, which was a monthly publication. Years later I was to grace the cover of *Ebony* magazine, in a sexy bathing suit. One of my first appearances in *Jet* referred to me as "Sixteen-year-old high school student Freda Payne Farley." The magazine included an article about me headlined: "The Girl Television Discovered." It was accompanied with a photo of me on *The Ted Mack Amateur Hour*.

"How did they even know about me?" I thought to myself.

From the '60s up to the '90s, if you look at the masthead of *Jet* magazine, the Executive Editor was Robert Johnson—not to be confused with the man who started BET (Black Entertainment Television). They had the same name, they are both out of Chicago, but they are two different people.

As the Chief Executive Photographer of *Jet* magazine, Ike

Sutton used to go around with Dr. Martin Luther King, as his photographer. If you see photos of Dr. King with Marvin Gaye, Richard Pryor, Sammy Davis, Jr., or Aretha Franklin from that era, chances are it was Ike who photographed them. Ike regularly traveled with them, and he was part of their entourage. That was his assignment as a press photographer.

After winning all of these talent contests, I was becoming known as an aspiring singer, and things were starting to happen in my budding career, and I was just a teenager at the time. I found myself in a wonderful position to launch a professional performing career. The best was truly yet to come, and it was awaiting me right around the corner.

CHAPTER TWO

"Duke Ellington and Pearl Bailey"

Duke Ellington and his orchestra were performing in Detroit when I first met him. At the time they were headlining at The Riviera Theatre, which was located on West Grand River Boulevard.

Just by coincidence, Duke's son, Mercer Ellington, was at a cocktail party and our neighbor, Allen Early Jr., was also there. Allen was an attorney, and he was known as one of the best criminal attorneys in Detroit. In addition to that, he was very good friends with my parents, and he liked me and he loved my singing.

At this cocktail party Allen met Mercer, and he started telling him all about me. He bragged about me so much that he finally talked Mercer into coming to my house to listen to me sing. When he did, and when he heard me, he was instantly impressed.

I sang "That Old Black Magic," and "From This Moment On," which were jazz standards that I knew, and had been performing on the talent shows. Those were my two big numbers; they had won me several of the competitions. After I finished singing, Mercer said, "I want my dad to hear you sing. We are playing at The Riviera Theater here in Detroit. Maybe I can make arrangements to bring you by. If your mother can bring you down to The Gotham Hotel, you can meet my dad, and he can hear you sing."

The Gotham Hotel was known as the black-owned hotel in Detroit where performers and other people of color would stay when they were in town. They preferred to stay there. Although there was no segregation or "Jim Crow" laws in Detroit at the time, people of color preferred to stay where they felt welcome. And it was priced more reasonably than some of the other hotels in town like The Sheraton or The Book Cadillac Hotel. So, that is where the Ellington band was staying during their engagement.

I liked The Gotham Hotel also. My dad, Fred Payne, used to take me and Scherrie down there on Sundays after church to have dinner. To me at the time, that was truly dining in style. Back then it was a big deal to dine at The Gotham Hotel.

I remember the time when I was seven years old, and I ordered Trout Meunière Almandine in the restaurant at The Gotham Hotel. The fish was sautéed in butter, and I absolutely loved it! I thought that was so delicious.

Mercer picked my mother and me up, and brought us to The Gotham Hotel to meet his dad, Duke Ellington. We walked into the room and sat in the sitting area of his suite. Duke then invited me into a separate room, where there was a spinet piano. It was just him and me alone in the room; nobody else was there.

Duke said to me, "Now Freda, let me hear what you've got!"

He sat down at the spinet and played one of his songs, and I sang along to his music. I recall the songs I sang for him that day were "I've Got It Bad and That Ain't Good," and then I sang "Mood Indigo," which are both Duke Ellington classics. A song like "Mood Indigo," with its long held notes, truly shows off a singer's musical ability. It also shows off the perfect pitch and the timbre of the voice.

When I finished singing, he turned around and looked at me and said, "That's really good. You remind me of Lena Horne. I like your voice. I would like to hear you sing with the band. The only problem is that we are leaving Detroit tomorrow morning at 6:30, headed for Pittsburgh. We are playing at The Holiday House there. Maybe, if your mother or your dad, or someone can drive you to Pittsburgh, I will be happy to invite you up on-stage to sing with the band. Because, if you are as good as what I just heard, I think that would be nice."

That is exactly what we did. We drove to Pittsburgh, Pennsylvania with my mother, and Mack Ferguson who was my mentor and family friend. Mack was a pianist himself, and we did gigs together in Detroit. We worked together a lot. He was about 30 years old or so. He mentored me and schooled me about a lot of things in dealing with people in show business, and otherwise.

When we arrived in Pittsburgh, we went directly to The Holiday House. It was a hotel, and it also had a cocktail lounge, and a formal showroom. We checked into the hotel, and it was something of a magical experience to be there. Years later, I would wind up headlining at The Holiday House. What an amazing coincidence that was. It was like "*déjà vu*" to be back there.

For that particular engagement Duke was playing in one of the big performance rooms at The Holiday House. The place was almost like a resort, with a big outdoor courtyard. Part of the grounds adjoined the larger part of the hotel, where the main lounge and banquet rooms were located. I remember that it had zigzag style sidewalks throughout the yard.

When we got there, Duke invited me to come to his room to discuss what songs he wanted me to sing with the band, and to plan it out. While I was there, he received a phone call. I heard him talking to somebody but I didn't know who it was. Amidst the conversation I heard him address the other person as "sweetheart" at one point.

As he got ready to sign off on the conversation, he again used that same word, telling the other person, "Okay, I'll see you in a minute, sweetheart."

I didn't say anything, because I didn't know who that was.

But after he hung up the telephone he said to me, "That was Billy Strayhorn."

Billy wasn't a member of Duke's orchestra, but he was Duke's songwriting partner. He is especially known for all of the songs he wrote himself including: "Take the 'A' Train." He literally wrote that song while waiting for the "A" train on the New York subway. He wrote that song to impress Duke Ellington, and it worked. "Chelsea Bridge," "A Flower Is a Lovesome Thing," and "Something to Live For" were among Billy's most famous songs. Billy was also known for writing the highly popular jazz standard "Lush Life," while still in his teens. He was very gifted as a songwriter. Billy was openly gay, in an era when it was decidedly not common for someone to admit he was homosexual. Lena Horne absolutely loved Billy Strayhorn. They were the best of friends.

The lyrics of the song "Lush Life," are slightly pointing towards the gay lifestyle, in a very subtle way. It is also about drowning one's sorrows in "jazz and cocktails," while looking for love in a smoky bar. It is known as a true jazz classic.

Duke said to me, "I am going to introduce you to Billy."

The moment we walked out of his room, we were instantly outside in a courtyard. Then I noticed from the opposite building a guy who was walking toward us. He was slightly chubby, but not fat. He wore glasses and stood about five-foot seven-inches tall. It was summertime, so the weather was nice outside.

As he walked toward us, Duke said to me, "Freda, meet Billy Strayhorn. Billy, this is Freda," and we shook hands. At the time I didn't realize how important Billy was, but I had certainly heard his name.

Later on that day I said to Mack Ferguson, "Mack, Duke was talking to Billy Strayhorn on the phone, and he called him 'sweetheart.' What does that mean, a man calling another man 'sweetheart?'"

Mack explained, "Oh, that is just some musician talk."

Back in those days even gangsters in the movies—like Edward G. Robinson and Humphrey Bogart—would refer to one another as "sweetheart." It was not so much an endearment as it was slang.

They called Billy Strayhorn "the shadow of Duke Ellington." He was Duke's "right hand man," and his devoted friend. He was known to be an important part of the entourage. Meeting Billy was definitely an experience.

That evening Duke made good his promise, and he introduced me from the stage of The Holiday House. He brought me up in the middle of the show to sing with The Duke Ellington Orchestra. As I recall, I sang, "I Got It Bad and That Ain't Good," and "Mood Indigo."

It was really an exciting experience for me. Not only was I singing on-stage with the great Duke Ellington, but his band members were a "who's who" of the jazz world as well. There was sax player Johnny Hodges, trombonist Juan Tizol, and tenor sax player Paul Gonsalves. To this day I can hear a jazz song on the radio and if Johnny Hodges is on the track, I can distinctly recognize his style.

Puerto Rican-born Juan Tizol was known for bringing a slight Latin flavor to several of Duke's signature songs like "Perdido" and "Caravan," which he is credited as having co-written.

How did it feel for me to be on-stage in the company of these great musicians? It was truly like Kismet, and I was in a wonderful dream. Too bad this wasn't recorded!

After the show was over Duke said to me, "Well, maybe we can work something out. We are going to leave here in a couple of days, and we're driving on the bus to Las Vegas. That's where I go next to perform. I would like to have you up on-stage with me again, in Las Vegas, if you want. I will be back in touch with you."

So after that, Mama and Mack and I drove back to Detroit wondering what was going to happen next. A few days later a big envelope arrived at the house. And inside of it was a ten-year contract from Duke Ellington, making me an offer to sing with his band. We read the contract. My mother read it. I read it, and then our lawyer, Allen Early Jr. read it. While we mulled over the terms we packed our bags for Las Vegas. Since Duke had said to me, "Come sing with us in Vegas!" I wasn't about to miss this opportunity.

Although I was not on Duke's payroll, I wasn't going to pass up the chance to sing with him in Las Vegas. This could be the biggest thing to happen to me in my budding singing career. So, Mama and Mack and I, packed the car and drove to Las Vegas. This was in 1961, and it took us almost two days to get there from Detroit. We had to make one stop to rest up at a motel and get a good night's sleep, before we got back on the road.

We went through all of the states between Michigan and Nevada. We went through parts of Missouri, Colorado, Texas, New Mexico, and Arizona. Taking turns driving, the three of us sat in the car for hour-after-hour and watched the changing scenery whiz by us outside the window. We were on a mission. In a way it was definitely a geographic experience, especially when we got to Colorado and saw The Rocky Mountains, and then The Grand Canyon in Arizona.

I was driving by then, and I remember getting a speeding ticket in Arizona. We had to go to this little rural courthouse and pay a fee. It was definitely one of those "speed trap" kind of situations they had set up there.

Mama tried arguing with the judge. "She's just a 17-year-old girl, this is her first infraction. Couldn't you just…?…She just didn't know…"

The judge wasn't having any of it. In the end, we just paid the penalty and left town. We had Duke Ellington waiting for us in Las Vegas! Nothing was gonna stop us from accomplishing our mission.

During this road trip, we experienced some racial prejudice that we were not used to in Detroit. Of course we knew it existed. At the time, Mack was married to a white woman, and this was a time when interracial marriage was deemed illegal in some states. So, he certainly knew about racial prejudice. It wasn't until 1964, when President Lyndon Johnson signed into law The Civil Rights Act, that things began to change. This exact subject has been addressed in a couple of recent movies: *Loving* and *The Green Book.*

According to Mack at the time, "We couldn't even consider living in the South." In one small town along the way, Mack went into a roadside restaurant to scout it out and check the menu. He was told that we could not eat in the restaurant, but that we could have a take-out order and leave with it. We ordered burgers or sandwiches and took them "to go."

When we finally arrived in Las Vegas, Nevada, it was about 9:00 in the evening. I will never forget my impression of the town when we took our first ride down the famed Vegas "strip." It was one brightly lit and colorful neon marquee after another, and it looked like a wonderland. I remember saying, "Wow! Look at all these lights!" I was in awe. That was back when "Vegas" was the old legendary "Vegas" when the mob still ruled it. And frankly, I miss those days.

Since we arrived in the evening, it was like a brightly colored neon forest in the middle of the desert. I read the hotel and casino marquees as we drove by them: "A Floorshow! The Flamingo! The Sahara! The Sands! The Desert Inn! The Thunderbird! The Dunes! The Riviera! The El Rancho! The Stardust Hotel & Casino! The New Frontier!" And on, and on-and-on. It was truly amazing to behold.

Back then several of the casino marquees featured the names of their own exotic sounding French revues. The Dunes had *The Casino de Paris,* The Tropicana had *The Follies Bergère,* and The Stardust played host to *Lido de Paris.* Ooh-la-la: Las Vegas!

Finally, it was time to find someplace to stay. I remember we kept stopping at several motels looking for accommodations. There were mainly the big and expensive casinos and hotels on the "strip," but as we got away from the casinos there were several less fancy motels as well. In our search for rooms, we would pull into one motel after another. The signs outside would clearly say the word "Vacancy," but when Mack would go into them one-by-one, he was told that there were no vacancies at all.

Mack would go in, and he would come back to the car and announce, "They said they have no vacancies."

"But the sign says 'Vacancy!'" I said in astonishment.

We didn't know what was going on. After about the second or third time, as a 17-year-old kid even I could see what was happening. I was thinking to myself, "Is he stupid or something? It's obvious they don't want us to stay there."

We saw a black man walking down the street. He looked like he could have been one of the workers in one of the hotels, like a janitor or something. So Mack and my mother stopped him, and told him of the dilemma we had been experiencing.

Mack said to him, "Hey man, we've been trying to find a place to stay. We just drove in from Detroit. We've been traveling for two days and we're tired, and they keep telling us there is 'No Vacancy,' when the sign clearly says 'Vacancy.'"

He explained, "Well, don't you all know? They don't allow 'us' to stay on 'The Strip.' All of the colored folks stay on the west side of town. They call it 'The Dustbowl.'"

"You mean they practice this kind of discrimination here in Las Vegas?" my mother said in complete disbelief.

He said, "Yes, ma'am."

My mother said to him, "But we're here with my daughter who is going to be singing with Duke Ellington upon his invitation. He is appearing at The Riviera Hotel in the lounge. Duke Ellington must be staying there at least."

The gentleman said, "Well, no ma'am. He can't be staying there. He can work there, but he can't stay there. They must be staying over at The West Motel. It is on the west side of town, owned by Dr.

West. If you call up there you will probably find the band there, and Duke."

Dr. West was a prominent black dentist in Las Vegas, and he owned his own motel. Well, Mack called The West Motel from a pay telephone, and sure enough, the whole band was there, and Duke was there as well. That neighborhood was definitely called "The Dustbowl" back then, and indeed it was located on the west side of town.

We were used to the more liberal atmosphere of Detroit. The idea of the "progressive" western United States having segregation like this came as something of a shock to us. After all this is 1961, not 1861! We would have expected this kind of behavior in the South. But in Las Vegas? Since black entertainers regularly played in Vegas hotels and casinos, we simply had no idea.

I was surprised to find out that Duke and his band were indeed booked at The West Motel. Before this all happened I would have never thought that stars like Duke Ellington weren't welcome to stay at the hotels and casinos where they were the headliners. That was quite the "reality check" to discover this was the way things worked.

We booked rooms at The West Motel. And, right next door to the motel was a casino that was also black-owned, called The Moulin Rouge. That was the first black-owned casino in Las Vegas.

Two important things happened during this trip to Las Vegas. I got the opportunity to sing with Duke Ellington there. Just as he had promised, I got up on-stage with him, one night only. As I recall, the song I sang was: "It Don't Mean a Thing If It Ain't Got That Swing." It was so wonderful to be up on the stage singing with all of the jazz guys you read about in history books, in Las Vegas no less! These were the "real deal" jazzmen who played with Duke, and it made the experience even more exciting. My featured singing went exceedingly well. In fact, well enough to make Duke genuinely want to hire me as a featured singer with his orchestra.

The second important thing that happened was that we discussed the contract that Duke had offered me. When Allen Early Jr. looked at the contract for me, the first thing he said was, "You know, this contract extends beyond your 21st birthday. It won't end until you are 27. That is too long. It needs to be shorter." Allen was concerned that for ten full years, I would just be an employee of a big band leader, and that might prove limiting. The next issue was the pay scale. It started out with me getting paid $175.00 a week for a year. The second year it would go up to $250.00, then the next year to $350.00, the next year to $450.00, and so on.

Since I was underage, my mother would have to sign the contract as my guardian, thus giving her consent. Therein lies the problem. My mother said to Duke, "Well, Mr. Ellington, let's say four years from now my daughter has traveled all around the country and maybe to Europe, and my daughter has become a big name. Let's say that happens, would you adjust her salary to $3,000.00 or $4,000.00?"

Duke looked at my mother as if to say: "Hell no!"

After going around-and-around about this contract, Duke threw in the towel and said to my mother, "Just forget about it." That was the end of that.

Ultimately, Duke hired a singer by the name of Milt Grayson to be the featured singer for the rest of the run. Later, Milt married Ann, the sister of my friend Roxanne Spino.

However, meeting and singing with Duke Ellington left a lasting impression on me. This man was a very iconic musician and star, and for me it was an honor. At that time he was beyond well-established. His music had touched me even as a child. I remember my Uncle Johnny playing his Ellington record collection on those old breakable 78 rpm discs. From the age of four and five years old, I knew who Duke Ellington was. I knew of his importance. He was the leader of the premiere black jazz orchestra in the world. I was so impressed just to have been in his presence. I felt like "I was steppin' in high cotton," as the old saying goes.

In stature, Duke was not short. He stood six-feet one-inch tall, and he was impressive looking. Another thing that I instantly noticed about him was that he was a perfect gentleman. But I also had a feeling that he liked me as well, more than just as a singer, too.

The Duke Ellington Orchestra was booked for a whole month at the lounge of The Riviera Hotel & Casino. This was a typical booking, since Lionel Hampton played the lounge, Stan Kenton played the lounge, and The Woody Herman Band played the lounge at The Flamingo. The big bands didn't play the big showrooms, usually the bands played in the Vegas lounges.

The Vegas lounges were sophisticated nightclubs unto themselves. They served cocktails and appetizers, whereas the big rooms had "the dinner show" at around 7:00 pm, and the 10:00 show was "cocktails only." In the casinos, if you were gambling they would serve you complimentary cocktails, to encourage you to spend more of your money gambling. You could hang out in the lounges and listen to some incredible music from the top bands in the country.

I was 17 years old at the time, and honey I was fully developed! I was a very zaftig, sophisticated looking 17-year-old. My mother said, "I can just see you on the road with all those old men in the band. I know that I would have to chaperone you!"

Fast forward to 2009, when I had been booked to perform with the present incarnation of The Duke Ellington Orchestra, which is now comprised of all young players. At the time his grandson, Paul Ellington, jokingly said to me about Duke, "I don't know what my granddad was thinking about when he sought to sign you as a singer. I think that he might have had other things in mind at the time!"

I laughed and said, "Oh Paul, I think you have a dirty mind!"

Looking back on this situation, I don't think it would have worked out at all. Can you imagine a 17-year-old girl traveling with an all-male band? And, if Duke Ellington actually had designs on me, I certainly had no idea.

As my mother would say, "All men are dogs! Some are big dogs, and some of them are just littler dogs."

Unfortunately, I never did get to regularly sing for, or to record with, Duke. It would have been amazing if it had happened.

After our dreams of working with Duke Ellington vanished, my mother and I decided to stay in Vegas, and Mack Ferguson was with us the whole time. What happened was that we moved out of our motel rooms, and we rented a house. The house was a modest home on the west side of Vegas. It was owned by a man by the name of Deek Watson, and Deek was one of the original members of the 1940s singing group, The Ink Spots. He owned two homes in Vegas. One home he lived in, and the other one he rented out.

It was more economical to rent this little house than it was to continue to pay a weekly fee at a motel. There were two bedrooms, a living room, dining room area, two bathrooms, and kitchen. We stayed there for three or four months.

If this trip to Vegas was going to work, we needed to find a venue for me to perform. The first gig we found was at a place called The Black Magic Lounge. We played there about three weeks. After that Mack Ferguson went checking around on The Strip, and he went to a hotel that was located directly across from The Sands Hotel & Casino. It was called The Sans Souci, which was a casino and hotel. Mack got us a booking there billed as: "Freda Payne & The Mack Ferguson Trio." In the main room was singer Miriam Makeba. Miriam had become famous because she was Harry Belafonte's protégé. She also appeared on *The Ed Sullivan Show* on TV.

Miriam and I developed a friendship, and she was a very sweet and innocent girl when I met her. She was from South Africa, and she was 21-years-old at the time. She was later married to trumpet player Hugh Masekela. And after that, she ended up marrying political activist Stokely Carmichael.

One of the things that I remember about this trip to Las Vegas, was seeing The El Rancho Casino & Hotel on fire. It had been one of the very first casinos on the strip, located across the street from The Sahara. There was a huge out-of-control fire that took The El Rancho, and literally burned it to the ground. I remember driving my two-toned white and coral colored Ford Fairlane 500 Galaxie past the hotel as it burned and I could feel the heat of the fire in the air. That car had been my graduation present from my parents when I was only 16, and that was the car we had driven to Vegas. It did not have power steering. That was an option that had just been introduced, but it would have cost more for that option. Back then I didn't need it because I had the energy of a teenager.

While we were in Las Vegas I met this guy by the name of Johnny George. He was a disc jockey at a radio station in Vegas. Johnny was an Indiana "Hoosier" who had his own radio show. He was Caucasian, and he had blondish reddish hair. I was closer to 18 years old when I met him. We dated briefly until one night, I lost my virginity to him. I felt it was time for me to become a woman, and we were even talking about marriage.

Hormonally, Mother Nature was taking over. I could feel my body changing. In certain cultures I would have been married off to someone at this time. But my focus was on my career, not marriage.

I was convinced that I was in love with Johnny George. This was the first time I was in love, and I was ready to experience more of life. Well, let me just say, I *thought* I was in love!

Then Johnny actually talked about us getting married. Things were moving rather fast, and when my mother got wind of this, she was scared that we would just go off and elope. This was magnified by the fact that Johnny was a full ten years my senior.

At one point, my mother did go back to Detroit, leaving just Mack and me there. Then Mack went back to Detroit for a week, and then returned to Vegas. That was when he handed me a large book full of songs called a "fake book," and he said to me, "You had better learn these standards, because you are going to have to know these songs. It's important to learn as many standards as you can, because this is going to sustain you." A lot of musicians have what is called a "fake book," which contains hundreds of songs, the lyrics and the music. Anybody who is in the business will know what a "fake book" is, as they are very useful to singers and musicians.

He was right, because once we got this gig at The Black Magic Lounge, those were the songs that we performed, and those were the songs that people were most likely to request in a nightclub setting. Then we were booked at The Sans Souci Hotel. After that engagement ended, Mack and my mother and I drove back to Detroit. It was still 1961.

When I was 17, it certainly was a *very good year* for me! Not only did I get to sing with Duke Ellington and his orchestra, but I also sang with Pearl Bailey, too. How this happened was again through our same neighborhood attorney, Allen Early Jr. who was at yet another cocktail party. While there he met a man named Bob Bailey—no relationship to Pearl, they just happened to have the same last name. Bob was married to Ann Bailey, and Ann was one of the chorines in Pearl's chorus line.

In addition to that, Bob was the road manager for *The Pearl Bailey Revue*, which was on a national tour of theaters. It was a whole touring company, and Pearl traveled with her husband, Louis Bellson, and his complete 17 piece orchestra. She also had six background singers.

One of them was leaving, or was fired, I was never quite sure. At the cocktail party Bob Bailey told Allen Early, "We're looking for a replacement background singer for Pearl's tour."

Allen proceeded to tell him all about me, to the point where Bob said, "If this little girl is good enough, have her come to the audition." I was still 17 at the time, and I had just graduated from high school. Since this was a big break for me, he probably figured he wouldn't have to pay me much money at all—which is just what ended up happening.

Bob Bailey also told Allen, "We are thinking about putting together a chorus line at The Moulin Rouge in Vegas. Can Freda dance?"

And Allen replied, "Yeah, she takes ballet lessons," which I had done, and modern dancing as well. With that I was invited to audition, along with several others. It was to be something of a double audition. I was auditioning to sing on the road with Pearl Bailey, and I was also auditioning to dance as part of the chorus line at The Moulin Rouge. After I sang, I changed my clothes and did the audition as a dancer.

To my surprise and delight, I was offered both gigs. The dancing gig in Vegas at The Moulin Rouge never materialized. Since I was instantly offered the job in Pearl's touring show, I took it. Two days later I was on the bus with *The Pearl Bailey Revue*. At the time, I was the only amateur in the cast, the rest of them were all seasoned professionals. My salary at the time was all of $125.00 a week. It was so inadequate that I still had to have Mama send me money from home just to make ends meet!

There were certain things that I had to do, as part of the job. These requirements came with a whole new list of weekly expenses. Out of my own money I was required to buy my own very specific make-up, and I also had to buy a certain highly expensive perfume. In real life, and at the age of 17, I didn't ever wear much make-up. I wasn't used to buying make-up like that—let alone expensive make-up. However, as a musical stage performer, every night on-stage I had to be fully made-up for the spotlights. And this was also the first time I wore false eyelashes. I wore them because Pearl insisted on it.

Pearl had her own unique set of guidelines and requirements she required of the cast. She was one demanding diva! One of the rules was that you couldn't just use the shade and type of make-up that best suited your own complexion. You couldn't wear whatever scent or cologne that you favored or usually wore. You had to wear the cologne she wore, which was Replique by Rafael of Paris. I bought a little bottle of Replique toilet water, and that was the main reason why I had to send home for money! A small bottle of that cost something like $35.00, which was a fortune on my salary, and that was just the cologne.

You also had to wear a very specific color of make-up that Max Factor made, called Pan Creole 27. Pearl Bailey's skin tone was several shades darker than mine. There was also one white girl in the chorus. She sang in the background, but she was required to wear Pan Creole 27 as well. That dark shade of make-up made the poor background singer look like an Indian or something. It looked ridiculous!

But, that was what I had to wear! It was way too dark for me. It was so unnatural, it made me look like I was wearing a shade of make-up that had too much red in it for my complexion.

However, it was the same color that Pearl wore, and that was the object. According to her, "I want all the ladies to wear the same color that I wear, so we can blend." That was the kind of an insistent diva she was. I am sorry to use that language to describe her, but she was challenging to work for. It was like perpetually walking on eggshells.

As a matter of fact, Lena Horne mentioned this same kind of issue with make-up in her autobiography. At the MGM movie studio, she had to wear a darker colored make-up than her own skin tone, so that she appeared darker on camera.

Lena also wrote extensively about how she was perfect to be cast in the film version of *Showboat*, as the mulatto girl Julie. The studio made her believe that she was going to play the coveted role of Julie. Instead, Lena was passed up by the studio, and Ava Gardner was cast as Julie instead. Lena would have been absolutely tailor-made for the role, and she was devastated when she was replaced by Ava. They told her that they were afraid the movie could not be presented in theaters in the South because of discrimination. The parallel in this story and working for Pearl Bailey is the fact that the studio had to put a darker make-up on Ava Gardner to make her look mulatto. To achieve this, so that she could play opposite Howard Keel and look darker than him, they also used something similar to Pan Creole 27 on Ava. Due to the darker make-up I had to wear in Pearl's act, I identified with both Ava and Lena in this instance. In fact, Lena and I had exactly the same color tone to our skin.

On top of having to buy the Max Factor make-up that Pearl wanted, and her favorite scent of perfume, we also had to pay for our own hotel accommodations. I did have a roommate, who was another lady they assigned me to room with. From my vantage point she was a much older woman who was one of the background singers, and she was also my chaperone on the tour. She was in her 50s. She was a nice African American woman, and we would get a room, and share it.

I had to buy my own food on the road as well, they didn't have any catering, and that was another added expense I didn't need. All of our transportation was on a tour bus. It wasn't a luxury tour bus like they have today. It had a toilet, but no bunks to sleep on, no lounge area, and no kitchenette. It was more like a converted school bus. Transportation seemed to be the only thing that we were not required to pay for, from my inadequate $125.00 a week salary.

In my eyes, Pearl Bailey had a huge persona. She was a genuine superstar, and she carried herself like she was fully aware of her fame. Her status in the business was very much like Queen Latifah. Pearl was a big star who regularly headlined at The Flamingo in Las Vegas. She was in movies alongside Bob Hope, George Sanders, Bing Crosby, Harry Belafonte, Natalie Wood, and many more. She worked in the top nightclubs in the country, and she would play in prestigious places like Carnegie Hall. She later starred in the show *Hello Dolly!* on Broadway. She was also one of the stars in the 1959 film version of *Porgy & Bess*, with Sidney Poitier, Dorothy Dandridge, and Sammy Davis Jr., directed by Otto Preminger.

My impression of Pearl, when I got to meet her in person, was that I found her to be a very forceful and "in command" kind of woman. She was also someone who had no problem speaking her own mind. If you did anything that she did not approve of, she would curse you out in a heartbeat.

There was a softer side of Pearl Bailey, that I occasionally got a glimpse of when we were all together. She wasn't mean all of the time. Once she invited me into her dressing room for a friendly visit, and some "girl talk." Another lady, who was her assistant, was also there. I can't remember the exact subjects we talked about, but I do remember having a couple of nice conversations with her where she let her hair down.

People who were in the general public absolutely loved her. But, people who are professionals, on the inside of show business, and who personally knew her, had a different point of view.

Looking back on my time with Pearl—in retrospect—I hoped that my partially negative feelings about her weren't shared by others. However, in time I spoke to several other people who were also aware of Pearl's ability to be a demanding diva. There were very few people I've run into who have said, "Oh, that Pearl Bailey, what a lovely person!"

I know that Queen Latifah portrayed Bessie Smith in an HBO TV film, but I have always said, "If anyone plays Pearl Bailey in a movie, it should be Queen Latifah." Not that Queen Latifah is anything like Pearl Bailey, but she has the attitude, the spirit, and everything. She could play the hell out of Pearl Bailey. I don't know why she hasn't done it. She has a reputation for really diving into her roles, and I think she is tailor made for that role!

Mary Wilson always maintained that Florence Ballard was another one who could have played Pearl Bailey. That is probably why Florence didn't get along with Berry Gordy. One thing about Berry—as we all know—he is a big control freak. It is either his way, or the highway. He is that kind of person, but it has worked out for him.

On the positive side of the coin, I have to say that Pearl did not spare on expenses. For example: the costumes for her show. We had dark-colored, custom-made and custom-fitted dresses to wear, and she ordered us these new blue hats from Beverly Hills. They were wide-brimmed blue "picture hats." At the time, those hats were extravagantly expensive at $50.00 apiece. Now in today's terms, that would be like buying $400.00 or $500.00 hats for the ladies in your cast.

I remember, Pearl saw me bending mine a little bit to make it fit better, and she went off on me: full force! "Do you know that I paid $50.00 apiece for those hats!" she yelled, cursing me out. "Don't you be bending those hats! You aren't accustomed to wearing anything that fine, are you?"

When I was like 13 or 14 years old, I remember buying two books on etiquette on my own, because I always felt that I needed to be prepared for high society. I still have those books to this day. One of them was the Amy Vanderbilt book on etiquette, and the other one was the Emily Post etiquette book. I read them both to prepare me for situations in life that I would surely encounter. And it has paid off.

While I was on tour with Pearl Bailey's revue in Cincinnati, we went to this very stylish Chinese restaurant. We were sitting at this long table because there were about ten of us in our party. So, I was looking at the menu, and people started ordering. As our first course we had our appetizers—egg rolls and coconut shrimp—that you would use your hands to eat. After that they brought out little bowls with warm water in it with a slice of lemon floating in the water, and placed them in front of each of us. I remember there was a white guy who was a professional, who was part of our party, and he said, "What is this? Tea? It doesn't look like tea, because it doesn't have any color to it. It is just warm water. Do we pick it up and drink it?"

Without missing a beat, I said to him, "Those are 'finger bowls' to clean your fingers!" I felt so proud of myself. Here I was at a table of all professional adults, but I was the only one at that table who knew what those little bowls with water were there for. As the only one who knew what a "finger bowl" was, I felt so proud of myself because I was already "up" on it. This was thanks to my books on etiquette—like Emily Post's best-selling guide! I knew they would come in handy!

When I think about it, had I signed with Berry Gordy and Motown Records, there wouldn't have been much about etiquette that their famed Miss Maxine Powell could teach me, that I didn't know already. Miss Powell was a Detroit legend who is famous for polishing acts like The Supremes, The Temptations, and Martha Reeves & The Vandellas, and preparing them to rub elbows with royalty. I was already ready for high society!

The first gig I was on with Pearl was in Cincinnati. We spent a week there. Then we went to New York City for a week at The Apollo Theater. This was my first time actually working at the world famous Apollo, and I was very excited to be playing on this legendary stage.

Pearl had a brother, whose name was Bill Bailey—no relationship to the famed blues song "Won't You Come Home Bill Bailey." This Bill Bailey was a very talented tap dancer, but he was also a heroin addict. We would play both matinee and evening shows at The Apollo. I remember one matinee when Bill came on-stage to do his featured dance number, and he was clearly stoned out of his mind. At one point he literally sat down on the stage because he was so high he couldn't stand up. If you have ever seen anyone on drugs on the street, sometimes they just collapse because they are so high. Bill was dancing one minute, and then he just collapsed onto one of the risers. Pearl had to come out and escort him off the stage.

Once he was off the stage, just like the old saying goes: "The show must go on!" And it did, just like the incident never happened.

I asked someone, "What is going on with him?"

"He's a junkie," was their reply.

I had never seen a heroin addict before I went to New York City. I had never been exposed to anything like that. Apparently he had gotten some heroin and injected it before he went on-stage. Sadly, he was obviously addicted and out-of-control.

Somehow, Pearl tolerated him and his druggy behavior. It was funny, she was very strict about maintaining professionalism at all times, but she put up with Bill's drug nonsense. Watching her at that particular matinee, dealing with her brother Bill, was the one instance I saw the compassionate side of Pearl. Usually, she was tough as nails!

Pearl's husband, Louis Bellson, was quite a handsome guy back then. Since it was his band we were performing with, he was on-stage throughout the whole show. I remember watching him and thinking, "How in the world could he have ended up married to Pearl Bailey?" She was such a ballsy chick. There was no question who was in control in that marriage. Louis was very mild-mannered. I guess certain men like to be bossed around by their women. They like a strong woman. That certainly describes Pearl's marriage to Louis Bellson.

I wasn't with Pearl for long. Much to my surprise, Pearl ended up firing me! After we left New York City, our next engagement was The Howard Theater in Washington D.C. We got to The Howard Theater, and that was when Pearl got sick, and the whole tour was forced to shut down while she recuperated. I don't remember exactly what it was that she came down with, a bad flu or something like that. However, she was sick enough to go to the hospital. She was there for about a week with an undisclosed condition.

She ended up firing me because she claimed, "You were the only member of the cast who didn't send me a 'get well' card!" I was astonished! And so was my mom! So, that was the end of that!

To have this happen was inconceivable to me. I was never that close to Pearl. She complained to me about the lack of a "get well" card, and then she fired me on the spot! I was in complete shock.

Looking back on my short time with her, I can honestly say that I didn't have a lot of one-on-one time with Pearl while I was part of the tour. When I think of her, I remember one occasion when I was in her dressing room, and just sitting there watching her looking in the mirror and doing her make-up. It was a brief run with her, but that is my Pearl Bailey story.

After that tour with Pearl Bailey, I returned to Detroit. That same year, I had my tonsils out. I was still 17 years old at the time, and I remember that I was worried it would change my voice. But it fortunately didn't. Before that I was always getting some sort of cold, or a sore throat. It had gotten to the point where my doctor said, "Maybe it would be wise to just get your tonsils out once and for all." So I did, and fortunately it did not alter my speaking or singing voice at all.

On September 19, 1960 I turned 18 years old, and I decided that I would move to New York City. I felt like I needed to go there to find better show business opportunities. I had walked away from the Berry Gordy situation, I turned down Duke Ellington's contract, I had toured with and been fired by Pearl Bailey. I had some first class experience under my belt, and I was ready for the big time. I had gone about as far as I could go in my hometown of Detroit. It was time for more, and I felt that moving to Manhattan offered me more opportunities for career advancement. New York City: here I come!

CHAPTER THREE

"New York City"

It was 1961, and it was time to try my wings. If I was going to become a nightclub jazz singer, a Broadway performer, a recording artist, or whatever I set my sights on, New York City was the place to go. So I packed my bags, and my parents drove me to Willow Run Airport in Detroit.

I remember sitting at the boarding gate at the airport with my parents. Just a few seats down was a lady who introduced herself to me, because she recognized me. Her name was Beverly Davenport. Beverly was a Detroiter, who had recently moved to New York City. She knew of my reputation having seen me on Detroit television shows and local talent shows.

She was warm, friendly and she spoke very well. After she introduced herself she asked me, "Why are you going to New York?"

I replied, "I am going there to see what I can accomplish in New York as far as my show business career is concerned."

She asked, "Where are you going to stay?"

"The YWCA in Manhattan," I said.

She then replied, "I have a small apartment on 103rd Street between Broadway and Amsterdam Avenue. Maybe you could stay with me and we could split the rent and utilities?"

My parents were listening to our conversation, and they were a little apprehensive at first, but Beverly seemed like a well-groomed Christian woman. She was just 21 herself, and she worked for Pacific Bell telephone company in New York. Also, we noticed, Beverly had a limp. She later explained to me that she had Polio as a child, and her hip was somehow deformed. It caused her to walk like one leg was longer than the other. Beverly was an attractive woman, with a lovely brown complexion.

It sounded like a great opportunity to live with Beverly, and a better economical situation. So, that is where I went. She had a studio apartment with two twin beds, a kitchen and a very small bathroom. In today's terms you would call it a "studio with kitchen." There was very little closet space, so I just had to make do with what there was. In New York City, space is so limited that the apartments are tiny.

I stayed with Beverly for my first six months as a Manhattanite. It was a tiny New York studio apartment on the first floor. She had one little TV, and at that time there were only three channels we could get: 2, 4, and 7. The TV had a little antenna that we had to wrap aluminum foil around to improve the poor reception. As a result, I wanted to go out and explore the city. We used to go downtown in the West 40s to a little place called The Champagne Colony. It was a piano bar that was located downstairs off the street. The Champagne Colony was sort of a gathering spot for people in show business, and the "locals." There was a piano player there, and sometimes people would get up and sing. It was like an "open mic" situation and you would see people like Johnny Nash, and many unknowns too. That is where I met Johnny Nash, and a man by the name of Kent Drake. Kent was a singer, and he was a Johnny Mathis look-alike, only he was taller and very masculine. He was "straight," and boy was he "straight!" Kent Drake and I became friends, and we had an on-and-off affair for a couple of years.

After living with Beverly Davenport for six months, I began to feel a bit cramped. It was busy, noisy and the neighborhood was not all that safe. At the time I had a Wollensak reel-to-reel tape recorder that I brought with me to New York, and somebody broke into the apartment and stole it. That was when I decided it wasn't that safe staying there. One night I met a girl around my age by the name of Carol Preston who used to hang out at The Champagne Colony as well.

There were so many talented people I met that first year in Manhattan. The Champagne Colony is also where I first met the writer Luther Dixon. Luther had written and produced several hits for singers on the Scepter Records and the Wand Records label like The Shirelles and The Chiffons. Scepter Records was founded and run by a woman by the name of Florence Greenburg. Also signed to that label was the legendary Dionne Warwick.

Florence was so well-respected in the business, that in 2011 there was a Broadway show called *Baby It's You*, and it was written about Florence Greenburg and her amazing life and career. And, Luther Dixon was a prominent character in that musical.

The musical director of *Baby It's You* on Broadway was Rahn Coleman. Rahn has also been my musical director and pianist off-and-on for the last 35 years.

Luther was attracted to me, and wanted to get me signed to the Scepter label. However, because of his relationship to Florence—they were having an affair—he was afraid she would be jealous of me.

Luther was quite a nice guy and he gave me my first autumn-colored mink stole. When I told my mother about it, she said, "He gave you a mink stole, he must want to marry you!"

I said to her, "Just because a man gives you a mink stole, that doesn't mean you have to marry him, or that he wants to marry you!" So, marriage to Luther was never brought up again.

Carol Preston was a registered nurse, African American, and very attractive. She was fair skinned, had freckles, and she was very petite. Carol had an upbeat personality, was very smart, and kind-hearted. She came from Springfield, Massachusetts. She also liked to go out and have a good time going to the clubs and the jazz joints around town. Sometimes we would stay out all night and get in at 4:00 or 5:00 in the morning. Carol would sleep a couple of hours, get up, get dressed, and go to work. I don't know how she did it on so little sleep.

As a nurse, Carol worked at Manhattan General Hospital, and she treated drug addicts. Occasionally she would tell me the names of famous musicians who were on drugs, who were her patients, and she would treat them with methadone. I was fascinated and shocked to hear how many talented musicians were throwing their lives away on drugs. This list included a jazz and blues singer by the name of Esther Phillips. She was big in the '60s and '70s, and she had such a unique voice, she was a true song stylist. Years later she had bought a house in the LA neighborhood called Mt. Olympus. When Esther passed away in 1984, I sang at her funeral service in Los Angeles.

Having known Carol for several months, one night at The Champagne Colony she said to me, "I am getting ready to move to an apartment at Second Avenue and 33rd Street. Maybe you could be my roommate. Would you be interested in that?"

"Yes," I replied. And, so Carol became my next roommate.

Since Beverly's apartment was more of a studio, and Carol's was a one-bedroom, it was seriously like "moving up" in accommodations—but not that much. It was however, a third floor walk-up. I remember lugging my suitcases up those three flights of stairs. It wasn't easy, especially if you had groceries or other packages. Back then, I was 19 and 20 years old, so that was never a problem.

Living at East 33rd Street and Second Avenue seemed like a safer neighborhood to me. It was also very conveniently located. It was easy for me to get around town from that neighborhood. I would take a bus or a taxi to get over to the West Side of Manhattan, when

I went to see a talent agent, or to go to the theater district.

Carol and I liked to go to this restaurant on West 48th Street, called Sapphires. It was located between Broadway and Eighth Avenue. The owner was an African American man by the name of Danny Simms. Danny was infamous at the time. He was not only a restaurateur, but he was also into real estate, and he was *also* known in some circles as a pimp. Danny had a reputation of hanging out with Italian mobsters, but he legitimately owned that restaurant. Not many black men owned their own businesses in midtown Manhattan back then, but he was one of them.

A lot of black and white entertainers would come to Sapphires after hours, or during the evening. I would be with my roommate, Carol, and we would go there to get a bite to eat, or just to hang out. It was a happening place.

One night Carol and I decided to go to Sapphires for a late night snack, after a little bit of "club hopping." Danny knew I was an aspiring singer, and that I was trying to get my career going. This particular night Danny came over to me, and he said, "Freda, I want you to meet this guy who is sitting over there. His name is Quincy Jones, and he is appearing at Basin Street East, with his big band, and he is going places. I think he is a person you ought to know. Let me take you over to meet him."

So, he brought me over to where Quincy's table was. Quincy then invited me to join his table. He was there with a guy by the name of Jerome Richardson. Jerome was a saxophone player in Quincy's big band. Quincy and I got to talking, and one thing led to another.

Quincy then invited me to go see his show the following night at Basin Street East. So I did that, and then afterwards he took me to a restaurant called The Brasserie on East 53rd Street off Park Avenue. That was back when The Brasserie was *THE* high-stepping place to go late at night, after the theater, or after the show. You had to walk down seven or eight stairs into the restaurant. The dining room was one big open space, and the way it was designed, everybody who was there could see you making an entrance. At the time the clientele was predominantly all Caucasian, and the women wore their sables, their chinchillas, and their minks. That was the time when women sported their diamonds and all of their finery.

We got our table, and we sat down. I recall that Quincy ordered *Steak Tartare*, and he explained to me, "Now remember, this is raw beef, taste it and see if you like it." I tasted it, I liked it, and I've been eating it ever since.

If you never have had *Steak Tartare*, it isn't just raw beef. It is ground raw sirloin beef, which also has diced shallots, capers, olive oil, one raw egg, Worcestershire sauce, Kosher sea salt, some finely chopped Italian parsley, freshly grated lemon zest, and fresh ground black pepper. You wouldn't see *Steak Tartare* in anything less than a Five Star restaurant that has high quality standards.

In later years Quincy wrote an entire page of his autobiography about me. He was definitely one of the loves of my life. He was so young and handsome. Quincy was quite a looker back then. He was just as cute as he could be.

My first intimate rendezvous with Quincy Jones was at the apartment which I shared with my roommate Carol. After that, there were other intimate rendezvous in different places, hotel rooms and such.

Quincy would take me out to all of these great music clubs around town. Finally, one night he heard me sing, because we went to a club where the members of the audience were encouraged to get up on-stage and sing with the band. It was a situation where they saw me with Quincy, and they knew I was a singer. The band leader said, "Freda, come up and sing with us."

Quincy said, "Yeah, get up there, I want to hear you sing." After I sang the song "If I Were a Bell," from the Broadway musical *Guys and Dolls*, Quincy was immediately impressed with my vocals.

In Quincy's autobiography he wrote about me, "I went to my office, finished some work, and made a call to a gorgeous honey with not a brick out of place named Freda Payne...I met this pound cake at Danny Simms' club in New York and we'd fallen in love...she was a really talented singer...and [she] killed it on 'If I Were a Bell.'" (1)

One of the people who helped me out in the early days of my career was a man by the name of Carl Carruthers. He had heard me singing when I was doing a club date up in Harlem, at the nightclub called The Baby Grand.

Carl had worked with Nat King Cole as his road manager and valet. He heard me sing one night at The Champagne Colony and was impressed. He invited me to The Copacabana one night to see and meet Nat King Cole. Carl was a person who took an interest in me and my career. He told me that I needed to get an agent. So, he took me to G.A.C., which was one of the biggest booking agencies in the business, along with William Morris, and M.C.A.

Carl introduced me to Sidney Bernstein and he came to hear me sing one night. I did a showcase performance at a small club in Greenwich Village, and after he heard me, he was immediately impressed with me and my voice. I ended up getting signed to G.A.C. by Sidney Bernstein. It was Sidney who was the agent that brought The Beatles over to America for the first time, and got them booked on *The Ed Sullivan Show*.

It was Sidney Bernstein who got me signed to my first recording deal, at ABC / Paramount Records. The president of ABC / Paramount was a man by the name of Sam Clark. My first single was a Bossa Nova recording called "Slightly Out of Tune," which had been a hit for Stan Getz, originally called "Desefinado." Sid Feller was the producer of that song, and it was released as a 45 rpm single in 1962. It was released as "(Desefinado) Slightly Out Of Tune" with "He Who Laughs Last" on the flip side. "He Who Laughs Last" was written by Carole King, who at the time was an aspiring songwriter.

"Slightly Out of Tune" was a very popular song back then, and was recorded by several established singers, including Ella Fitzgerald. Although the single did not become a huge hit for me, it received radio play, and this was to lead to my first album deal.

At the time I was still taking dance classes as I felt that I needed an outlet for exercise, so I went to Luigi's Dance Studio on Broadway, and I took Modern Jazz classes. Also, I took Afro-Cuban classes with dancer Savilla Forte. Savilla was a former Katherine Dunham dancer, and she had a studio located on West 44th Street and Seventh Avenue. Actress Nichelle Nichols who is known for her 1960s TV fame, was also a participant in that Afro-Cuban class. It was a couple of years later that she was cast, along with William Shatner and Leonard Nimoy, on TV's *Star Trek*. That is where she found stardom playing the role of Uhura. Back then she was an aspiring entertainer like me, although she was ten years older than me.

I then proceeded to land several singing jobs including one at The Baby Grand Club up in Harlem. Nipsey Russell was the in-house comedian and the on-stage host for the club. He was there almost all of the time. That particular club was Nipsey's mainstay when he was not doing other gigs.

After "(Desefinado) Slightly Out of Tune" was released, that was when the company decided to put me on their jazz label, called Impulse Records. It was comparable with being on Blue Note, or on Verve Records—pure jazz. Impulse was a label that had mainly jazz musicians signed to it like John Coltrane, Duke Ellington, McCoy Tyner, Sonny Rollins, and many more heavyweights of the jazz world.

My debut album was called *After The Lights Go Down Low and Much More!!!*, and it was 100% jazz. Because this was a jazz label, the musicians who were on my debut album were Ernie Royal, Phil Woods, Seldon Powell, Zoot Sims, and Hank Jones on piano. Hank was also Ella Fitzgerald's piano player. Several of these musicians were Count Basie's prime players in his orchestra, including Ernie Royal and Phil Woods. Side One of my debut album was "big band" jazz, and Side Two was me with a jazz trio.

The album's arranger and conductor was Manny Albam, and the producer was Bob Thiele. The entire album was recorded on September 17, 18, and 19, 1963. The final recording session on the 19th of September was actually on my 21st birthday. What a great 21st birthday present that was!

On the back of the album, the liner notes described me as being, "Freda Payne—a young and vibrant personality—a singer with a feeling for ballads and rhythm songs. Here is Freda's first album—a collection of familiar songs and new music composed by the jazz *avant-garde* musicians. Freda—enhanced by the talented arranger Manny Albam—displays a unique and personal vocal style." (2)

One of the tracks was called "Blue Piano," and it was composed by Duke Ellington, Bob Fields and two others. Amongst the other songs on the album were jazz standards including "'Round Midnight" by Thelonious Monk, and "I Cried For You." I was now referred to as "recording artist Freda Payne." I loved it!

Several months after my album was released, Quincy called me to say, "I would like to book you on a show at The Apollo Theater in Harlem." It was a whole staged revue that had Billy Eckstine head-lining along with The Quincy Jones All-Star Orchestra, comedian Redd Foxx, the dance duo Honey Coles & Cholly Atkins, and I was the female vocalist on the bill. Quincy gave me arrangements he had already done for other artists like Ray Charles, Sarah Vaughn, and Dinah Washington. Some of the arrangements were penned by Billy Byers. Of course I accepted this offer and it really turned out to be a great show. We were booked for a week at The Apollo, followed by a weeklong engagement in Chicago at The Regal Theater.

With regard to the songs that Quincy wanted me to do, I was surprised when he said to me, "I want you to do this song by The Supremes called 'Where Did Our Love Go.'"

And I said, "Well, why do you want me to do that song? It's an R&B song."

He replied, "Because that song is a Number One hit."

So he had Billy Byers do an arrangement of the song for me. At the time I was doing jazz songs in the show like "One Mint Julep" and "Secret Love." The song "One Mint Julep" he had arranged for Ray Charles and Sarah Vaughn, and "Secret Love" he had arranged for Dinah Washington. I also performed "Teach Me Tonight," which was also Dinah's arrangement.

It felt so strange for me to sing a pop song like "Where Did Our Love Go." Although I was apprehensive, he was insistent that I do it. So I did. Quincy was right, the audience immediately recognized the song and they loved the way I sang it.

It was so exciting working with Quincy. I had fallen in love with him. However, there was a huge "catch" to this situation. I knew it was all for naught, as he was a married man at the time, with a young daughter. I just felt that I was one of the links on his chain of women. It reminds me of Aretha Franklin's song "Chain of Fools." Little did I know, he was really in love with me, too. But, that is water under the bridge.

It's ironic that Quincy now has a documentary on his life that has been airing on Netflix, and I was never mentioned at all in the film. The only place I was shown, was a quick shot of my face, when it spoke about the women in his life. I was quite insulted by that. They should have mentioned that I was with him at The Apollo, *and* I am the only one still alive!

During this era, I worked at a supper club in Brooklyn, called Club Elegante. It was located on Ocean Parkway, and was owned and operated by Joe Scandore. He featured a revue as part of the supper club entertainment. The first time I worked there was with the comedian Timmy Rogers, and The Four Tops. They still had not yet been discovered by Berry Gordy for Motown. There was also a jazz dance act called Norma Miller & Her Jazz Men.

By the way, Norma Miller was still around at the age of 99. PBS-TV has featured her in a documentary about The Savoy Ballroom. She now resides in Florida.

The act at Club Elegante was Norma with four guys. Norma would enter the stage like a showgirl with a long train of ostrich feathers. The Jazz Men were her chorus boys. It was a really good flashy dance act. I loved watching them. There were also two tall Vegas-style showgirls with chocolate brown complexions, who were gorgeous twins.

Then I was the featured chanteuse on the bill. I wore beautiful evening gowns, and I sang standards like "The Second Time Around" and "He's Got The Whole World In His Hands." I also sang several contemporary songs including "More," "King of the Road," "You're Nobody 'Til Somebody Loves You," and "Somewhere" from *West Side Story*. Because of my performances at Club Elegante, Joe Scandore wanted to manage me and my career. He also managed many other artists at the same time including comedians Pat Cooper, Pat Henry, Don Rickles, and Totie Fields.

Because of Joe Scandore, I started getting booked to sing on late night television's *The Tonight Show*, with Johnny Carson. In fact, I was booked on *The Tonight Show* on several different occasions, as well as *The Merv Griffin Show*. One of the *Tonight Show* appearances I did was with Harry Belafonte who was playing "guest host" while Johnny Carson was on vacation. I was invited to be one of the show's guests that week. Dionne Warwick and Petula Clark were also guests that same week. The episode I was on included Paul Newman, Dr. Martin Luther King Jr., folk singer Leon Bibb, ventriloquist act Aaron & Freddy, and comedian Nipsey Russell. Recently, that week of shows hosted by Harry Belafonte were edited together as a documentary called, *The Sit-In: Harry Belafonte Hosts The Tonight Show* (2020).

Joe put me into another one of his revues, also featuring The Four Tops, but this time around the headlining comedian was Flip Wilson, who was relatively unknown at the time. He was just starting out in the business.

Around this time I was booked to work with a revue called *Larry Steel's Smart Affairs*. Larry Steel was an entrepreneur and producer from Chicago. The revue was booked in nightclubs across the country, and it featured chorus girls who were very elegant as well as great dancers. Their lead dance captain and choreographer was a man by the name of Lon Fontaine.

Also, while I was performing at the club, the *Larry Steel's Smart Affairs* show would feature a headliner who would draw a crowd, such as Sammy Davis Jr., Sam Cooke, or Marvin Gaye. There would always be a comedian like Slappy White, or George Kirby, or Timmy Rogers, included on the bill.

During the Marvin Gaye engagement, there was a slight rift between Marvin and me. At the time I had a solo spot where I sang three songs. One of them was "Who Can I Turn To (When Nobody Needs Me)."

In the show, Marvin did a medley of standards, and one of the songs in the medley was that same song. His musical director, Maurice King, came up to me and said, "I want you to drop 'Who Can I Turn To' from your spot. You can find another song to do, as Marvin sings it as part of his medley."

I was not at all happy to hear this. I only had three songs, and I had paid for musical arrangements for them, and I wasn't about to drop it from my part of the show. So, I went to Marvin to complain about this suggestion I drop my featured ballad.

"I don't know if you noticed," he said to me, "but I sing a portion of 'Who Can I Turn To' in my medley. I think you should do another song."

"But Marvin," I argued, "that song is part of my act, and I am going to continue to do it."

Marvin looked at me, and dropped the dispute. It wasn't like he was mad at me, but I wasn't going to budge from my position. In the long run, I continued to sing the whole song, while Marvin did a couple of lines of "Who Can I Turn To" in his medley.

Because I stood my ground about the song, I felt that Marvin admired me for standing up to him and not dropping the song. In later years, after "Band of Gold" became a hit and I became a star, a friend of mine by the name of Douglas Young, told me that Marvin admired me and my singing so much that he considered doing a duet recording with me. Although it never transpired, it was flattering to know that Marvin Gaye thought of me in that light.

Larry booked me on several of his shows during this period. He had a standing appearance during the summertime in Atlantic City, New Jersey at a nightclub called The Club Harlem, which was located at 32 Kentucky Avenue. Leroy "Pops" Williams was the owner of the club. He was an older man at the time, probably in his early 80s and everyone just called him "Pops." This was around 1964. This was long before gambling came along in Atlantic City.

The Club Harlem was quite well known and it was well attended during the summer months. If you were in Atlantic City during those years, you certainly would have gone to The Club Harlem for the shows. They had a lounge in the front of the club with a wrap-around bar, and it featured a quartet that really was jammin' until 4:00 in the morning. The keyboard player played on an organ, and it was a happening place. A big band was in the showroom with 12 - 14 players, and that band was led by Johnny Lynch. You had to walk through the lounge to get to the showroom in the back.

In the main showroom was "a floor show," and that was where I was featured. We did two shows a night, and sometimes three shows on the weekends. On Saturday night into Sunday morning there was a breakfast show that started at 6:00 in the morning! The Club

Harlem was especially well-known for this well-attended breakfast show, and we always drew a crowd. We drank countless cups of coffee to stay awake. By the time we were done with that breakfast show, it would be daylight when we would exit the club, and boy were we ever beat! But the crowds were great, so it was a lot of fun.

When we had our closing night for the season, we would "bury" the show. That was where everybody would change places, and perform in someone else's spot. It was something that was done back in those days. I once performed in Lola Falana's spot, as her—costume and all! Lola, back then, was a chorus girl, just getting started in the business. And one of the male dancers performed as me, in my own gown, and it was Donald Fontaine—no relationship to Lon Fontaine by the way.

Lon Fontaine was the lead dancer for the troupe, and he choreographed most of the routines for the revue. Lon did other shows and he later choreographed acts for many other entertainers, including The Temptations, and Gladys Knight & The Pips. Lon and I became very good friends, and we went on to work together when he choreographed my act. In 1970 after having my first big hit, "Band of Gold," I performed that act at The Venetian Room in The Fairmont Hotel in San Francisco. That same year I also did it at a club called P.J.'s, which was a nightclub located in West Hollywood. My act, which I performed at all of these engagements, was choreographed by Lon. But, Lon worked mainly in nightclubs and stage shows, and he got his big start with Larry Steel's revue. Lon lived in Los Angeles. Years later, he moved to New York, where he lived until his death.

Unique to The Club Harlem was something that was at every table. Instead of clapping for the acts, there were these little wooden "knockers." Each table had a little stick with a ball on the end of it, and the patrons would knock on the tables with these little mallets instead of applauding with their hands. The knockers had handles that were about four or five inches long. It wasn't mandatory to use the knockers, but these little mallets were used to favorably acknowledge the act. This was something unique and charming from an age-gone-by. The Flame Show Bar in Detroit used knockers as well.

I performed at The Flame Show Bar myself in 1962, and this was when the heavyweight champion Joe Louis was doing a comedy act. I was booked there by Leonard Reed who was a promoter from New York, and he used to be part of a tap dance act called Shim Sham Shimmy.

In 1971 I came back to Atlantic City to headline at Club Harlem for a couple of nights. This time around I wasn't a member of a revue, by then I was an established singing star with hit records. It was fun to be there and reminisce. Although The Club Harlem closed in 1986, it is still fondly remembered to this day.

When I was 21 years old, I went to an audition in New York, at The Latin Quarter nightclub, on Broadway. The Latin Quarter was owned by Lou Walters, the father of TV commentator Barbara Walters. I went to this audition on a dare. The audition was to be one of the dancers at The Latin Quarter. I won the audition, and they offered me the job.

However, I ended up turning them down. I said, "I just wanted to see if I could dance well enough to get it." They wanted me, but I just didn't want to do it. I loved singing night-after-night, but I wasn't so sure I would enjoy dancing in a chorus line night-after-night. After that I decided to put my dancing aspirations behind me, and concentrate on being a singer instead.

In 1963 I was booked to perform at The Playboy Club in Chicago. I was the opening act for comedian Don Adams. Don later went on to star in his own hit comedy TV series, the "secret agent" spoof *Get Smart*. I recall that he was very personable on-stage, but I found him not to be very friendly towards me backstage. I remember sitting in the Green Room with him, and he barely spoke to me. It is funny how some comedians are the same warm and friendly people they appear to be on-stage, while others are completely different on a one-to-one basis. Don Adams was one of those from the latter category.

In the early '60s, I was in the famous nightclub Mister Kelly's for the first time. It was one of my off nights from singing at The Playboy Club. Mister Kelly's was the club where big headliners like Sarah Vaughan, Woody Allen, Ella Fitzgerald, and Eartha Kitt would perform in Chicago.

That particular evening I said to myself, "I am going to go to Mister Kelly's to see what this new girl singer, Barbra Streisand, is doing." She was working with a trio: a piano, bass, and drums. She was becoming very popular as "the new kid on the block," and people were taking notice. I remember walking down the street, and going to the club by myself to check out her act. I wanted to see and hear this new singer that everyone was talking about. And, it was walking distance from The Playboy Club where I was performing, which was also Hugh Hefner's residence.

When I saw Barbra Streisand, and heard her sing, I said to myself, "Wow! She's really got a great voice!" It was heavenly.

Mister Kelly's wasn't a really big place, but it was the premiere nightclub to appear at in the Windy City. Streisand wasn't a big star yet when she was at Mister Kelly's in 1963, but right after that she went on to play at The Rivera Hotel in Las Vegas where she shared the bill with Liberace. Word-of-mouth began to spread that she was an amazing talent to watch and a rising star. When I saw her, she was on her meteoric rise to the top. Not long after that engagement at Mister Kelly's her career really exploded. It was the following year, in 1964, when she starred on Broadway in *Funny Girl*, and after she finished that play she was a bona fide superstar.

I remember that one critic wrote about her at the beginning and pointed out that she was not the prettiest girl, and she had that distinctive nose of hers. However, claimed the reviewer, "once she opened her mouth and began to sing, diamonds and pearls came out." Her singing voice was absolutely flawless. She had immaculate control of her voice, and her intonation and pitch were perfect.

My mother and I went to see Barbra Streisand on Broadway in *Funny Girl* in 1964, and her acting and vocals were nothing short of amazing. She was perfectly cast as the character she played, vaudeville star Fannie Brice, and in my eyes she not only fulfilled my expectations, she exceeded them. You have to be incredibly good to be on Broadway, and Streisand fulfilled that assignment with flying colors.

While on Broadway, Barbra's understudy was Lainie Kazan, and that launched her singing and acting career as well. That was the beginning of Lainie's fame, and that was when she started to take off too. *Funny Girl* was such a successful show on Broadway, Barbra went on to reprise her role in the West End production of it in London in 1966. After that, she starred in the movie version of the musical along with Omar Sharif.

In November of 1963 I was booked to perform with Lionel Hampton and his band, at The Riviera Hotel & Casino in Las Vegas. Also on the bill with me were the world-famous Nicholas Brothers.

I will never forget November 22, 1963, because that was the day President John F. Kennedy was shot in Dallas, Texas. It occurred at 10:30 in the morning Las Vegas time. I had just gotten up, and I turned on my TV to the tragic news. I was staying at a motel right off the Strip, called Bali Hai. The Nicholas Brothers stayed there, as well as trumpet player Maynard Ferguson. Maynard was a well known trumpet player, who had his own big band. As I recall, he was performing at The Flamingo Hotel & Casino, in the lounge.

I worked with Lionel Hampton on two separate occasions. They had me there for the first run, and then the following year they called me back again. When "Hamp" worked in Vegas it was usually for a two or three week run.

Lionel was an adorable, very likeable, very kind, sweet man. I really enjoyed working with him. His wife, Gladys, was always with him. She was unquestionably "the boss" in that marriage. She was one of those really strong ladies who ran the show. Gladys actually managed Lionel, and he had an agent by the name of Joe Glazer, who was my agent at the time as well. That was the connection which made that booking happen. Joe owned A.B.C. booking agency, and another agent there was a man whose name was Oscar Cohen. Oscar used to book me as well. Sometimes Oscar was referred to as "Joe Glazer's son," but to this day, I don't know if that was really true. I think he was an adopted son.

Back then they would have major stars performing in the lounges in the Vegas hotels. Sarah Vaughn would be singing in the lounge. Della Reese, and Louis Prima & Keely Smith would be singing in the lounges, too. It was only acts who had reached a certain plateau, who would be in the big showrooms, such as Lena Horne and Pearl Bailey. Lena would not have played in the lounge, she would have been in the main showroom at The Sands. Frank Sinatra would have been in the main showroom at The Sands as well, and Joey Bishop, Dean Martin, Sammy Davis Jr., and people of that major Hollywood kind of stature.

There were many people who would play in the big room at The Riviera. Edie Adams was a big draw back then. She was in movies, like *It's a Mad, Mad, Mad, Mad World*, and she was the widow of comedian / actor Ernie Kovacs. Edie was a headliner, and she had an elaborate Las Vegas act with dancers and lots of glitz and feathers. I got to know her back then, and she was a really nice lady. She would invite me up to her suite for a glass of champagne, and she was delightful.

I used to go and see the other shows in town such as *The Follies-Bergère* at Tropicana Hotel & Casino, and *Casino de Paris* was at The Dunes—which is now long-gone. These shows featured bare-breasted showgirls, tumbling acts, and magicians. The Stardust Hotel had their own version of the French themed stage show called *Viva La Paris*. They would all have partially nude showgirls who would wear high headdresses towering over their heads like they were ten feet tall. They looked like elegant chandeliers in motion, moving in coordination to musical accompaniment. The really tall showgirls were called "horses" back then. They were more like walking mannequins. The other chorus girls were the real dancers.

I had met blues and jazz singer Dinah Washington on several different occasions, including at The Apollo Theater with Quincy Jones. One of the first times I met her was at The Rivera Hotel, and I was working with Lionel Hampton. She had come to see the show. Dinah had been a singer featured with The Lionel Hampton Band back in the 1950s, so she was well-acquainted with Lionel and the band. What happened was that I was arriving at the hotel, and I was walking through the casino, towards the lounge to get to my dressing room when I encountered Dinah. At that time, Lionel had a valet by the name of Leo. Leo was a nice guy, a gay man who was very sweet to me. We became great friends.

When I saw Dinah Washington, she was standing outside the lounge of the casino. Dinah was talking with Leo, and I just walked up to him and said, "Hi."

Leo spoke up and said, "Dinah, this is Freda Payne. She is working on the show with us."

Dinah narrowed her eyes and looked at me, and in a most accusatory tone said, "Freda Payne! What is your phone number doing in my husband's phone book?"

I looked at her in horror and disbelief. Dinah Washington was like that. She took no prisoners. You were either with her or against her. She was also known to pick a fight with men!

I thought to myself, "Lord! Is this woman going to pick a fight with me right here in the casino?" What was I going to say to her? Her husband was football player Dick "Nightrain" Lane who played for the Detroit Lions. I had given my number to him because he said he knew of some people who could help me in my career. He had never "hit" on me; he was just a nice person.

Well, Leo jumped in and tried to calm her down by saying, "Dinah, Freda is not like that. She is a nice girl. I am sure you are blowing this out of proportion."

Then she sort of backed off. While this was transpiring, I was thinking to myself, "If this woman takes a swing at me, I am going to kick her ass!" I might be a lady, but I am from Detroit, and I am tough!

I became friendly with the songwriter / arranger Artie Butler. Artie was the musical arranger of such big songs as The Shangri-La's "Leader of the Pack" and Neil Diamond's "Solitary Man." He is also the writer of the music for the song "Here's To Life," along with Phyllis Molinary.

Artie had some great stories about Dinah Washington. He told me that he was once in a recording session with Dinah, and they were there with a full band and strings. It was in the summertime, so Artie had on a pair of pink slacks. According to him, Dinah stopped the session and said, "Listen, if you are gonna play on my session, you had better take off those damn pink slacks! I don't want no man wearing no pink slacks in my session!"

The next time I encountered Dinah Washington was just weeks before she passed. That was again in Las Vegas, at The Thunderbird Hotel & Casino. I worked there with *The Larry Steele Revue*. We had just closed the show, and Dinah was the next act to appear at The Thunderbird, so I decided to stay over, just so I could see her perform.

I was watching Dinah's show with a lady by the name of Mokihana, she was Hawaiian. She was a large woman, and she sang at the hotel as well. She was playing the role of Bloody Mary in the big room of The Thunderbird Hotel in the musical *South Pacific*. We became friends, and she and I, and one of our male friends went to see Dinah's show together.

After the show we went over to see Dinah and to say "hi" to her. She was cordial to me this time. She also knew Mokihana, so she must have figured if I was with her I was "cool" and presented no threat to her.

So this time around, Dinah presented a super friendly side of herself, and she said, "Why don't you come over to my bungalow, and hang out for a minute."

She was staying on the premises at that time, and she had her own private bungalow. We walked outside to her bungalow. Dinah changed into some lounge clothes, and she sat in the middle of her bed and rolled a joint. I smoked pot and got high with Dinah Washington that evening. It was just "us girls," sittin' and talkin' shit, and smokin' pot!

After that trip to Vegas, I returned to my Mom's house in Detroit and I stayed for a while. Then I went back to New York, and then returned to Detroit. I was there when the news came that Dinah Washington had died. It was December 14, 1963. I went to the funeral home where her body was on view to the public, and I went to pay my last respects to a great jazz and blues singer.

I got in line, just like everyone else who was there that day. There she was in her casket. She had on a mink stole, and they had a little bejeweled tiara on her head, because she was known as "The Queen of The Blues."

Dinah's passing was officially classified as being an accidental death. She was taking diet pills or some sort of other prescription where you were not supposed to have alcohol with it. Apparently she had a couple of shots of vodka while on the pills, and it killed her.

Dinah had finally found the man she loved. Her career was at an all-time high, she looked great, and she was happy. How tragic that she passed away at such a peak in her career and life. She was only 39 years old at the time.

When I got back to New York City, it was to a new residence. During this period I moved to the YWCA The YWCA was located on 51st Street and Eighth Avenue, kitty-corner and down the street was Madison Square Garden. It was later relocated to 33rd Street and Seventh Avenue.

That was an adventure staying at the YWCA, and it was actually a lot of fun. I met a lot of interesting people there. When I think about it, I remember the cafeteria there. You didn't have to be staying there to eat at the cafeteria. There was a guy by the name of Peter LaSally, who became one of the executives who worked on *The Tonight Show*, right after that. Also, while I was staying at the YWCA, The Alvin Ailey Dance Company was in residence on the second floor of the building. That was where he held his classes, and they had their rehearsals there.

One of Alvin Ailey's lead dancers was a man by the name of James Truett. I took classes in Modern Dancing with him, in the Alvin Ailey style. I remember one of the dancers who was in the class with me was Altovise Gore, who later married Sammy Davis Jr.

While I was living at the YWCA I got a booking to perform at The Concord Hotel in the Catskill Mountains. It was a resort in northern New York State, and in the winter they had skiing. I worked on the same show as O.C. Smith. It turned out that O.C. Smith and I became acquaintances, nothing personal, we were just good friends. He called me and asked me if I wanted to perform with him at The Concord Hotel in the Catskills. It was the middle of the winter at the time, and I gladly accepted the invitation. When O.C. picked me up at the YWCA to drive to The Concord Hotel, it was in his little red Volkswagen bug. We drove up to The Catskills in the snow.

O.C. and I were performing in the lounge, and in the main room were comedians Steve Rossi and Marty Allen (who performed as Rossi & Allen), and their opening act was singer Linda Hopkins.

This was years before O.C. scored his big hits "Honey (I Miss You)" and "Little Green Apples."

In the main room was where Linda Hopkins was appearing. This was the first time that I was introduced to her, and we became life-long friends. She later starred in the 1985 Broadway musical *Black and Blue*, and she received a Tony Award nomination for it. Ruth Brown won the Tony Award for her role in that same show, which started a bitter rivalry between the two of them. Also, I later worked with Linda in a touring company of the Broadway musical *Ain't Misbehavin'* in the 1980s. Over the years Linda and I have become very close friends.

This trip to the Catskills was the very first time I was introduced to snow skiing. I took some lessons from a ski instructor who came from Switzerland. He was Swiss / German. I did have a little "flirtation" with the slender, blue-eyed, ruggedly handsome ski instructor. However, after ski season ended he went back to Switzerland. We exchanged letters for a few months, and then it tapered off.

I went to Los Angeles in 1964 because I was booked at a club, with Don Rickles who was the headliner, called Slate Brothers Club, which was actually owned by the two Slate brothers. It was located on La Cienega Boulevard, a couple of blocks south of Santa Monica Boulevard, on the west side of the street.

While I was there, *The Tonight Show* with Johnny Carson had left New York City for a two week series of shows in Los Angeles. They were trying out a West Coast perspective. For that stint, I was booked to perform on the show for the first week and then again for the second week of *The Tonight Show*. The national exposure was great for me, to say the least. On this particular night the other acts who were booked on the show included: Zsa Zsa Gabor, comedian Allen Sherman, Howard Duff, Ida Lupino, and Marlon Brando. It was a big thrill to be there with all of these bona fide Hollywood stars. We would tape *The Tonight Show* in the afternoon, and then I would go back to the club to do my evening show with Don Rickles.

I remember being in the Green Room of *The Tonight Show*, and Marlon came over to me and asked me if I wanted some champagne. Usually I don't drink alcohol before singing on a show, but if Marlon Brando asks you if you if want a glass of champagne, how can you refuse him? So, I said, "Yes."

We were all sitting in the Green Room and I was in my gown which was a blue floral print. Marlon Brando was sitting across from me, and as he picked up the bottle of champagne that was there for all of us, he asked me, "Excuse me, but are you Puerto Rican?"

At this point I thought, "This is kinda cute of him." But I responded, "Why, no. I'm Negro."

As he sat next to me, we had a brief conversation.

Then he said to me, "What are you doing after the show? Do you want me to give you a ride back to your hotel, in my limousine?"

"Well, I'm not staying in a hotel; I am staying with some family friends."

"I could certainly take you to where you are staying," he offered.

"That would be nice," I said, "but I am performing tonight at a club called Slate Brothers, and I am going directly there after the show."

Marlon said, "I can give you a ride to the club after the show."

"That would be great, because I was going to have to call a taxi," I replied.

We finished the show, and I got into Marlon's limousine. *The Tonight Show* emanated from NBC Studios in Burbank, and he dropped me off at the club in West Hollywood. I went inside, and put my things down in the dressing room. Then I went to Don Rickles' dressing room to tell him about my experience of meeting Marlon Brando. Well, Don Rickles got very excited, and said to me, "Did you invite him to stay to see the show?"

"He might have had something else to do, because he didn't

mention staying for the show, so I didn't mention it to him."

I just didn't think of it, and I figured if Marlon Brando wanted to see the show, he would have asked me if I minded. I wasn't about to be forward enough to invite him. I was just in my early 20s, I wasn't going to do something like that.

However, a day or two later one of the newspaper gossip columnists, I think it was Dorothy Kilgallen, ran an item that Marlon Brando and I were involved with each other. See how shit happens!? Gossip! Rumors! His reputation was that he was into exotic women of color.

It made me think: "Should I have dated Marlon Brando, because I was his 'type?'" Oh well, that's water under the bridge!

One of the press members who wrote about me frequently during this era was syndicated columnist Walter Winchell. While I was in Los Angeles, Walter phoned me to tell me that Lena Horne was going to be performing at The Coconut Grove in The Ambassador Hotel. The Coconut Grove was a very famous Hollywood nightclub, and Walter took me and socialite Susan Statler—of the Statler Hotel family—out together. It was the three of us, Walter, Susan and I sat at a little ringside table. That was the first time I had the opportunity to see Lena Horne performing in person.

My impression was, "Oh, my God! She's not like a 'sex kitten,' like I was expecting her to be, she is more like a force of nature! She is a woman who came out onto the stage with confidence, and assuredness of who she is—and don't you ever forget it!"

The audience was immediately bowled-over by her presence. I felt like I was in a dream. I said to myself, "Here I am sitting with Walter Winchell, and watching Lena Horne. You can't make this up!"

After Lena's performance was over, Walter turned to Susan and I, and said, "We can go upstairs to her suite. Would you like to meet Lena?"

Naturally, I immediately replied, "Why yes!"

We got up to her suite, and I got to meet her. I was so excited, and she was very nice. She was gracious, but it was not like she was overly friendly either. But I was just so happy, and I felt blessed to be in her presence. I was starstruck!

After all, I was five years old when I first became aware of Lena Horne and who she was. I remember asking my granddad back then, "Granddaddy, who is the most famous colored entertainer and movie star in the world?"

He said without hesitation, "Lena Horne."

And I said, "Well, why is she so famous?"

"Well, she is very beautiful. She looks like she is white, but she is not. She is like us, colored, and she's got a whole lot of talent. She sings, she acts. The only thing is: she has skinny legs, that's why she wears all them long gowns."

I had always wanted to meet Lena Horne, so for me, this meeting at my young age was something of an epiphany. It was a like a mystical thing. It wasn't just a dream, it was like a dream becoming a reality. Here I was meeting someone I had idolized since I was a child. Up to this point I had only seen her on TV, on *The Ed Sullivan Show* and other TV variety shows. Then I had seen her in the movie *Stormy Weather*, and I saw her on Judy Garland's 1960s variety show. Judy and Lena had done a duet on that program together. Meeting Lena that night at The Coconut Grove was simply magical to me. I will never forget that evening at The Ambassador Hotel.

The next time I saw Lena was in 1997, and it was at The Avery Fischer Hall at Lincoln Center to honor her on her 80th birthday. They gave an all-star tribute to Lena. I performed on the show to honor her, as well as Liza Minnelli, Rosemary Clooney, Sheryl Lee Ralph, Rita Moreno and many others. (In 2015 Avery Fisher Hall was renamed David Geffen Hall.)

While I was booked at Slate Brothers Club in West Hollywood, one of the performers whose act I caught, was the handsome song crooner Jack Jones. He was booked to appear at the same night-club, and I saw his show. I was very impressed with him. This was back when his hair was thick and medium brown, and he was the up-and-coming new male singer on the scene. It was great to see his act, and I could tell he was really going places.

Working with Don Rickles was a great boost for my career. The kind of audience that Don would draw would be comprised of the "who's who" of Hollywood. Among the people I met there, who had come to see Don, were director Stanley Kramer, Peter Falk, John Cassavetes, Gena Rowlands, and Carol Burnett. The biggest stars all came to see Don's act, and I was there to entertain them as well.

Then I was booked to appear at a West Hollywood nightclub called The Losers.

The Losers was located right on the southwest corner of Santa Monica Boulevard and La Cienega. It was a small, intimate club. Barney Kessel was the guitar player, and it was his group, The Barney Kessel Trio, who accompanied me there.

During that time, I was performing one night and the club was so darkly lit that I couldn't see any of the audience members, with the exception of people in the front row. At one of the tables, just away from the stage, someone suddenly lit a match to light a cigarette, as that was back when you could smoke in a nightclub. As the match was lit, the orange glow of the flame illuminated the person's face for a brief second, and I could plainly see it was Frank Sinatra's face. I instantly recognized him, and I almost froze, but I kept on singing.

After the show was over, the owner of the club grabbed me and said, "Come with me, Freda., I want you to meet Frank."

I was awe struck. I thought to myself, "Oh my God! Frank Sinatra!"

Seconds later I was standing in front of Frank. He was sitting at a table with a woman I did not recognize. The club owner said, "Frank, this is Freda Payne."

Frank smiled and said, "Quincy Jones sent me here, and told me to see you perform. He told me that you were very good, and Quincy was right, you *ARE* very good."

When I first met Sinatra I was instantly impressed that he was so pleasant and nice. For me, that was quite a memorable Hollywood experience.

There was a guy by the name of Lou Brown who was Jerry Lewis' musical conductor for years. Lou and I became pals, and it was Lou who first introduced me to Jerry, and we also became good friends. At the time Jerry was beginning work on the film *The Disorderly Orderly*. Lou Brown had mentioned to Jerry that I was going to be performing at The Losers at the same time as Jerry's filming schedule.

So Lou said to me, "I would like to get you a part in the movie. You can be an 'extra' or something, and maybe we can even get you a speaking line or two in the film."

Somehow Jerry's agents talked to my agents, and they worked out a deal for me to be an extra, and I even had a line of dialogue in it. I ended up playing a nurse in the film. I was on the set for about two weeks. At one point during the filming and nightclub singing, I nearly lost my voice!

It turned out to be a great learning experience for me, and since it was my first film role, it also required me to join the Screen Actors Guild (SAG). I had already been a member of the American Federation of Television and Radio Artists (AFTRA) since 1959, when I was 16 years old. I had originally joined AFTRA because I had been singing on radio commercials in Detroit. SAG and AFTRA were separate unions at the time. Only recently have they merged together.

It was wonderful to be cast in a major Hollywood film production, and it was a great introduction into the movie business. At the same time, I felt that several of the other actors were jealous of me, because I had been cast simply because I was one of Jerry's friends, and not a full-time actor. As I recall, I was the only woman of color in the film.

Although it was fun, it was also very exhausting for me at the time. I was literally doing "double duty," as I was performing at night at The Losers, and every morning I was getting up at 5:00 a.m. to report to Paramount Studios. Once I checked in at the studio, they would transport me and the other members of the cast to our location, which was The Doheny Estates. We also worked in and around The Doheny Mansion, and on the grounds.

I saw *The Disorderly Orderly* recently, and let me tell you, from today's perspective, it seems so incredibly corny. It was super corny, and I had exactly one line in it: "Well, just hold on a minute, I'll ask Dr. Smathers." Then you could spot me in the background several times. I would either walk through some of the scenes, or I was involved in some of the slapstick pranks that happened in the film. At one point some pills had been spilled on the hospital floor by Jerry, and I was one of the nurses who was seen slipping and tripping over them in the hallway. To this day I still get residual payments for *The Disorderly Orderly* that I made back in 1964. The checks are rarely above $20.00—and some are only $9.00 and some change!

This was an exciting period of time for me. Although I was only in my early 20s, I had already sung in nightclubs, had a debut album released, sang on national television, and now I was in my first Hollywood movie, and I was ready for more.

CHAPTER FOUR

"Europe and Motown"

I was first brought to Europe to perform in 1965. The agency I was signed to put me together with a promoter by the name of Jeffrey Patterson, who was from Australia. Jeffrey was a nice guy, a tall and stately man with a really good personality. For several months he had me working at Officers' Clubs throughout Germany. Several top American performers were brought to entertain the U.S. troops and officers who were stationed there. It was my first trip to Europe, and the first ground I set foot on there was in the city of Frankfurt, Germany. Those Officers' Clubs would get some big names to go over there to perform, like Della Reese, O.C. Smith, Nancy Wilson, and people like that. Della was really big at the time, but she worked those same Officers' Clubs that I did because it was for the military hierarchy.

They put me in nice hotels, and the pay was sustainable. I have nothing but great memories of this tour. Jeffrey also had Cab Calloway flown over to Germany to perform at the time, and we were staying at the same hotel. There were some excellent musicians on the show. They were all German, and highly professional.

I remember when Jeffrey and I drove together from Frankfurt, Germany to Paris, France, in his Mercedes Benz. It was a very nice car, but in Germany at the time, having a Mercedes was like having a

Ford or a Chevrolet in America. Even the taxi cabs in Germany were Mercedes Benz, too, and the busses as well. Still, I was impressed to be seeing the European countryside in the passenger's seat of a luxurious Mercedes Benz.

Jeffrey and I would stop occasionally in some of those little towns in France, and there was no such thing as a "fast food" restaurant in France at that time. It simply didn't exist. We would go to a little village and stop, and we would walk into a little pub or a little cafe. The only food you could get was one of those long French sandwiches. They call it a *baguette*, and it would be either ham, or a Camembert or Brie cheese sandwich. I would get a sandwich, and something to drink. It was all so quaint and charming.

When we arrived in Paris we went directly to the section of the city known as Pigalle. It wasn't the nicest part of Paris, but it was where all of the hotels were cheaper. The famed Parisian nightclub landmark The Moulin Rouge is located in Pigalle. I remember that the hotel we stayed in, The Hotel Blanche, wasn't as nice as the ones we had while we were in Germany. Even so, it was an exciting adventure to find myself in the middle of Paris.

I remember the first time I experienced the French bathroom accessory: the *bidet*. I didn't know what the hell it was, or what it was for.

I thought to myself, "If this is the toilet, where do I poop!?! And how do you flush it?"

I thought it was another toilet. I found it confusing and it wasn't until I made a phone call to the front desk to discover that the regular toilet was in a room down the hall. That's how cheap that hotel was. You had to go outside of your room to use a common bathroom. By that alone, I could instantly tell that hotel wasn't all that great.

When I had called downstairs to the lobby, I said, "What is this toilet in my room?"

The concierge said, "Mademoiselle, that is not a toilet. That is a *bidet*! That is for you to *douche*! You *douche*!"

Well, I knew enough French from high school to know that the French word "*douche*" means "wash." So, I asked someone else to further decipher this mystery.

"Why does this guy keep saying, '*douche*?'" I inquired.

"Well, that is for you to wash your vagina," was the reply.

I said, "Okay" That was a funny bathroom lesson I learned in France.

In that hotel the only meal that was available was in the morning. You were able to order what is known as "continental breakfast" in your room. I knew enough French to recognize *Le Petite Déjeuner*, which is coffee, a small orange juice, and a buttery croissant. That is just the perfect amount of food to get the day in Paris started.

One of the main reasons to come to France is for the cuisine, and we certainly sampled a lot of that. In addition to the great French food we had in Paris, there was a restaurant there that was owned by an African American former U.S. soldier in Pigalle. It specialized in American-style soul food. I remember they had the full soul food menu including chicken livers and rice, collard greens, fried chicken, pork neck bones, and barbecued ribs. That is where a lot of the entertainers would come and hang out. I forget the man's name, and I forget the name of the restaurant, but I do recall that is was on Rue Fromentin in Pigalle during that trip.

On that European tour Jeffrey had me booked not only in Germany and France; I was also booked in Oslo, Norway for a special engagement at the *La Chat Noir Theater*. "*La Chat Noir*" means "The Black Cat" in French. When I arrived in Oslo, it was a revue of all-European acts, and I was the sole American singer on the bill. There was a French comedian, an Adagio dance duo, and a magician doing tricks on-stage. After we were done with the show, we all went to a late night restaurant together. As we laughed and talked, the conversations at our table would be comprised of several European languages at once, and I didn't understand any of them: French, German, and Italian. I understood some French, but not enough to participate in an ongoing conversation.

Since I didn't speak any of these languages, I would order wine and something to eat, and just enjoy everyone's company while they chatted away. I would order a "split" bottle of red wine, which was enough for two glasses, which was just right for me.

Intermittently someone would look up from their conversation and say, "I am so sorry, we should be speaking in English."

"No problem," I would say with a smile.

So they would speak to each other in English with me for a while. Then someone would start telling a story in a different language, and off they would go. And I would return to my wine and *Steak Tartare*, or *Steak au Poivre*.

If you are familiar with the terms "the midnight sun" and "the aurora borealis," Norway was that part of the world where they are visible. In Scandinavia for that part of the year, it is totally daylight up until 11:30 pm at night during the summer months. This is also true in other northern cities at that latitude, including our own Anchorage, Alaska. Summer was the time of year I was there, as opposed to the winter when darkness prevails.

There is a song that made a reference to this, written with music by Lionel Hampton and lyrics by Johnny Mercer, called "Midnight Sun." Well, during this trip I was certainly experiencing a totally different climate and weather pattern up in the far north.

Then I also worked in Stockholm, Sweden. I was booked at a big restaurant / supper club called Bern's. Harry Belafonte had worked there, and Marlene Dietrich, as well as The Supremes and lots of great headliners. They kept me working there for a good three or four months. The guy who booked me there was a man by the name of Leif Madison. He wanted to keep me in Stockholm, and make a big star out of me in Sweden and Europe. It was flattering, but at this point I was becoming way too homesick to stay there beyond the six or eight months I was in Europe.

While I was in Stockholm, I met heavyweight boxing champ Muhammad Ali. There was an afternoon luncheon reception that was given in his honor, at Bern's. He was very charming, and according to him, he wanted to date me! I was interested, but I was too busy at the time even to go out to lunch with him. If I did not have a rehearsal at the same time, I would have gladly gone out with him.

I said to him, "I can't accept that invitation, I'm too busy focusing on my career. I have shows and scheduled rehearsals I have to concentrate on."

My second album was recorded in Sweden, called *Freda Payne in Stockholm*, and it was released in 1965. I sang "live" in the studio with The Don Gardner Quartet. Toots Thieleman played harmonica on the song "Bluesette," which he wrote. That was when I first met him.

I also recorded songs like "False Love," which was the English language version of the Swedish lullaby *"Du Har Lå Din Kärlek Fä Försvinna."* It wasn't so much a jazz album, it was a combination of R&B, pop and jazz. "Once Upon a Summertime" and "Bluesette" represented the more jazz oriented songs, while "See See Rider" and "On Broadway" represented the rock & roll / R&B side of the album. I also recorded the blues song "Nobody Wants You When You Are Down And Out."

While I was on my European tour, I was booked to perform in Spain as well. I played at a club in Madrid. It was a nightclub called The Pasapoga. I was there for two weeks, and I recall very distinctly that while I was there, that's when Nat King Cole died.

I remember seeing a local newspaper, which was all in Spanish, and there was a picture of him on the cover. I was at the nightclub and one of the musicians was reading the paper. I asked him, "Why is Nat King Cole on the front cover of that newspaper? What is this about?"

"Oh, he died," was the reply. "He had cancer."

I will always remember that moment in Spain.

In each of the European cities I played on this trip, the club would have their own musicians—a local "house band"—to accompany me. It would be me with a jazz trio, or sometimes I would have a full 12 or 14 piece band with me, backing me up, and I would be the "featured" vocalist on the bill.

Some of the nightclubs would have a dance team on the bill as well. There would be a tap dance duo, or some sort of act. The great tap dancing duo, The Nicholas Brothers, would have been the kind of act to be on these shows. Some of the acts would be reminiscent of their nightclub dance routines.

I remember working with a dance team of two black guys that had an act, and in it they did a little bit of gymnastics, a little bit of tap dancing, and some singing. There was another entertainer I do remember who billed himself as "Jack Hammer." He was a black American entertainer who was also working on the Officers' Clubs circuit.

One night after the show, Jack Hammer and I were hanging out, and having dinner. Afterwards we went back to the hotel and talked in the lobby. We had a conversation about what was going on in America with Dr. Martin Luther King and the Civil Rights Movement.

Jack said to me, "Dr. Martin Luther King has to become a martyr to be revered almost like Jesus Christ, to be fully appreciated and praised." Mind you, this was still 1965, not 1968 when King was assassinated.

Then he said something that shocked me, and I will never forget it. Jack said, "He is going to have to be assassinated to become martyred."

I was shocked when he said this. It was like a prophecy! When it happened three years later, his words echoed in my ears.

This whirlwind trip to Europe proved to be full of surprises and adventures. One of the true surprises came when I suddenly found out I was pregnant. I felt frightened and very confused. What was I going to do? I said to myself, "I can't go back to America pregnant!"

What had happened was that I had an affair with a handsome young man in Madrid, Spain. You hear about all of these college students in their early 20s on their spring break, running around Europe and "sowing their wild oats," so to speak. They were everywhere, drinking and partying, and having one night flings with someone they will never see again. It was "The Swinging '60s!" The decade of "Free Love." Well, that is what happened to me. That was what I did in Madrid.

In the hotels, on the main floor there would be a little area with comfortable chairs, like a parlor. That way you could have a conversation with someone without inviting them to your room. People would meet their guests that way, and order a drink or tea or coffee. It was very European, and Madrid was very conservative and proper.

Regarding my surprise pregnancy, the guy in question was a Russian exchange student. We had a very short affair.

We went out once, or maybe twice at the most. I won't mention his name, but as I remember him, he was charming and he dressed very conservatively in suits.

It was like that classic jazz song, "My Old Flame," with its line, "I can't even remember his name." Well, this was a case in point!

Not long afterward I experienced all of the classic signs that I was pregnant. I kept repeating to myself: "There is *absolutely* no way I can go home pregnant! I simply can't go through with this."

When my engagement at The Pasapoga came to an end, I stayed in Madrid for a couple of weeks, just to enjoy the city. In Spain and Italy the stores would routinely close in the afternoon for "*siesta*," and then they would reopen three hours later.

After Madrid, I went to England. What ended up happening was that I stayed there for six weeks before going home. I was ready to go back to the US, but that was when I found out that I was pregnant. I knew that I couldn't go home in that condition, let alone being pregnant by a Russian Exchange student, so I postponed my trip back to the United States.

When I arrived in London I met an American woman who was a known blues singer over there. She was an African American, and her name was Patrice Redding. I told her about my dilemma, and she invited me to come stay with her. She also told me that she would immediately start looking around to find me a doctor who would perform an abortion, as it was also illegal over there at the time.

She eventually found a contact, and I had an abortion there. It was done in a clinic, and it cost the equivalent of $3,000.00 US dollars which was about 750 Pounds Sterling then. It was very expensive, and the clinic was very exclusive, like I was going to a spa. They came and picked me up in a Rolls Royce, and I was taken directly to the clinic. They performed the abortion, and I was there for only a few hours, and then I was returned to Patrice's apartment.

Had this not happened, there would have been no other reason for me to have stayed in London that long. But I did. I ended up hanging out in London for several weeks. In no time I was back in top form, and I went out to all of the fashionable discos in the area. It was an era of the popular chic discotheques in London, and I sampled them all.

While in England, I worked in Manchester, at a very exclusive private club, sort of like one of the Playboy clubs in America. I stayed in a charming old hotel. I remember that in my room the ceilings were very high, and the room was really big. That's how it was in those big old hotels.

During all of this time, since 1957, I had not seen or talked to Berry Gordy. I certainly knew what he had been up to. He had scored a lot of success with Martha Reeves & The Vandellas, Smokey Robinson & The Miracles, The Marvelettes, The Temptations, Mary Wells, The Four Tops, and—recently—The Supremes. Berry's music empire, Motown Records, had become a big deal on the international record charts. The aristocrats and the royals were into Motown music as well!

While in Manchester I happened to read in the local newspaper that *The Motown Revue*—billed as *"The Motortown Revue"*—was appearing at an old classic theater. I thought to myself, "I wonder if Berry is traveling with them? I'm going to call up the theater and see if he is there."

I called up, and I was connected with the stage manager. I said to the person who answered the phone, "Is Berry Gordy there by any chance?"

"Yeah, he's here," the stage manager confirmed.

I said, "Can I speak to him please? This is an old friend of his from Detroit." They put him on the phone. "It's Freda! Freda Payne. I'm here in Manchester, Berry."

He was very excited to hear from me. "What are you doing in Manchester?" he asked.

"I'm in town singing. I'm working in a club here, a private club."

"Well, I want to come and see your show," he said. So I gave him all of the information, and he came to see my show.

In the act I was doing contemporary standards like "You're Nobody 'Til Somebody Loves You," the song "More (The Theme from *Mondo Caine*)," Jacques Brel's "If You Go Away," and that kind of material. I was singing all standards or middle-of-the-road songs. Everyone was going crazy over Barbra Streisand's song "People" at that time, so I sang that, too.

Berry loved my show, and he said to me afterwards, "Do you want to come and see *The Motown Revue*?"

"Absolutely," I replied.

The Motown Revue at that time included not only The Supremes—with Diana, Flo, and Mary, as well as "Little" Stevie Wonder, The Miracles with Smokey and Claudette Robinson, Martha Reeves & The Vandellas, and Jr. Walker.

In the meantime, I was comfortably staying in Manchester at my old and classically appointed hotel in town. So, Berry decided to invite himself to my hotel, since the Motown troupe was staying at the newer Britannica Hotel. Well, there we were in my big old hotel room with the high ceilings. At first, Berry was really cordial and nice with me. Berry sat on the bed and I sat on a big easy chair across from him. Then his tone became more flirtatious.

Finally Berry said to me, "Why don't you come over and sit on the bed next to me." I wasn't really into him, but Berry kinda talked me into it. He was sitting there, and he literally proceeded to entice me into having sex with him. He didn't force himself on me, or anything like that. Although I wasn't into it, I eventually gave in to him. I was attempting to hold the line, and not to cross it. I was trying not to go from being business friends, and being intimate. But what happened next showed me that he wasn't having it like that. So, I relented, and we made love at my hotel.

I was all of 23 years old back then, and I decided, "Why not?" Then the next day I visited him at his hotel, The Britannica. By the way, The Britannica Hotel is still there. I remember the rooms were much smaller compared to my hotel. The Britannica was a new hotel, with lower ceilings and more compact rooms.

Billy Davis, who was Berry's friend and assistant, was there at the hotel as well. Billy worked as Berry's valet, packing and unpacking his clothes in each new city *The Motortown Revue* visited. Billy has since died of AIDS. But back then he was an important part of the troupe.

That day when I went to see *The Motortown Revue*, Berry took me backstage. I saw Diana, and Mary and Flo and said "hello." I didn't know them well, but I certainly knew who they were, because of their recent hits on the radio.

Then I was hanging out with The Miracles. Smokey Robinson is the one who kept saying out loud, "Wow, you should be with us at Motown. Berry, Freda ought to be with us!"

"Maybe she should," Berry replied. Then he asked me, "When are you coming back to Detroit?"

"Well, when I finally leave here, maybe about two or three weeks from now, I am returning to Detroit."

He said, "Get in contact with me when you get back to the States. Maybe we can do something. I'll have Ralph Seltzer send you a Motown recording contract."

"I will call you when I get back to Detroit," I replied.

Berry's sister Loucye passed before I returned to Detroit. I knew that Berry was very close with all of his siblings, and they were all involved in the family business of Motown Records. I remember sending a condolence message to Berry from Europe. About two or three weeks later I came back to Detroit and, as promised, I got in touch with him.

Was this going to be the next phase of my career, as a Motown singing star, alongside The Supremes, The Marvelettes, Marvin Gaye, Mary Wells, The Temptations, The Four Tops, and Martha & The Vandellas? For a short period of time, it looked like this was what was going to happen.

As Berry had promised, Ralph sent me a Motown recording contract, and I read it over. I let my lawyer, Allen Early Jr., read it over as well. Then my mother read it over. After Allen read it he said, "I just want to change a couple of things that are obvious to me."

My mother agreed with him. It wasn't anything drastic. It was no major thing that needed to be done to it. There were just a few things that would have been appropriate for anybody to question, or at least inquire about. What kind of professional entertainer would sign a contract without allowing his or her lawyer to look at it? It is not an outlandish occurrence at all.

I sent the contract back to Motown with Allen's suggestions for it. And I got a call back from Berry.

My mother answered the phone, and she said, "It's Berry, he wants to speak to you."

I said, "Okay," and she handed me the telephone.

Berry said to me, "First of all: nobody changes my contracts."

Innocently I said, "You let The Four Tops change your contract, because I had heard about that."

"Well, that's different. That's because I'm friends with Levi Stubbs. I just have to say this: we can stay friends, but we can't do business. Things are moving too fast around here, and I don't have time to have you questioning everything!"

Right then and there I saw his "alpha male" side.

I was rather amazed to hear him say this, but I said to him, "Okay." There was nothing else for me to say.

After I hung up the phone, I was a bit disappointed, but I wasn't devastated. It wasn't like I thought, "Oh my God, that was my one big chance!" I knew that there were other opportunities awaiting me. But I was shocked that Berry had taken that position.

Perhaps if I had come back begging for him to reconsider, he might have. But I had been in the business for a while at this point, and I figured: "Well, I certainly don't have to do that!"

At the time, I could clearly see that I didn't have any choice in the matter. My mother was questioning this deal with Motown Records, and obviously Berry wasn't that serious about signing me if he couldn't even discuss the terms of the contract.

So, that was it. The possibility of me signing with Motown Records instantly vanished. And I think that Berry Gordy also realized at that point that there might have been a huge conflict between me and Diana Ross. I really do believe that. And, he was probably right!

Looking back on that time I can clearly see why Berry was interested in offering me a Motown recording contract. This had to do with what was going on with the label's premiere female star, Mary Wells.

I spoke to Martha Reeves recently about this. She told me that this was the period where Mary Wells was getting ready to leave Motown Records. At Motown, Mary had a string of hits, especially her Number One song "My Guy." She was so popular that she once toured with The Beatles.

Mary Wells ended up getting a new manager, and together they found a loophole in her contract with Berry. Since Mary had signed her contract before she was 21 years old, she and her new manager found a way to nullify it. With her impending absence at the company, Berry was interested in finding a new solo female singer to take Mary's place on his roster.

The ironic thing that took place was that Mary Wells went on to sign a new recording contract in New York with ABC / Paramount Records. That was the company I had my first record deal with. Apparently, Mary thought she would become a bigger star by leaving Motown Records and Berry Gordy. It didn't turn out that way at all.

As it was, I think that Berry got a lot of inspiration from me, and a lot of ideas from me. When he came to see me in Manchester, I was doing the song "You're Nobody 'Til Somebody Loves You" in my act. Not long afterward, that same year The Supremes did the song in their new nightclub act they debuted at The Copacabana. Berry knew that if The Supremes were to crossover to a white audience, he would have to have the group sing more middle-of-the-road songs and standards to be accepted by more people.

One would think that I knew a lot of the Motown stars when I was growing up in Detroit. Not really. I guess you could say we were in the same church, but we sat in different pews. I lived in a whole different neighborhood than where the majority of the Motown artists came from. I was not from "the projects." My mother always owned her own home.

I once saw The Supremes at The 20 Grand nightclub. They were there to see a show. I remember that night seeing Diana, Mary and Florence sitting there at a table, just a little way away from me. We were there to see Tammi Terrell who was performing. I looked over at the table and Diana was eating popcorn. The 20 Grand was *THE* club in Detroit, along with The Flame Show Bar.

I didn't know The Supremes well at this point, and I had no relationship with Florence. Of course I got to meet her. She knew who I was, and naturally I knew who she was. She was very kind towards me, and I was very kind towards her as well, because I admired what they were doing, especially when I heard all of the gossip about what was going on within the group, and how Diana was treating her.

I got more information about that from Motown's legendary Earl Van Dyke, who was a member of the famed Funk Brothers. The members of The Funk Brothers were the core musicians on all of the Motown recordings. Earl later became my musical director and pianist for 12 years—from 1971 to 1983. It was then that he told me about stuff that he had witnessed directly, about Diana's actions towards Florence. And Earl did not like Diana at all. He said, "She's a real bitch." Earl told me about all sorts of things that Diana deliberately did to hurt Florence. He told me this in confidence.

I heard all sorts of firsthand stories about what Diana was like back in the day, when she was striving to climb to the top. If she had been kind and considerate, I don't know if the result would have been any different. She certainly hurt people along the way, without any regard for their feelings.

I didn't know Mary Wilson very well during the 1960s. Mary told me once that Berry would talk about me, and that he would "talk bad" about me. I have no idea exactly what he said. Berry is the kind of person who can't take rejection. It has to be "his way" or it's "no way." He is unrelenting. He is going to do what he is going to do, and there are no apologies along the way.

Today I see all of the surviving Motown acts, and they have all done quite well. They are working in great venues, and they are celebrated as legends, icons, and classic professional acts. Recently, there have even been two Motown-based musicals on Broadway— *The Motown Musical* (2013), and The Temptations story: *Ain't Too Proud to Beg* (2019). In Detroit, one of the prime tourist attractions is Motown's Hitsville Museum. To this day, Motown Records has the reputation of being the musical beacon on the hill.

Sometimes I wonder, "What would have happened if I had signed with Motown? How far would I have gone?"

I could have signed with Motown Records right then and there, if I had really wanted to do that. But, it just didn't seem to be in the cards for me. Looking back on it, had I signed with Motown, I wouldn't have been able to have some of the amazing kinds of experiences that I ultimately had.

We never get to see what might have been had we taken another path. Because I am a Christian, and I believe in God, I just have to leave it at that. I could have been part of the Motown legacy, but I chose another path to travel. In other words: it was "the road I didn't take."

CHAPTER FIVE

"Broadway, Sinatra, and The Psychics"

It was the beginning of 1966, and I was back in New York City. I was still living with Carol Preston on Second Avenue, at East 33rd Street. One night we were out somewhere, and she introduced me to a man by the name of Robert Potter. He was about five-feet nine-inches tall, and of medium build. He had dark brown wavy hair, and he was very handsome. He sported a mustache, and his complexion was a nice caramel color.

Robert and I almost immediately hit it off. At first I was attracted to his good looks, and his manners. When he kissed me, my knees buckled, and we started dating. I began to spend more-and-more time at his place than I spent at my own apartment.

He lived in The Lincoln Towers apartment complex which had several high-rise buildings, and his address was 180 West End Avenue. His apartment was a one bedroom on the 30th Floor. It was very nicely appointed. He was a bit on the quiet side, but very polite. Robert shopped at Brooks Brothers a lot, so he was usually conservatively dressed.

At the time I was being managed by Clarence Avant. He later became known as "The Black Godfather" in the late 1970s. There is a Netflix documentary on him and his life. I met Clarence around 1966 and began working with him. He was something of a deal maker in show business, and he later became the CEO of Motown Records. Clarence was known as the man who launched the careers of Bill Withers, Alexander O'Neal, Charrelle, and others. As a manager, Clarence worked not only with me, but with Jimmy Smith, Sarah Vaughn, and TV and movie composer Lalo Schifrin as well. Later, Clarence had his own record labels: Sussex Records and Taboo Records.

It was Clarence who got me my third and next recording deal, this time with MGM Records, and to produce my album he hired a man by the name of Al Wilson. In the past Al had produced recordings with Bob Dylan, Simon & Garfunkel, and Eric Burdon & The Animals. My third album, *How Do You Say I Don't Love You Anymore?*, had the songs arranged and orchestrated by Benny Golson. Benny was a well-established, well-known jazz saxophonist. I was very elated to be working with someone of his caliber in the jazz world.

For me it was kind of a middle-of-the-road album. I even sang some pop tunes on it, including my versions of The Righteous Brothers' "You've Lost That Lovin' Feeling," and The Beatles' "Yesterday." I was happy with the MGM album. The arrangements were good and the quality was there. It was much better produced, and had a much better sound quality than the Swedish one I had done the year before, while in Europe. On the cover I was in sort of a "sex kitten" kind of pose wearing a little pink negligee, and I am holding a white telephone, like I am making a late night call to a boyfriend—to tell him "I don't love you anymore!" Unfortunately, my MGM album came and went without making much noise on the record charts.

Speaking of boyfriends, I didn't know anything about Robert's "full disclosure" resume. When I asked him about his business dealings, he told me that he owned a couple of brownstone buildings up in Harlem. After five or six months of dating him, I finally found out that his explanation about the buildings he owned in Harlem was just a cover for what he really did. His business partners were living right across the street in The Lincoln Towers complex. They were Jerry and Vivian Nagelberg. Vivian was a very fair skinned Negro woman, and Jerry was white and Jewish. They were a married couple. Under that mild-mannered façade, it turned out that they were the kingpins in an illegal drug business, and Robert worked with them. Jerry and Vivian ran a coffee shop right downstairs on West End Avenue, across from their apartment building. They also owned some real estate as well, but their main source of cash flow was from the drug business.

After I learned of Robert's dealings, and what his relationship with the Nagelbergs really was, he would open up to me about how they had contacts with actual police officers, who basically helped them out. There were also certain people working in the banks, who helped them to "launder" the drug money. They would often take short vacations to Miami Beach, staying at The Fontainbleau Hotel, and sometimes it would be Puerto Rico, or Nassau where they would go.

Of course, I would be invited to go along. I recall one of those trips to Miami Beach, where we stayed at The Fontainbleau Hotel. The hotel would be full of New Yorkers coming down to Florida for a vacation. We would sit out in the sun by the pool, or go out to the beach. As a foursome, we would go out for dinner every night.

There was an incident that happened on the Fourth of July, 1966. This is something I will never forget. I was in New York, and I had gone with Vivian Nagelberg and her niece, whom they called "Little Vivian," and we drove out to New Jersey. We had gone to the home of jazz singer Betty Carter for a Fourth of July barbecue. Betty was a very well-respected jazz vocalist. She had recently done a duet with Ray Charles on the song "Every Time We Say Goodbye." Betty was married and she had five boys.

Robert stayed in New York, and he was planning on joining us in New Jersey when he finished one of his business deals.

We hadn't been there but about an hour, and someone phoned Betty from The Roosevelt Hospital in Manhattan, and asked to talk to Vivian. It was a nurse calling to inform Vivian that Robert had been admitted to the hospital for stab wounds on his leg, and a slash wound on his nose.

Apparently, even though he had lost a lot of blood, he was conscious enough to have given the nurse Betty's phone number, as he was originally going to join us at the barbecue. Upon hearing the news about what had happened, I was in physical shock and deep concern. After all, I loved this man.

This spoiled the whole day, so we came back to Manhattan immediately. When we got to the hospital, Robert was able to tell us what had happened.

According to him, one of Vivian and Jerry's associates who worked in their organization assaulted him. He and Robert had frequently clashed in the past. He felt that Robert was trying to take advantage of him, so the man pulled a knife on Robert. Apparently that led into a physical fight, in which Robert fell backward, while his attacker continued to stab him. Robert was able to fight him off, and he was able to call for an ambulance. I was so stressed that I became physically ill in the car because my nerves became unhinged.

Robert survived all of this, and he and I had become engaged during that first year we were together. Regardless of what he was involved in, I was totally in love with him. I remember when my parents came to visit me from Detroit, they were wondering how Robert could afford an apartment in a very upscale apartment complex in Manhattan, on the 30th floor no less. Even without knowing about Robert's dealings with the drug world, my stepfather was instantly suspicious. My mother was skeptical as well, as she had good instincts about men.

Also suspicious was my manager, Clarence Avant. At one point

Clarence came to me and said, "I have been asking around as to what Robert is really up to and what he is about. And, all sources seem to point to the fact that he is nothing but a small-time hustler." Clarence demanded that I stop seeing Robert or, if not, he couldn't manage my career any longer.

Well, needless to say, I didn't quit Robert, so Clarence just walked away, and stopped managing me. I turned my back on Clarence, which was a BIG MISTAKE! Piece-by-piece, I could see that being with Robert was to my detriment. But I was in love, and I couldn't see the forest for the trees. I thought Robert loved me as well.

I was later to find out that he didn't love me like I thought he did. He ultimately betrayed me in the worst kind of way. Here's what happened: I had gone to Detroit to fulfill an engagement at The Elmwood Casino in Windsor, Ontario, Canada, directly across the river from Detroit.

The Elmwood Casino was a big Detroit area attraction. While appearing there I was billed in their advertising and programs as "Recording and Dancing Star Freda Payne." I remember seeing that ad, and I thought to myself, "I'm not gonna dance, I am just going to sing!" Apparently they recalled me as a teenager doing dance recitals. It was fun to be playing my hometown, although it is technically a ten minute drive across The Ambassador Bridge into Canada.

While I was in Detroit, I was staying at my mother and father's house. One day, I was thinking about how Robert was doing, so I thought, "Let me just give Robert a call. I am missing him so much."

I called his apartment about four or five times. After not getting an answer, I had a hunch in the back of my head, "I wonder if Robert is over at Sonia's house?" Sonia was a woman he had fathered a child with before he had met me. The child they had together was about two years old at the time, and I was suspicious that he had not fully cut off ties with Sonia.

Somehow, I had acquired Sonia's phone number when I had

been doing my detective work of going through his pockets. I thought I would just give her a call, and ask if she had seen Robert. Well, was I ever in for a BIG SURPRISE!

I placed the phone call, and guess who answered? Robert. Back then you couldn't tell who was calling you, because there was no such thing as "caller ID" as we know it today. I was about to hang up from the call when—much to my surprise—he answered the phone.

I said to him, "What the hell are you doing over there?" I was totally unprepared to get the answer I received.

He said, "I am married, that's why I am here."

I was so startled I dropped the telephone, and then after I picked it up, I loudly slammed it down on the receiver. I phoned him back immediately. Then I found out from the both of them that they had eloped in my absence. I felt like someone just put a dagger in my heart. I couldn't believe what I had just heard from him. Then Sonia got on the phone and confirmed it.

My survival instincts kicked in, and instead of doing something to escape the reality of this and the pain, I decided to face the reality of "what a fool I have been!" I swore I would not get drunk, and that I would not go smoke a marijuana joint, or do anything else to numb the pain, because I wanted to go through this stone cold sober.

Sometimes, being in love with the wrong person is like an addiction. You have to face the facts and stop the addiction "cold turkey."

My mother said to me, "Baby, I know you are surprised and deeply hurt, but just take this as a life lesson. Freda, you can't trust him anymore. Even if he were to come back to you on his knees and crying, you can never trust him again."

This incident so reminded me of that standard song written by Harold Arlen, "Mama was right, there's 'Blues In The Night!'"

It's funny. Back then I had gone to see a psychic, while Robert and I were engaged and everything was on good terms. And the psychic said to me in my reading, "I cannot see marriage in the cards for you and Robert."

This was in spite of the fact that I kept telling her, "Well, I'm engaged. Look, I've got a two carat diamond engagement ring on."

She just calmly said, "I've been reading you for 45 minutes, and I just don't see marriage in the cards, young lady."

It wasn't more than two and a half weeks later that Robert betrayed me by marrying Sonia, and essentially "stabbing me in the back." I would have never dreamt that this was possible. I felt betrayed and emotionally shattered.

I did go to see this same psychic reader privately in her apartment, upon my return to New York from Detroit. I told her what had happened, and she was not surprised. She read my cards again and she said, "Only about a year from now, they will break up and the marriage will end." And she was right!

She told me that after the marriage ended, he would try to reconcile with me. She was right. He did try to return and get back with me. But, after this episode the thrill was gone, and I no longer had faith in him anymore. I had learned my lesson, and that was the end of Robert Potter.

I became friendly with a girl who lived in the same building I did, located in the area of Manhattan which at the time was known as Spanish Harlem. I had a small studio apartment there. She had a one bedroom apartment with a roommate, on another floor in the same building. She was a professional dancer. Her name was Sandra McPherson, and everyone called her "Sandy." We became friends and discovered the irony that we were both staying in the same apartment building. She came to me one day and said to me, "There is a building located on Central Park West on the corner of 97th Street. The apartment is on the 19th Floor, and it has two bedrooms. We could move there, and be roommates." So we moved in together and split all of the expenses.

Sandy became my best friend. As a professional dancer, she

danced with Tommy Johnson and another girl named Arlene, and they had a trio nightclub act. Sandy also danced in several Broadway shows. And, she eventually became a dancer with the George Faison dance troupe. In fact, Debbie Allen—who has become a very successful choreographer, director, actress, and producer—came out of George Faison's troupe as well. Sandy was also one of the dancers in the 1978 movie version of *The Wiz*.

I remember one time Sandy telling me, "You know that girl Debbie Allen, in George's troupe with me? I think she is going to become a really big star, because she is really good."

"What do you mean, Sandy?" I asked.

"She's going to become like a Mitzi Gaynor." That was really saying something because, at the time, Mitzi was a huge star, who had movies, television and even her own headlining Las Vegas revue. Needless to say, we can see how far Debbie has come as a TV and film producer / director. She was one of the producers of the movie *Amistad* (1997) and the TV series *Grey's Anatomy*.

Our apartment had an alcove dining room, a living room area, and one bathroom. In New York City it is so expensive, you would typically have two or three people living there so that they could share the rent. That was how it was back then. And now the rents are probably ten times higher than it was back then.

Since Sandy was a professional dancer, and since so many of our friends were in show business, I was always hearing about who in town was casting what Broadway show. The Broadway community is a small circle, and since everyone talked to everyone else, there was always a buzz about what was going on, and who was leaving or coming into what show.

At the time, Sandy was already one of the original members of the cast of the new hit Broadway show *Hallelujah Baby!* If you look on the Original Cast album cover, Sandy's name is listed as one of the chorus dancers.

One of my friends was Emily Yancy. It was Emily who was the first understudy to Leslie Uggams in *Hallelujah Baby!*, which had recently opened and was a hit. What happened was that Emily had auditioned for the Broadway company of *Hello Dolly!* with Pearl Bailey and Cab Calloway in the starring roles. Emily was offered the job of playing one of the supporting roles in that show, and she accepted it.

Since Emily was leaving *Hallelujah Baby!* to move to *Hello Dolly!*, they were holding auditions for a new understudy to take her place. Sandy, who was a member of the company, in the chorus, then encouraged me to go and audition for the understudy role. At first, I totally rejected that idea, because I felt that I was not qualified. After all, this was a lead role, with lots of dialogue, and it was Broadway. That was a big deal.

Sandy said to me, "You have it all. You can sing just as well as Leslie. And I believe you can act as well. You should go for it!" And so, I did.

Prior to this show, Leslie Uggams had never been a lead in a Broadway show herself. She had mainly been working on TV shows, including *Sing Along With Mitch*, the Mitch Miller show. Originally the producers had approached Lena Horne about playing the starring role of Georgina Johnson, but they couldn't reach an agreement.

Leslie was known for her TV work, and she was performing at The Club Harlem in Atlantic City, while casting for the show was underway. So, the producers went down to Atlantic City, to scout out Leslie. They were impressed, and they cast her in the role of Georgina Johnson.

Well, when I first auditioned, I just went in and I sang a song which is called "Every Time," and the producers were very impressed with me. But, when it came time to read my lines of dialogue, it didn't quite work out well. The producers felt that I was not experienced enough with stage dialogue, and in reality I wasn't. In other words, they were impressed with my singing, but not with my delivery of lines of dialogue. This was Broadway, and you really had to be on top of your game. They were very critical, and I understood it. To be cast in a Broadway show, you really have to be polished.

So, I didn't get it that time. Instead, the producers hired a girl by the name of Norma Donaldson, and she had a lot more experience in the acting field. Well, about two months later, my roommate Sandra said to me, "Guess what?"

I said, "What?"

"The producers let Norma go because she was not up to their standard of carrying the lead role. They decided to try Norma out for one show, because Leslie is about to take a break for a night or two to have some minor surgery."

Well, what happened was that they let Norma go on, and by the Intermission of the show they had to call Leslie back in to finish the second act.

That just goes to show you how cut-throat that Broadway is: you can have a great audition, but when you actually set foot onto the stage—in front of an audience—that is the moment of truth. You can either come up to the standards of a Broadway star, or not. Norma did not, at least not in that particular show.

So, what ended up happening was that the producers of *Hallelujah Baby!* requested that I come back in and audition for the role again. At the time, it was Billy Dee Williams who was the stand-in for the show's male star, who was Robert Hooks. Robert Hooks was a big time star back then. Robert was the male lead in *Hallelujah Baby!*, and he was also one of the stars of the *NYPD* TV show with Jack Warden as its main star. This was back when that TV show was still broadcast in black & white. Robert was doing movies, and he was one of the founders of The Negro Ensemble Company in New York, from which several prominent black stars have come, including Samuel L. Jackson and Louis Gossett Jr.

Billy D. was already an experienced actor by that time. Since Robert was busy during the days with his TV show, it was Billy who took over the two matinee performances during the week—Wednesday and Saturday.

Apparently, Sandy knew Robert Hooks, because everyone in the theater community knew each other, and they were friendly with each other. Sandy was also friendly with Billy D. So, she asked Billy D. if he would come up to our apartment to coach me, and to run some of the lines of dialogue with me. Billy D. gladly agreed, and he came over and coached me, and told me what to do. He helped me read the lines more effectively, and showed me certain techniques.

When it came time for me to audition for the producers at the theater, it was Billy D. who was on-stage with me. This time around the dialogue was much more smooth and natural, because we had been rehearsing together.

Well, it worked beautifully! I was hired right there on the spot. Suddenly I was Leslie Uggams' understudy in *Hallelujah Baby!* I was given a script and I had a couple of weeks to learn my lines.

This had come about because of Sandy, and her insistence that I audition. One of the other professional people I met through Sandy was David Baumgarten. He was the President and CEO of APA (Agency for the Performing Arts). He became a good friend, and he became my agent. When we met, David instantly liked me and saw I had talent and a future.

Because I was cast in *Hallelujah Baby!* I had to be represented by a theatrical agency, so I was signed to APA as an artist in 1967. My first theater agent there was Bruce Savan, and he negotiated my contract with the show. This was also when I first joined Actors Equity, the union that handles all of the Broadway shows, regional theaters, plays and musicals.

David Baumgarten would invite me out to dinners and lunches, at many fine restaurants in New York. In fact, he would take me to some of the best ones in town. He introduced me to a man by the name Claude Phillipe, and he was the owner of the restaurant called Le Pavillon. It was there that I had soft shelled crabs for the first time, and I loved them. They were absolutely delicious.

David would take me to some of the most exclusive and expensive French restaurants in town, including La Cirque, Lutèce, as well as Le Pavillon. He also loved Scandinavian restaurants, and he took me to Scandia and introduced me to Swedish food, which I loved. He would also take me to eat at Sardi's in the theater district, and the famed Manhattan restaurant: 21. David and I certainly had some great meals together!

David was also romantically attracted to me, but he knew I didn't feel that same way about him. He was about 55 years old, and I was 25 at the time. Although I was never personally involved with him, he took me under his wing.

Meanwhile, I was invited by David to go on a little trip, and a brief vacation. That particular week he had invited me and a lady by the name of Helena Harris to go to Colorado with him for a couple of days. Helena was a lady who was born in Germany, and she lived in Manhattan in an apartment on Park Avenue in the 60s. Helena was the girlfriend of Claude Philippe, who had a country house in upstate New York.

In Barbara Walters' memoir, *Audition*, I was surprised to read that Barbara and Claude had at one time been lovers. She wrote glowingly about him.

Helena spent almost every weekend at Claude's country home, and David Baumgarten and I would often be invited as well. We would drive up there, and spend the whole weekend in a beautiful country setting. Claude would do all of the cooking and we would have gourmet meals and very fine wines. At his country house Claude had cows on the property. He also had a black dog up there who was some sort of a sheep dog. It was a wonderful setting, and I loved going there for a little weekend escape from the city.

Helena was a petite woman, and wore her reddish-brown hair very short, and she would always be very fashionably dressed. She was into the designs and clothing of the French couture designers Courrèges, and Coco Chanel.

So that particular week in July, David and Helena and I all went to Colorado Springs, Colorado. We stayed at The Broadmoor Hotel there, which was lovely. I still have a clear memory of us there, sitting around the pool, and laying in the sun.

I remember Helena saying to me, "Oh, Freda! You've got a beautiful tan. You are tanning so fast!"

She was just making a comment about how jealous she was that I had achieved a healthy color quicker than she did. Well, of course I was tanning faster, I have more melanin in my skin than she had! This was aside from the fact that I am already tan.

One day, while we ate in the dining room of The Broadmoor Hotel, David said to me, motioning towards a particular table, "See those people over there?"

"Yes," I replied.

"They are the Rockefellers."

Those were the caliber of people we were spending the weekend with. The Broadmoor Hotel was that kind of a posh place, and it was definitely considered to be a very "high end" resort in every way!

Since I had just been hired to be in *Hallelujah Baby!*, I had my script with me, reading and studying my lines. I carried my script with me wherever I went that weekend just to keep running my lines.

There was a man there who was an acquaintance of David Baumgarten and Helena, and his family owned the majority of the stock in Pacific Bell telephone network. I was clearly sitting in the presence of wealth and attainment.

While we were in Colorado, over the television came the news that there was rioting going on in Detroit. I remember calling home, and making certain that my family was safe. Scherrie was still living at home with my mother and stepfather. I confirmed that they were all fine, and out of harm's way. That was a huge relief.

The riots actually started about a block or two away from where we used to live on Atkinson between 12th and Woodrow Wilson streets. Our address had been 1699 Atkinson Street, when we lived in that neighborhood. By 1967, Mom, my dad, and Scherrie lived on Monte Vista, right between Meyers and Seven Mile Road, so that was a different part of Detroit than where the riots were taking place.

My dad and my mother owned a bar on 12th Street between Collingwood and Calvert, called The Collingwood Bar & Lounge. Daddy had to sleep at the bar during the riots with his gun to protect it. And, he put a sign outside the bar which said, "Black Owned." Thankfully, it was never harmed.

I was especially relieved to find that the riots didn't touch the area where my family lived. When the riots had finally started to die down, Scherrie had her movie camera, and she took some film footage of the homes that burned down.

I felt so safe in Colorado, and yet there was a touch of guiltiness. Detroit was my hometown, and all of this destruction was taking place near where I grew up. It was a really weird feeling, with my emotions trapped somewhere between relief and guilt. It was a strange sort of "double whammy." Here I was having a great time, in the lap of luxury with a bunch of very affluent white people, and on TV I was watching my hometown on fire and African American people rioting, and several being killed. The death toll was 33 black people, and 10 white people.

After we came back to New York from Colorado, I started my new job understudying Leslie in *Hallelujah Baby!* During the run of the show I had to be at the theater six days a week. Of course I was working on my lines, and memorizing the whole show. I had memorized all my lines, and all of the singing and dancing numbers, and it was exactly three weeks after being hired, when the producers told me that I was going to go on for a performance, and to be the star of the show. They gave me a five day notice to prepare. To get me ready for this, we had rehearsals in the afternoon every day so I would get the "blocking" and all of that down, and the timing for the costume changes.

Finally the night came when I was set to go on. It was a Tuesday night, so it was enough time for my parents to drive to New York City from Detroit, and they brought Scherrie. I went on, and I did a flawless performance—both vocally and acting-wise—and I received a standing ovation. When the curtain went down for the final time, everybody in the cast came over and congratulated me, because they were so happy that I pulled it off so well.

Then after that, a week or so later, I went on again. They called me and told me to get prepared to do the show. This time I was only given a few hours notice. The stage manager telephoned me at 11:30 a.m. and said, "You're going on again tonight. Maybe you should come in early to get prepared."

I went on the second time, and by now my confidence level was at a high point. Ultimately I went on five more times after that. So, I can officially say that I got to do a lead role in a hit Broadway musical in New York City.

The first time I had done it, I felt absolutely elevated. It was euphoric! Back then they had a full orchestra with strings in the pit to accompany me. I had all of this wonderful music to sing to, and the score playing. It was simply amazing. The second time I went on, it was as exciting as the first! The euphoria that comes over you when you step on the stage in a hit Broadway show is hard to match. This was definitely a great career plateau for me as a performer.

When I was in this show, my character was the first person the audience would see on-stage when the curtain went up. I played the role of Georgina Johnson, and at the very start of the show I had a little monologue, and I was also the last person on-stage. It was a wonderful experience that I will never forget as long as I live.

The show had great music, and it had a really wonderful plot. The story that *Hallelujah Baby!* tells is about how this lady, Georgina Johnson, evolved through the ages. It starts in the 1920s, and then it evolves scene-by-scene and act-by-act into the 1930s, the 1940s, the 1950s, right on up to the 1960s. Although the times changed, Georgina maintained that she was her own woman, and she remained unchanged through it all. "I remained Georgina Johnson" she proclaimed, and through every decade she stayed 25 years old.

The play told the story of her life, as she moved across each of these different time periods, during decades where society was progressing at a rapid rate. Although the character of Georgina would evolve in the show, her changes were done with different wigs and costumes. In the first scene, I would have a '20s style rag covering my hair, then it moved up to being more of a short Afro hair style. Then in the next scene it would be a different thing. Finally, when it got up to the 1960s, she looked like she was more contemporary and sophisticated. There was also a scene where Georgina was seen as a chorus girl in a nightclub like the famed Cotton Club. This required me to do a little bit of a choreographed routine that was one of the show stopper numbers. The song was called, "Feet Do Your Stuff." It was me and several chorus girls and chorus boys. It wasn't any serious dancing, but I did have to sing and dance a bit.

When the first scene starts, I am seen as a maid working in somebody's house, in the South. You find out that I am living in a world where I have no power over my life, and where there is prejudice and segregation. It depicted the typical segregated South situation where the white man is the boss, and we are the workers.

That was the early 1900s, into the 1920s, then it went into the 1930s and things got a little better. Then came the 1940s, and 1950s, where Georgina has evolved into a successful singer in a nightclub.

When it finally ended up in the 1960s, it was the time of the Civil Rights movement, and Georgina was involved in a love triangle with a white man, who was played by Allen Case.

One of the odd, or unique, things that happened in the play was that none of the characters aged at all during the course of the play. It had that kind of fantasy aspect to it. According to the liner notes on the Original Cast vinyl album, the plot of *Hallelujah Baby!* follows "what's been happening between Negroes and whites during the last 60 years. It is about people, and it is about time." And it was also how attitudes changed.

Of course Georgina grows and evolves through the decades. Then the male lead evolves on his own path in life. He goes from being a porter, then he moves up the ladder, and then he eventually ends up a figure in an organization like the NAACP in the 1960s.

The show had a great cast, including some up-and-coming stars. Garrett Morris, who later became famous on *Saturday Night Live*, was in the chorus of the show. Recently, he is one of the stars on the hit comedy TV show, *Two Broke Girls*. Back then, he was a chorus boy in *Hallelujah, Baby!*

The show was a very prestigious and glamorous Broadway production. It had music by Jule Styne, who wrote *Funny Girl*. It had lyrics by Betty Comden and Adolph Green who wrote *On The Town*. And the "book" of the show was by Arthur Laurents who wrote *West Side Story*. According to Laurents, the show was originally written with Lena Horne in mind for the role of Georgina, but when she passed on it, Leslie was cast in the starring role. Here I was—for six performances—on Broadway playing a role that was written for my idol, Lena Horne! What an amazing twist of fate.

In the 1960s, tackling the subject of interracial dating was still very controversial. The fact that Georgina was having an affair with a white man—Allen Case's character, yet she still had a relationship with a black man—Robert Hooks' character, was a new topic for a Broadway musical. In the plot of the show, her relationship with Robert's character also spanned several decades, so he evolved and grew right along with her.

As a side note, at the time, Leslie Uggams was actually married to a white man from Australia, Grahame Pratt. They are still together, and have been married all these years.

Hallelujah Baby! went on to win the Tony Award for "Best Musical" in 1968, and another Tony for "Best Score." Leslie Uggams was awarded the Tony for "Best Actress in a Musical," and Lillian Hayman won for "Best Featured Actress in a Musical." Lillian had the show-stopper number, "I Don't Know Where She Got It." Also, it won for "Best Original Score," "Best Direction of a Musical," and "Best Producer of a Musical."

When I was put under contract to do the show, I was hired not only as an understudy to the lead role, but I was also a "swing dancer" as well. If, for any reason, a dancer in the show can't dance for a given performance, a "swing dancer" steps in for them. During the time I was in the show, I only had to do this once. It was the scene which depicted the entrance to a ballroom gala, but we had to do some "leaps" and "*grande jattes*" into the ballroom, and moves like that.

The dancer I was subbing for was Hope Clark, who was the dance captain for the chorus girls, and she was quite a wonderfully strong dancer. This was an amazing time for me, and it was a true career high point.

The theater that we were in was called The Martin Beck Theater, and it was on 45th Street, right off Eighth Avenue. In 2002 that theater had its name changed to The Al Hirschfeld Theater, to honor the famed Broadway cartoon illustrator.

Each night, after the shows were over on Broadway, everybody would go to a restaurant on West 46th Street called Joe Allen's. We would go there just to hang out after the show, and there was no telling who you would run into there. Another place we would go would be an Irish pub on Eighth Avenue between 44th and 45th Street, around the corner from the theater. That was a big theater district hangout of ours. I loved being part of a hit Broadway show!

We often hung out at that pub, where we would get a little snack, or an Irish coffee, or whatever we were in the mood for at the time. Also, Joe Allen's was, and is still, a favorite post-Broadway show hangout.

Hallelujah Baby! didn't have an exceedingly long stretched-out run on Broadway like some musicals do. It opened on April 26, 1967 and closed on January 13, 1968. I was there as part of the cast for somewhere around six months. This was really a fun time for me, and I stayed with the play until it closed.

In 1968 I auditioned for Bob Fosse's film version of *Sweet Charity*, which was set to star Shirley MacLaine in the title role. The part I read for was that of Helene, one of Charity's fellow hookers in a sleazy dance hall. Ultimately, the part was awarded to dancer and actress Paula Kelly. Although I could certainly sing the part with no problem, I have to say that Paula's dance experience was a lot stronger than mine. I would have loved to have landed this role, but looking back on it, the producers made the right choice by choosing Paula, because her dancing in *Sweet Charity* was impeccable. And, she was a good singer too.

The next theater production I did in New York City was *Lost in the Stars*. This was an Actors Equity production that was up on 103rd Street on the West Side. It wasn't a Broadway show. I played the role of "Linda" in this play that takes place in South Africa. It had some music in it, but it had a lot of straight acting in it as well. They eventually made a movie out of it, starring Brock Peters as a Zulu preacher. In the plot of the show—as filmed, the preacher goes to Johannesburg to find his estranged son, played by Clifton Davis, where he encounters his girlfriend who is pregnant, played by Melba Moore.

In this particular production that I was in, my big number was a song called "Who'll Buy?" The music was written by Kurt Weill of *Threepenny Opera* fame. Weill, along with Bertolt Brecht, was the writer of the classic song "Mack The Knife." This was just a short run, two or three weeks at most.

I remember being downstairs in the dressing room of the theater, and there were several people in the room with me. That is the day that Dr. Martin Luther King was assassinated. It was April 4, 1968. It was one of those things like remembering exactly where you were when John F. Kennedy was shot. It was just like that.

I remember all the rioting in the streets that occurred in Washington D.C. and the fires that were burning up in Harlem. For African American people, Dr. Martin Luther King was someone who they could look up to, as he was not only a Civil Rights leader, but he was someone who could be viewed as a savior. It felt like losing a member of your family when he was assassinated.

After *Hallelujah Baby!* closed, and *Lost In The Stars* ended, I resumed working in nightclubs. The circuit I was on found me working in Miami, in Puerto Rico, in Vegas, and at Paradise Island in Nassau, in the Bahamas, back in the days when that really was paradise, and there was only one casino there. I even headlined for two weeks at The Plaza Hotel in Manhattan, back when they had a showroom there.

On my travels during this era, I got to run into several performers I loved and admired. Before my engagement at The Plaza, Michelle Lee was booked there and I went to see her show. She was married to actor James Farentino at the time, and I met him too.

The next time I saw Frank Sinatra was in Florida where he filmed *Lady in Cement*, playing the role of Tony Rome. At the time, I was performing in the lounge at The Fontainebleau Hotel. This was circa 1968. I was staying there at the hotel as well as singing in the lounge. Sinatra would come into the lounge with his entourage to see my show.

At the time, Frank was staying in the penthouse while he was in town working on *Lady In Cement*, along with Raquel Welch. I was really impressed with him, and he was very complimentary about me and my singing. After my show he would invite me up to his penthouse, so naturally I took him up on his invitation. Sinatra was a perfect gentleman, and he never made a pass at me sexually. But he would invite me to just come up and hang out with him. I would be sitting there, and a parade of his friends would stop by to see him. I remember a man by the name of Prince Romanoff, and comedian Pat Henry whom I already knew through my former manager Joe Scandore. I had worked with Pat at hotels in The Catskills.

Sinatra was very warm and friendly, and we would have several conversations on a "performer to performer" basis. During one of my conversations with Frank he said to me, "Freda I like you. You're a really good singer, and you are a lady." I will never forget that compliment from the one and only Frank Sinatra.

On one occasion Frank said to me, "They want me use Dionne Warwick to be my opening act for an upcoming appearance at Carnegie Hall. But I don't know. When she sings, she uses too much vibrato in her voice. What do you think?"

Here was Frank Sinatra genuinely looking to me, and asking me for my opinion, which was instantly flattering. I said to him, "Yeah, but Dionne sounds good to me. I don't think she has that much of a vibrato. I think she would be a good choice for you."

The next thing I knew, I opened up the newspaper, and there was an announcement that Dionne Warwick was opening up for Frank Sinatra! I was impressed to think that I might have had a hand in it!

Way before this dialogue with Sinatra happened, I had a conversation with a guy in New York I met. The guy was one of those "shady" characters in show business. He said to me, "If you ever run into Sinatra, and he 'hits' on you sexually, don't turn him down!"

I was aware of that, but he never made "a pass" at me. I was so flattered that he thought of me as "a lady." I always had a nice, friendly relationship with Frank Sinatra.

Little did he know, I was not Little Mary Sunshine, or a "goody two shoes." But when you are around a powerful person, you are kind of on-your-guard. You want to put your best foot forward, and you never want to do anything wrong, or say anything wrong. You are just happy to be there.

I also felt a certain sense of protection or security being around Sinatra. If anyone tried to mess with me, I would just say, "You'd better watch your step: Frank Sinatra is a close personal friend of mine. Don't even think about messing with me!"

After getting to be friends with Frank in Florida, every time he would see me, he was warm and charming towards me, and we always had respect for one another. On one occasion, at The St. Regis Hotel in New York, I was headlining at The Maisonette Room, and I was with my friend Lenny Bleecher. We were walking together into the lounge of the hotel, and Sinatra was with a group of people who were sitting at his table. I just happened to walk by. I spotted him, and just casually said, "Hi Frank."

He stood up from his seat, and announced to his friends, "Now, there goes a great singer!" I was so flattered.

When I think of him, I think to myself, "I really could have had it all by dating Frank Sinatra if that was what I wanted." However, that was not in the cards. What I had instead was a great friendship with a lot of mutual respect, that went on for years.

July 20, 1969 was the day man first landed on the moon. I was so impressed to hear this. While booked for a weeklong engagement at The Shamrock Hilton in Houston, Texas, there was a special event on my day off that was given in the ballroom of the hotel, honoring the astronauts who went to the moon. I was invited to attend, and I was able to meet the famed astronauts John Glenn and Neil Armstrong. Years later, John Glenn became a Democratic Senator from Ohio. That afternoon was a big thrill for me, to meet the first men who had landed on the moon and returned safely. I actually got an autograph from Neil, and for the life of me I can't find it.

Speaking of "in the cards," when I lived in New York City, there was a place in town called The Gypsy Tea Kettle. You could go there and get your fortune told. Actually there were a couple of them. One was at Lexington and 56th Street, and there was one located at Seventh Avenue and 50th Street, right by the subway entrance. That was the one I most frequently visited. It was like a hotel lobby, but you had to go in, and up on the second floor, there it was: The Gypsy Tea Kettle.

You could go there and get a reading for $5.00. I would get these readings from a guy there by the name of Larry Taylor. There were other readers I went to as well.

One day I went to Larry's apartment for a private reading, and he said to me, "You are going to sign a record deal, not in New York City. These are dark complexioned people, and they look like they could be your cousins."

"My cousins?" I said.

He thought for a minute and replied, "No, they are not your cousins. But they are of your race. And, it is not here, it is somewhere else. I am seeing somewhere in the Midwest."

I said, "Could it be Detroit?" Because I was thinking that it might be Berry Gordy and Motown Records approaching me again.

He said, "Maybe. You are going to sign with a record company, and you're going to get two big hit records, and then you are going to leave the company."

"That doesn't make any sense." I said, "I've been in the business for eight years now, and I finally get two hits? Why would I leave the record company if they gave me two hits? I wouldn't want to leave. I would want to stay and get more hits."

He then said, "Deception is involved. But you are going to go on from there."

Larry literally predicted it before it even happened, and he was 100% correct! I was going to have two huge hit records. I just knew the prophecy was going to come true. I had a feeling in my gut. The gypsy didn't lie!

CHAPTER SIX

"Invictus Records"

While still living in New York, my roommate Sandy and I had an apartment on Central Park West, and in the next building lived the singer Tamiko Jones. We had known each other in the business, and we were friends. One day Tamiko called me up and said, "Freda, guess who is here? He says he knows you from Detroit."

I said, "Who is that?"

"Brian Holland."

"Brian? We went to high school together in Detroit."

"Well, he is sitting right here," she announced, "and he wants to talk to you."

"Well, put Brian on the phone!"

So Brian got on the phone, and he said, "Hey there, Freda, what are you doing? What's up?"

I replied, "It's so good to hear from you, Brian! You guys have certainly become famous since we were all in school. And, especially since the last time I saw all of you guys."

He explained, "Well, we've done alright. We had a great run with Motown, and we just left Motown and Berry. We were with him for ten years or so, and we've formed our own record label called Invictus Records. What are you doing?"

"I'm not doing anything right now," I said. "Well, I was in this hit Broadway musical called *Hallelujah Baby!*, I was understudying Leslie Uggams. And after that I did a musical called *Lost In The Stars* off Broadway, but I'm not doing anything right now."

"If you are not doing anything, then why don't you come on over here? I would love to see you."

"Okay, I will be right over."

It was lucky that I was home at the time. I could have been at an out-of-town engagement or something. So I got up and walked over there. We sat in the living room of Tamiko's apartment and reminisced a bit. Then Brian started asking me questions like, "Are you with a record label now?"

I said, "I was with ABC/Paramount. I did a single with them, and then I did an album on Impulse Records. But they didn't pick up my 'option.' Then I was on MGM Records. I had one album on that label, and they didn't pick up my 'option' either. So I am not with any label at the moment."

"Why do you think the MGM deal didn't work out?" Brian asked.

"The reason that MGM didn't pick up my option was because I had split up with Clarence Avant, who got me the deal in the first place," I explained.

"Are you being managed by anybody now?" Brian asked.

"No, I just got out of my contract with my manager, Joe Scandore, and his partner Mel Shayne."

After I quit working with Joe Scandore, Mel had left, and Joe aligned himself with Shelly Berger, who later managed Diana Ross, and The Temptations. I am still friends with Shelly to this day.

So, Brian said to me, "Well, why don't you come with us? Maybe we can do something?"

I said, "You have your own record label now?"

"Yes, Invictus. We are just getting it together, and we've got a couple of groups already signed. We need a female singer on our roster."

"How did Berry take it when he found out you guys wanted to leave Motown?" I asked with genuine curiosity.

"Well, we sued him, then he counter-sued us back, and at the moment our lawyers are working out the details. That's why we went off on our own and established Invictus Records."

So, after that Brian called his brother Eddie, and then Eddie got on the phone and said to me, "Well, we would like to fly you into Detroit, so we can sit down and talk about it. We would love to have you with us at Invictus."

"Well, then I would love to be there!" I replied.

Since the time Berry Gordy brought Eddie Holland over to my house in Detroit in 1957, Eddie had been quite busy. Together with his brother Brian, and their friend Lamont Dozier, they had made quite a name for themselves as the songwriting and record producing team Holland-Dozier-Holland. They were responsible for writing and producing dozens of Motown hit records, including "Heat Wave" for Martha Reeves & The Vandellas, "It's The Same Old Song" for The Four Tops, "Come See About Me" for The Supremes, and "Can I Get a Witness" for Marvin Gaye. Now they wanted to work their magic on me! And I wasn't about to miss out on this opportunity.

They flew me to Detroit, and presented me with a contract. I proceeded to read the contract, clause-for-clause. I did not scrutinize their contract the way that I did with Duke Ellington, and Berry Gordy Jr., because I realized that I had all these people in my past who had made offers to me, but things didn't work out when it came time to signing a contract. After I was done going over it, I just signed it right on the spot.

I thought to myself, "I may as well sign with Holland-Dozier-Holland. What else am I doing now in my career? I should just take a chance and do it, before another opportunity passes me by."

At the time, I was just working in small clubs and some very nice supper clubs across the country, but making minimal salary. I knew that having a hit record would instantly bump my career up to the next level. Case-in-point: I was making approximately $1,500.00 a week as opposed to $5,000.00 or $10,000.00 a week if I had a hit record.

Eddie told me later, that he was expecting me to contest the contract, and want to make some changes to it, and to negotiate. He said to me, "I was all ready to have to do that with you, and I was willing to make any changes you requested."

Here was the one time I could have made some demands and changes to the contract, and have all my requests met. And it was also the one time I didn't question a thing on a contract, and just signed it on the spot. It was ironic indeed!

Had I negotiated better, and with improved terms at the beginning, I may not have encountered the problems I ultimately did. As it was, I signed my contract with Holland-Dozier-Holland and Invictus Records, and we started recording right away. All of my Invictus recordings were produced and recorded in Detroit. I stayed at my parents house on Monte Vista Street, while we were working on the recording sessions for my debut Invictus album, *Band of Gold*.

One of the people I worked with at Invictus was songwriter Ron Dunbar. He used to pick me up at my parents' house, and he would drive me to the recording studio. Sometimes it would just be a meeting at Eddie's apartment, and we would go over songs and listen to tracks, and then we'd start working on and rehearsing to the pre-recorded tracks. Then, if I had to record, he would take me over to the studio, which was on Grand River Boulevard. It was a converted theater building where they had built their own recording studio. They called it Holland-Dozier-Holland Sound Studios. For recording engineers, H-D-H hired Lawrence Horn and Barney Perkins, who had both worked at Motown Records.

I had to forget everything I'd been doing before I signed with Invictus, and learn everything anew. My formal vocal training did not apply to this style of music. Singing jazz songs and Broadway tunes are different than singing upbeat R&B songs. Eddie Holland was very patient with me, teaching me his method of singing and recording, and I just did exactly what he told me to do. In truth, though, it wasn't too difficult because, although I am a natural jazz singer, I can sing soul. I came into the Invictus sessions knowing that I could not impose my jazz chops to the R&B concept the way H-D-H produced songs. I just wanted to put out good product, record great pop songs, and do as I was directed to do in the recording studio, and I did just that. For instance, if they said, "We don't want any vibrato on this song," I would follow their instructions, and do exactly what they said.

We recorded a lot of material, and in 1969 they decided to release the first Freda Payne single on their label. It came out late in the year, in November. The first single was from the album ultimately to be entitled *Band of Gold*. The "A" side of the first single was a song called "The Unhooked Generation." That song was about being addicted to a person romantically. In the song's lyrics the singer becomes "unhooked" from this toxic love affair. I really liked it, and H-D-H thought it was pretty hot too, and they also expected it to really go up the charts. But it didn't go as far as everyone expected. Its one distinction was that it made it to Number 43 on the *Billboard* R&B chart, but that was it.

So, Brian, Eddie, and Lamont started thinking, "What are we going to release next?" In January of 1970 they decided to release the song "Band of Gold," which was supposedly written by Ronald Dunbar and Edythe Wayne. However, they weren't the actual writers.

There was a legal conflict. When Holland-Dozier-Holland sued Motown Records for not paying them what they felt they deserved, Motown in turn sued them back. Until the lawsuits were resolved, the three of them weren't supposed to do any songwriting. But, in fact they were the true writers of "Band of Gold," even though Ron Dunbar and Edythe Wayne were listed as the songwriters on the record label and the album as well. The song was pure H-D-H.

The song "Band of Gold" began to climb the record charts in the U.S. and the U.K. It went on, and went on, and finally it started to make some noise and receive some radio airplay. It moved slowly at first, and week-after-week it started to show up on some local playlists. Then it started to catch on more, and all of a sudden: BAM! Finally, it hit the U.S. *Billboard* charts in April of 1970, and went all the way up to Number Three on that publication's "Hot 100" chart, and Number 20 on the R&B chart. Also it hit Number Two in *Cashbox* in the U.S., and Number Two in Canada. In Australia it peaked at Number Five. The best of all: It topped the charts in Ireland, and it also hit Number One in Great Britain and stayed there for six straight weeks!

"Band of Gold" was so appealing to radio programmers and fans alike, that it instantly became my "signature song," and I have always been glad to have it. It ended up selling two million copies worldwide. The single version of "Band of Gold" was certified *Gold* after over a million copies sold in America alone. I would turn on the radio, and there I would be! The next song that was released as the next single, "Deeper and Deeper," also became a Top Ten hit for me, peaking at Number Nine on the R&B chart, and Number 24 on the Pop chart.

My album *Band of Gold*, including the title track, represented all of my initial recording sessions at Invictus. Based on the success of those two hit singles, they took the album up to Number 17 on the R&B chart in the U.S., and Number 60 on the Pop album chart.

The first time I realized that "Band of Gold" was really big, I was taping a TV special in Toronto, Ontario, Canada. It was an episode of *The First Edition* with Kenny Rogers. After that I also did a Barbara McNair special, and a Lou Rawls special which were all taped in Toronto. American production companies and stars were doing a lot of their TV specials in Toronto at that time, to eliminate the U.S. union costs.

I was in my dressing room, and a production assistant came up to me and said, "Miss Payne, there's a phone call for you from the BBC in London. They want to interview you."

"What?" I said with surprise.

So, I got on the phone with them, and the person on the other end said, "Why hello, Miss Payne. How does it feel to have a Number One record over here in the U.K.?"

"Really? Number One? Well, it feels great!" I genuinely exclaimed.

When they were interviewing me, out-of-the-blue they said, "Do you think that if this had been done by Diana Ross, it would have been an even bigger hit?"

"What a weird comment," I thought to myself. I said back to the interviewer, "I have no idea. Whatever Diana has done, she has done. This one was meant for me! So, now I have a hit of my own, and I love it!"

My new Invictus album was released at the same time that Diana had released her debut solo album on Motown, having just left The Supremes. The timing was perfect for the press to jump on the bandwagon and make critical comparisons, especially since I was now with Holland-Dozier-Holland, and they were the ones who made Diana and The Supremes into huge stars.

When the British music publication *New Musical Express* reviewed my album, they did so in an article called: "Can H-D-H Make Freda Into Another Diana Ross?" According to writer Allen Evans, "On their albums there are many similarities, like short talking patches, build-ups to climaxes, uses of almost identical backings of girl singers, groups, and strings. But the main thing is Holland-

Dozier-Holland, the multi-million selling song writing team who have started their Invictus label in opposition to their former boss Berry Gordy's Tamla Motown…Listening to the two debut LP's, I found that Diana changed a bit from her former days. Her singing is quieter, more precise…Freda on the other hand is right in there pitching…Freda is a most welcome newcomer to the world of stardom, which is so ill-populated these days." (3)

As soon as "Band of Gold" became a huge international hit in 1970, things started rolling faster-and-faster for me, and I was suddenly "on the map" in the music business. It began my most successful streak as a recording and performing artist.

I didn't realize it at the time, but "Band of Gold" was to become known as my career-long trademark song. From this point forward I wouldn't think of performing on a show and not singing it. It is instantly recognizable wherever I go, and I am glad to have it as my own!

In 2019, when *Rolling Stone* magazine published an article called "20 Biggest Songs of The Summer: The 1970s," music critic Al Shipley ranked "Band of Gold" at Number 16 on his list. According to the article, "Because the full lyrics are trimmed to fit the three-minute single edit, 'Band of Gold's' tale of a failing young marriage was heavy on emotion and light on detail. Years later, Ron Dunbar, who wrote the song with the Holland-Dozier-Holland team, was shocked to learn that the ambiguity of the story made it a hit with the gay community, which developed its own theories about why the groom couldn't make love to his new bride." (4)

Who would have guessed that "Band of Gold" made such an impression on people 50 years after it was recorded? That is the wonderful thing about having a huge hit record. You record it, you leave the studio, and all of a sudden it has a life all its own!

There were a lot of things going on behind the scenes when it came to the production and recording of the song "Band of

Gold." One of the other people involved in its creation was producer Tony Camillo, who not only worked with Motown and with Invictus Records, but went on to write several hits. Most notable was "Midnight Train to Georgia," which was a huge Number One hit for Gladys Knight & The Pips after that group left Motown Records and signed with Buddha Records in the early '70s.

In a letter that Tony Camillo sent to me in the year 2000 he wrote, "I am certain that you do not know the facts about the record 'Band of Gold.' It is the truth when I tell you that I am responsible for most of the creation of that record. I created every part that was recorded on that record and even created the melody. The only thing I did not create was the words. Eddie Holland told me he would not give me credit, if I did not sign a seven year contract with him. Both he and Motown were trying to get me to sign, but I refused to do so. Instead I wrote some of my own songs like 'I Feel a Song In My Heart' [for Gladys Knight & The Pips] and recorded them with the Motown rhythm section. I knew that Eddie was not someone I wanted to be with under contract. It was the right decision for me. It's what eventually made it possible for me to do my own thing as a producer." (5)

In a very short period of time, I was to release four albums on Invictus Records, and I had a string of Number One, Top Ten, and Top 40 hits on the charts. The success of these recordings kept me busier than ever. In addition to an exciting run of television appearances, I was also working in nightclubs and concert halls at the time. As soon as "Band of Gold" hit Number One, I had to come up with a new stage show to feature it as the centerpiece of the show.

For a new and stronger stage act, I turned to my dear friend, songwriter Lenny Bleecher, as that was his specialty. I had known Lenny from New York, when I lived there in the 1960s. His wife, Baba Baldwin, had her own couture dress shop on East 55th Street between Madison Avenue and Fifth Avenue. She was a Caucasian woman, and her clientele was mainly white society women. Baba was also known for having dressed Louis Armstrong's wife, Lucille. Baba was a very lovely person of French heritage, with a motherly personality and she was also on the stout side. Baba made every person she encountered very comfortable, and that was the motherly side of her personality.

Although Baba made mostly dresses for society women, Lenny wanted her to design gowns for me. Her designs were custom made, they were expertly tailored and very conservative. She ended up doing several gowns for me as well as several pieces for day wear including pant suits, and dresses. Up until now, most of my gowns had been done by Roxanne Spino.

As it ended up, Lenny played a very pivotal role in my life. I had known Lenny since about 1968. He was primarily a songwriter, and he also did special material for musical performers to present in their stage acts. He was very good at writing parodies of established songs. He wrote a very amusing set of lyrics for me to sing when I performed "My Favorite Things" on-stage. Lenny had a great sense of humor.

Performers had to have an act which was written out, and you would go to a writer like Lenny to put it all together so that you would have set monologues in between your songs. For instance, the light man had to know exactly what light color and intensity to use on each number to set the right mood on-stage, and things had to be scripted. Nowadays, it seems like many performers can ad-lib their way through a show and speak extemporaneously. But back then, agents would specifically ask you if you had "an act" before they booked you in their nightclubs.

When hit-making contemporary acts like The Temptations or The Supremes were booked into The Copacabana, they had to have a specific act with monologues, and songs. We all had to have a carefully structured act to fit into a nightclub setting.

That was how I got to know Lenny. He worked on my act, so that I had a solid set of songs and entertaining things to say on-stage. Actually, I knew him before he married Baba, in 1969. I had met him in the office of O.B. Masingill who was doing musical arrangements for me at the time. He was my arranger.

This was during a time when I was working with the famed Danish concert pianist and comedian, Victor Borge. He appeared in theaters in-the-round, starred in his own TV specials, and even played Carnegie Hall. At the time I was making appearances on *The Tonight Show*, with Johnny Carson, and in fact I had been on that show several times.

The next time I encountered Lenny, was in 1970 when he suddenly appeared again in my life. He had just married Baba Baldwin, and I had just had my hit "Band of Gold."

I was working on a guest appearance on *The Dick Cavett Show* on TV, and I was with my road manager, Bobby Lucas. We had a rehearsal at the studio, and we had a break before we began taping the show. So, Bobby and I decided to go to a local coffee shop on Seventh Avenue during the break. We were sitting there and in walked Lenny Bleecher. It was a serendipitous moment. Lenny and Baba had been out driving, and Lenny suddenly decided that he needed something to eat, so he pulled over and ran into this same coffee shop. What a crazy coincidence! That was how we reunited.

He said to me, "I have just gotten married to the most wonderful woman. You have to meet her. Let me go to the car, and get her." When he returned from the car, Bobby and I got to meet Baba for the first time.

At the time, The Three Degrees had scored a huge hit with "When Will I See You Again," and they were booked to perform at The Copacabana. Lenny was working on and writing their act, and Baba designed gowns for them.

After our reunion in the coffee shop Lenny and Baba and I

became very close friends. Lenny and Baba lived on West 86th Street, between Amsterdam and Columbus. They had an apartment that had three bedrooms, and a very large living room, which is considered a huge apartment in New York City terms. They lived there from the late '60s to the mid- to late-'70s.

I didn't have a hit record when I first met Lenny. I was a performer and a cabaret singer of note, but I didn't have a hit song of my own to center an act upon. I would work in showrooms at Miami Beach hotels like The Fontainebleau, The Diplomat, The Doral Beach Hotel, and The Americana. I also played at the St. James nightclub in Miami Beach, which was an all-black club that had a motel as well. I would also work in the Caribbean at various resort hotels. I appeared in Puerto Rico at The Caribe Hilton in San Juan, and I worked at all of the first class supper clubs.

So, even at the beginning of my show business career, I had to have professional sheet music and specifically orchestrated arrangements for the bands I played with. I had to have a carefully scripted act, so that I knew exactly how it was timed, how it unfolded, and what I said in between songs. I had to pay for someone to write an act for me and of course I paid for my own gowns. It seemed that every cent I made at this point, I put back into my career. I was just doing my best to hang in there until I had a hit record, or something else to propel me into the big time. Thanks to "Band of Gold," I had arrived!

In 1971, I was booked to perform with Jerry Lewis in concert at The Olympia Theater in Paris, France. I was what they called "*le grande vedette*" on the show, or in English: "the opening act." A gentleman known as Bruno Coquatrix was infamously known as the owner of the Olympia. He was quite a colorful character.

This particular performance was a really high-profile engagement, and the *crème-de-la-crème* of Paris was there. This included the Prime Minister of France, the Baron and Baroness Brandolini, and the royalty, the rich people, the celebrities, they were all invited. And to top it all off, excitingly handsome actor Omar Sharif was there as well. This was because Jerry Lewis back then was revered in France as being a master comedian, on par with Charlie Chaplin. The French respected him greatly as a comic genius—even more so than they did in America.

I remember opening night of this engagement. Having known Jerry for a few years, I went to his dressing room to say, "Good luck, Jerry, have a great show." And when I got there, I could see that he was so nervous his hands were trembling. He was such a consummate professional, I would have thought he would be much more comfortable performing live.

I thought to myself, "Damn, I thought I would be the one who should be nervous, and he is the one trembling!"

Somebody wisely told me to be sure and say something in French on-stage that evening to win over the audience. They appreciated American performers who at least made an effort to talk to them in their native language. After all, this was Paris! So when I wanted the audience to clap along with me, I knew how to invite them to do so by saying, "*frappe dans vous mains.*"

They loved me that night, and I was a big hit. Afterwards we went to the famed restaurant, Maxim's, and Omar Sharif was one of the invited guests. At the time I was represented by Rogers & Cowen as my publicists. So, the publicist decided that they wanted to stir up some gossip, and they came up with the idea of planting a press item that I was secretly dating Omar Sharif.

To accomplish this, Rogers & Cowen called Omar's representatives and asked them if it would be OK to plant this item. He confirmed that he was fine with that plan. So from that point forward, journalists would constantly ask me about my affair with Omar Sharif. When I was asked about it, I would reply, "Oh, it was just a publicity stunt."

However, no one ever believed me when I gave them this explanation! "Oh yeah, sure," they would reply, assuming I was trying to cover up the truth about a really hot affair with one of the top leading men in Hollywood.

One of the people who totally refused to believe my denials was publicist and producer, David Gest. He was one of my best friends, and he would say to me, "Well, after all, you had an affair with Omar Sharif."

I would tell him, "Oh David, it really didn't happen." But he absolutely refused to believe me. The more I denied it, the more he was convinced it had happened.

The other person who didn't want to hear anything about my denials about "my affair" with Omar Sharif, was Aretha Franklin. In the fall of 1997, I went to see Aretha in Toronto, Canada where she was in concert. That same week I was working in neighboring Mississauga, Ontario, doing a show. I was appearing there almost two months.

I was part of the cast of a "book" show called *Something to Remind Me.* It was a revue comprised of the music of Burt Bacharach & Hal David, and the music of Carole King combined. On my off day I received a call from Aretha's conductor and musical director, H.B. Barnum. I had worked with H.B. as well. He produced my act and wrote my musical arrangements back in the early '70s when "Band of Gold" was a big hit.

H.B. called to tell me, "I am working with Aretha here at a theater in Toronto. Do you want to come see her show on your off night? I am inviting you, as Aretha really wants you to come." So, I gladly accepted. After the show we all went out to a restaurant, and I was sitting directly across the table from Aretha.

The very first thing she said to me was, "Well, tell me Freda, how was it dating Omar Sharif?"

I was tired of denying the whole story all these years, so I just looked at Aretha and I said, "Oh girl, it was *nice!*" And I just left it at that.

When I was in Paris in 1971, when I was "supposedly" having a mad affair with Omar Sharif, I was introduced to several members of French society. One of the people I met was Andre Oliver, who was the business partner and close friend of Pierre Cardin, the famed couture French designer. Pierre was on par with Coco Chanel, Yves St. Laurant, and all of the premiere French fashion elite, and I was happy that we hit it off so well.

Andre Oliver instantly took a liking to me as a friend. When I met him, famed French discotheque owner and grand dame, Régine, was there as well. She had one of the top private discos in Paris, and she was quite a character herself. As a brilliant piece of public relations, Rogers & Cowan arranged for Pierre Cardin to play host at a private party for me. He loved the idea. This was all happening because of the success of "Band of Gold." It seemed that everyone in Paris now knew who I was.

So, Pierre threw this elaborate party for me at Andre Oliver's apartment. Needless to say, Andre's apartment was a work of art in itself. To top off the opulence: he had original Monet's on his walls! It was as decadent as can be. I knew that Pierre and Andre were gay, but I couldn't have cared less. Andre might have been gay, but I would have still gone for him. He was still a man, and a handsome one at that! I would have "jumped on his bones, in a New York minute!"

Although I was attracted to him, obviously nothing happened between us, other than a wonderful friendship. Again, the guest list for this party consisted of the *crème-de-la-crème* of French society. They all came. There were the Baron de Rothchilds, the Baron and Baroness Brandolini—who owned Fiat Motors in Italy, and the Prince of Thailand—who came dressed in his traditional Thai clothing. Of course Pierre Cardin and Régine were there, and all of their friends and associates, and the press as well. I have in my possession a black & white 8" x 10" photograph with the two of them from this party.

Since I was the guest of honor, and the guests were comprised of the most fashionable Parisians, I had to be dressed for the part as well. For this party, Pierre Cardin loaned me an original outfit to wear, so that I was dressed in the very latest full couturier fashion. Since I am not as tall as runway models, they had to hem the pants so they would fit me correctly. It was a black sequined jumpsuit that had to be shortened about five inches, with a black lace tunic over it, and a dramatic ruffle around the collar. I will never forget that *tres chic* outfit, or that night where I was made to feel like I was the toast of Paris. I was at the height of my newfound fame and it felt wonderful, like I was Cinderella, and I had just arrived at the ball.

In the meantime, amidst my trips back to Detroit, I happened to notice that Eddie Holland was a very attractive man. I wasn't really dating anyone seriously at this point, and I hadn't really thought of him in those terms before.

I said to myself, "You know what, he is a man who is 'in charge.' He is the president of this record company, and he isn't married. Even though Eddie is something of 'a player,' maybe we could be a great 'power couple.'" I knew there were a few women he was dating, including a woman he had a child with. But they were never married.

At the time I thought that Eddie and I could be like Berry Gordy and Diana Ross. Sometimes you cannot help what choices you make. Often they simply are based upon what opportunities cross your path. Eddie seemed like "fair game" and "a catch."

So, I figured, "Eddie Holland? What the heck?" And, I started flirting with him. Naturally, he took the bait. So Eddie started inviting me out to dinner, and then one thing lead to another. So, that was the beginning of my relationship with him.

Meanwhile, we also had to work together and that is always a delicate balance. It seemed that our whole relationship was like oil and water—completely incompatible with each other on so many levels. Our personalities were so different. I saw him as being a "diamond in the rough" as a man. I saw where he was missing out on a lot of things in life. I thought he could be so much more than he was allowing himself to become. Although he was only 32 years old at the time, he acted like he was 55 years old. He carried himself like he was an older executive. I thought he was very serious and that he should loosen up and enjoy life more.

Eddie and Brian did have some money invested in race horses, and he would invite me to go with him to the race track. But I thought there was so much more available to him at this point in his life.

I said to him, "You should be traveling to Europe. You should be playing tennis. You should be playing golf. You shouldn't just stay here in Detroit doing the same mundane things all of the time."

It was around this time Holland-Dozier-Holland wanted me to move from APA (Agency for the Performing Arts), and put me with another agency like ICM. I was totally against that plan, but they basically steamrolled their way in and signed me to a different company as my booking agent. They wanted me signed to the one they had worked with, and they created a lot of bad blood for me with my former agent David Baumgarten. He was the one who was behind me for all those years, and it was David who watched out for me. He was like my godfather. David was very hurt by this move, and irreparable damage was done. It was Eddie's ego that made him want to take me away from David. He felt threatened that David and I were too close.

Then Eddie, as the President of Invictus Records, formed a managerial company, called Creative Attractions. He appointed a guy by the name of Clarence Tucker to run it. At first they were optimistic about it, but I wasn't happy with their management decisions. One thing they did, which I really resented, came back to really hurt me then, and into the future. It caused some very negative feelings in the business.

Eddie had known about my friendly relationships with David Baumgarten and all of the other agents at APA. I was very close with them, and they had taken very good care of me for years. My friends at APA included my agents Marvin Josephson, Roger Vorce, Harvey Litwin, and Bruce Sevan who had negotiated my contracts for *Halleluiah, Baby!*

I had been signed to APA since 1967. They are the ones who handled my international bookings in Curacao, Puerto Rico, and Aruba, and booking me in all of these prestigious supper clubs like The Plaza Hotel in New York, and The Shamrock Hilton in Houston, Texas. They were the ones who lifted me up and kept me going all these years, including my touring with Victor Borge. APA had done so much for me, and I truly appreciated all of it. They had gotten me work and given me opportunities that made me into a top entertainer. They were there for all of the lean years in my career, now it appeared that I had my first big hit with "Band of Gold," and here I was leaving the people who were the most loyal to me. But my hands were tied, and my back was up against the wall.

APA had gotten me and my career to a certain point that I was very proud of, and here comes Eddie Holland wanting me to break off all contact with APA. This caused all sorts of problems and bad feelings.

That was one thing that Eddie did that simply wasn't right. Years later I brought it up to him, and he admitted it was his ego that motivated that. He also said to me, "I wish I could have been more mature about how I handled that situation."

At the time I was embarrassed, hurt, and mad, but Eddie insisted that it was his contractual right to be involved in deciding who my booking agent was. As my new agency, Creative Attractions had made a lot of promises to me about my career that didn't quite develop. Then there was a lot of "double booking." "Double booking" is when two different agents claim credit for booking a gig, and they would both charge me a percentage. This became a nightmare for me.

But I was in love with Eddie Holland, so I went along with this. Let me rephrase that: I *thought* I was in love with Eddie Holland. Whenever we had a disagreement, I would literally tell him off on a regular basis. When I "went off" on him, I would really demean him. And maybe I was unwise for doing that.

Eddie was now pulling all of the strings of my career. We had this lustful physical relationship together, and yet I felt like I was being disrespected, and undermined. I also felt that he was treating me like I had never left Detroit, and that I was just a naïve local girl.

He didn't realize I had become educated by my worldwide experiences. I had lived in New York and in Europe. I had grown in life and in the business.

Otis Smith, who was the Vice President of Invictus Records at the time, would often have to phone me to calm me down, and to calm Eddie down. I liked Otis Smith. He liked me as well, and he was a very experienced record executive. Otis went on to form his own record label which was called Beverly Glen Records. He was the one who recorded Anita Baker on her very first album called *The Songstress*.

On one occasion I said to Eddie, "You know what the problem is here: I left Detroit when I was 18 years old. I'm nearly 30 now. I've been to Europe, I played Broadway, I have been all over. That's the problem. You can't treat me like I just got off the bus."

That was a huge dilemma. So, the whole time we dated we fought. I would tell Otis all about it. Otis respected me, and understood what was going on.

Otis used to call me: "Freda Payne Superstar!"

They did have big plans for me and for my career, but it finally got to the point where I just couldn't take it anymore, and I became very unhappy with the situation. Here I had a huge hit record with "Band of Gold," and four successful singles off my second Invictus album, *Contact*: "Cherish What Is Dear To You (While It's Near To You)," "Bring The Boys Home," "You Brought The Joy," and "The Road We Didn't Take." *Contact* became the biggest-selling album of my entire career. Everywhere I went people knew my name. I had "made it," and yet I was miserable.

I remember Lamont, Eddie and Brian were right there in the studio with me for a lot of the sessions during the recording of my *Contact* album. The arrangements were wonderful and I enjoyed doing all the songs: "I'm Not Getting Any Better," "He's In My Life," and especially "The Road We Didn't Take," which was sort of prophetic.

According to Lamont, "The *Contact* album represents an important shift in that era. Up to that point, we had focused mostly on singles, but the album was becoming king, and concept albums were just starting to become important. Brian Holland and I worked closely together on seven of the songs for what would be the first real concept LP I'd set out to help write. Built around the themes of sadness and heartbreak, the album earned Freda a Grammy nomination." (6)

Originally, the song "Bring the Boys Home" was written for Laura Lee to record. But, Holland-Dozier-Holland gave it to me because they knew it would be a big hit. When "Bring The Boys Home" was released, public support for the ongoing Vietnam War was at its lowest ebb, particularly among African American families whose children were being shipped out *en masse* by the military and used as little more than cannon fodder in many cases. The song's sentiments and its message of bringing the American soldiers home certainly resonated with a lot of people at the time. "Bring The Boys Home" was my second million-selling *Gold* record, making it to Number 12 on the Pop charts, and Number Three on the R&B chart in the U.S.

The funny thing was, when *Contact* was released "Bring The Boys Home" was not included on the initial pressings of the album. Then, when "Bring The Boys Home" quickly climbed up the charts, it was added to the subsequent versions of *Contact*.

The *Contact* album itself was a true "superstar" package. On the cover I was photographed in a beautiful form-fitting A-line silk jersey, long sleeved burnt orange gown. My very modern necklace was a gold choker with a large gold rectangle featuring a dangling line of gold chains hanging from it. The cover folded out to include a "tear away" full length poster of me in the same outfit. The photographer's name was Steve Berman. The deluxe album package presented me like a true star, and I loved it.

Contact was enthusiastically received by pop and soul fans around the world. Ron Wynn in the *All Music Guide* claimed, "Freda Payne's second Invictus album was a significant success…sophisticated pop / soul with excellent production, arrangements, and material supplied by the Holland / Dozier / Holland team. They wisely didn't try to make her a sassy or hard-edged vocalist, putting her voice in string and horn-dominated charts and emphasizing her soothing, lightly sensual side." (7)

In *The Audiophile Man*, a reviewer found *Contact* to be "…sleek, well produced, shamelessly commercial but in a good way!…Payne isn't sassy here, she's smooth and sexy which suits her personality right down to the ground." (8) A music writer in *Central Michigan Life* proclaimed it, "…a well-worked album entitled *Contact*…lush orchestrations and velvet 'n' vigor vocals were the key to its successful sound." (9)

My *Contact* album made it to Number 76 on the Pop album Chart, and Number 12 on the R&B album chart in *Billboard* in the U.S. It was certified *Gold*, and it truly cemented me in the public's mind. It took me five albums to get to this point, but I felt like I had finally "arrived."

As 1972 started, I was thrilled to have *Contact* nominated for a Grammy Award in the category of "Best R&B Vocal Performance, Female." It was the 14th Annual Grammy Awards, and *Contact* was nominated against Aretha Franklin: "Bridge Over Troubled Water" (single), Jean Knight: "Mr. Big Stuff" (single), Janis Joplin: *Pearl* (album), and Diana Ross: "(I Love You) Call Me" (single). I was up against some pretty stiff competition: Aretha, Janis, and Diana no-less.

From 1968 to 1975 Aretha Franklin was nominated in this same category year-after-year, and she won this Grammy Award eight consecutive years in a row. Aretha was amidst her un-stoppable winning streak, and ultimately her soulful version of the Simon & Garfunkel classic "Bridge Over Troubled Water" took the "Best R&B Vocal Performance, Female" trophy that year. I might not have won a Grammy Award that year, but at least I was officially playing in the big leagues now!

In the early 1970s, I worked with the legendary Bob Hope several times. One engagement was in Ohio, and it was held at an arena. Bob was the headliner, and I performed as his opening act. I was very impressed with him. He was not only a legend in the business, but he was also a really nice man and a humanitarian—via all of his famed USO shows for the troops.

Another time I worked with Bob was in Detroit, at The Michigan State Fair, September 9 and 10, 1972. For this event, the show was held outdoors at a large band shell. It was quite an elaborate show for a state fair. We had a full big band to accompany us. It was the typical state fair setting, with prize animals, fried food booths, exhibits, cotton candy, and amusement park rides. I remember that my dressing room was in a trailer.

My mother accompanied me, and my biological father,

Frederick Payne, also came to see me perform as well. We were in the outdoor backstage area, and Bob Hope walked out of his trailer. I was standing right there with my father, so the natural thing to do was to introduce him to Bob.

Well, Fred had a few drinks, so he was a little animated and over-enthusiastic to meet Bob. When I introduced him to Mr. Hope, my father shook his hand, but he wouldn't let it go.

"How do you do, Mr. Payne," Bob said to him.

"Nice meeting you, Mr. Hope," my father replied.

Then, to betray the fact that he had consumed a couple of drinks, Fred said to Bob, "It is nice to meet a man like you, a man of distinct-ment," as opposed to "a man of distinction."

While all of this was going on, my father kept on shaking Bob's hand and not letting go of it. Perfect gentleman and comedian that he was, finally Bob said to my father, "You're sure keeping my hand warm!"

That very second my mother came rushing over. She could see the embarrassed look on my face, and she took my father by the arm and quickly ushered him away.

In 1970, when "Band of Gold" had first become a hit, I went to Los Angeles to perform at a nightclub called P.J.'s. It was located on the corner of Crescent Heights and Santa Monica Boulevard. During that time, I made friends with the owner of the club, Paul Raffles, and his then-girlfriend, actress Stella Stevens. Stella was very friendly with Jerry Lewis, and she dated him, although he was married at the time. She had been in Jerry's film *The Nutty Professor*, and she remained friends with him. Stella Stevens and I first became friends when I was working with The Lionel Hampton Band at The Riviera Hotel in Las Vegas.

P.J.'s became known as a hot West Hollywood nightclub that was frequented by the likes of Frank Sinatra, Mia Farrow, Joey Bishop, Paul Newman, and Steve McQueen. I was working at P.J.'s and I remember Diana Ross came to see me perform one night. I remember she was traveling incognito that evening. Choreographer Lon Fontaine was the one who mentioned to me that she was in the audience that night.

As I recall, I introduced her from the stage, announcing, "Ladies and gentlemen, Diana Ross is in the audience tonight." That evening I was wearing a "nude" color jumpsuit that was encrusted with pearls and crystals and beads, which was designed by my dear friend Roxanne Spino of New York City.

After that, my bookings became more-and-more impressive. I headlined The Venetian Room, located in The Fairmont Hotel in San Francisco with an act that my friend Lon Fontaine had choreographed for that particular engagement. I also headlined at the world famous New York City nightclub: The Copacabana. That was an exciting career high-point.

Unfortunately, that was also when the clouds were beginning to form between me, Eddie Holland, and Invictus. The main problem that I was having with Invictus, was that although I had several hits on the charts, I wasn't seeing any financial compensation for my work. I had never received an advance for my signing with Invictus. Nor was I seeing any royalty money from Invictus, even after "Band of Gold" became an international hit and was certified *Gold.* This started a bitter feud. I knew that I would eventually have to say "goodbye" to Invictus.

When I was playing at The Copacabana in New York, Eddie told Capitol Records, who were the distributors for Invictus, not to promote my record that had just been released, and that was "Bring The Boys Home." Apparently, Eddie and Capitol were having contractual disagreements and I was caught in the middle.

One of the promotion men who worked for Capitol was Sydney Miller. Sydney saw the situation unfolding, and he ignored the order not to promote "Bring The Boys Home." He felt that it was a big mistake on the part of Invictus, and he continued to do what had to be done in the promotion field. Sydney saw the potential of "Bring The Boys Home" as a hit, and he was right.

It wasn't long afterward that he was fired by Capitol Records for having ignored the order. But Sydney would go on to do bigger and better things, such as forming *The Black Radio Exclusive* (*BRE*), a music industry magazine, as well as holding national conventions that drew together radio and promotion men and women from all over the country. Sydney still is a friend of mine to this day. "Bring The Boys Home," in spite of all of that behind-the-scenes drama, became a huge hit.

My recordings were now so popular that my third album on Invictus was my greatest hits album: *The Best of Freda Payne*, which was released in 1972. I gave Eddie an ultimatum to either write me a check or there would be consequences.

After having this big huge hit with "Band of Gold," I was told, "You have no royalties."

"Well, you had better get me some royalties!" I snapped back at Eddie. I was furious. "If you can't pay me, you had better take out a loan and pay me something to keep me satisfied."

They weren't paying me anything. They weren't taking care of me. They hadn't given me any "signing" advances, bonus checks, royalties, or anything like that.

You would have thought that Holland-Dozier-Holland had learned something from their own complaints about Motown. Instead, they just repeated the same mistakes.

The fact that I had a Number One hit, and a Grammy nominated hit follow-up album, surely meant that I was owed something. It made me question and drill Eddie about it.

He said, "Well we spent a lot of money on promotion and things like that."

I said to him, "Eddie, you'd better pay me something! I saved you a fortune. Whenever you flew me to Detroit I saved you the hotel costs by staying with my parents. And on top of that, you didn't even pay me an advance for signing. 'Bring The Boys Home' is a huge hit. I hear it everywhere I go. If you don't have any royalties for me, you better get some money and pretend it's royalties, and give me a check!" The arguments went around-and-around, and I wasn't about to back down.

It was clear that I was going to have to sue them if I was ever going to see any money from my three albums on Invictus. Now how was I going to afford to hire a lawyer and take on Holland-Dozier-Holland? I didn't have to wait long for the answer. It was about to present itself.

When you find yourself at your darkest hour, that's when God sends his angels to find a solution and a remedy for it. That was when my angels stepped in, and the solution appeared.

So, what happened was that I was asked to do a benefit performance with Frank Sinatra at The Beverly Hills Hotel, in Beverly Hills, California. It was a fundraiser for United States Senator John V. Tunney, who was one of the U.S. Senators representing California. He had gone to school with Teddy Kennedy, and in fact Kennedy was the godfather to Tunney's children. Tunney's story was also the basis for the 1972 Robert Redford film, *The Candidate*.

The fundraiser was really a "swell affair," with tuxedos and white ties on the men, and diamonds on the women. The crowd that night was the *crème de la crème* of Beverly Hills. I performed on the benefit along with Frank Sinatra. He was the headliner, and he was the evening's host / organizer. It was wonderful to be working with him again.

At the time I had a dear, close friend who also became my road manager, and he was kind of like my mentor. His name was Bobby Lucas. Bobby had originally been a professional singer himself. He looked and sounded sort of like Billy Daniels, who was a male crooner from the 1940s and 1950s, and worked mainly in white nightclubs. Billy Daniels is best known for his recording of "That Old Black Magic." I met Bobby through Roxanne Spino, who designed many of my gowns. They were very close friends, and Bobby would occasionally help Roxanne in the designing and production of her gowns. He was very talented in many ways. In fact he used to do some of the beading on my gowns. Sometimes he would stay at Roxanne's for days at a time, beading and sewing.

When Bobby was in New York City, he would stay with Roxanne and her husband in their lush apartment at West 95th Street between Columbus Avenue and Central Park West. I used to go and hang out at their apartment with them and Bobby, and we would just sit and talk for hours.

When Roxanne designed and created gowns and outfits for me, she wanted them to be creative, colorful, and sexy. She would do gowns that were elaborately encrusted with beads, and jewels, and fine stones. Roxanne did a lot of gowns like that. Some of my most sexy gowns were hers. I was photographed wearing one gown she did for me, which is on the back of my *Payne & Pleasure* album. The sides of that gown were all cut out and were very flesh-revealing.

Roxie was African American, and she used to be a dancer with The Katherine Dunham Troupe. That was when she and Eartha Kitt were both members of Katherine Dunham's dance troupe at the same time. In time Roxie gained a lot of weight, so she started working in the background of show business. Her husband was Al Spino, an Italian guy. They had a son and a daughter. Their son Billy was Roxanne's from a former marriage, and the daughter they had together was named Vanessa, who was the youngest of the two.

Bobby Lucas was originally from Georgetown in Washington D.C. As a teenager he left home and went on the road with Billie Holiday. Bobby was a fan of Billie's and followed her around, visiting her backstage when she performed. He told me that one of the things they had in common, was that they both loved to read comic books. He would go out and buy them for her, so she loved to have him around. Bobby had been around show business for a long time. He was a very funny man; very witty, very bright, and he knew a lot of people. And, I discovered that he even knew Frank Sinatra.

We had an afternoon rehearsal with the orchestra the day of the show at The Beverly Hills Hotel on Sunset Boulevard. Frank had already run through his songs, so it was my turn.

After my rehearsal, Bobby was with me, and Frank took one look at him and said, "Hi, Bobby."

I looked at Bobby and said, "Frank Sinatra knows you?" He just smiled, and we all got a big laugh out of that.

After I finished my rehearsal for the John Tunney event that afternoon, Frank Sinatra said to me, "Let me escort you to your room." It was so nice of Frank to personally escort me to my hotel room. That was the classy kind of guy Sinatra was.

Bobby was the type of person who always made people laugh. He could walk into a room where no one was conversing, then Bobby would say a few witty words, and everyone would just crack up with laughter. He was very perceptive and observant, and also very psychic. I really miss Bobby a lot, to this day.

The Tunney benefit went very well, and the crowd was most appreciative of my singing on the show. The next day Bobby said to me, "Freda, did you see how Senator John Tunney was looking at you?"

I said, "No."

He explained, "His eyes were almost popping out of his head, and his mouth was hanging open when he was looking at you."

"Really? You know me - I was oblivious to that," I replied. "I was in the moment on-stage and just doing my own thing, being Freda!"

"I am sure that your looking 'drop dead' gorgeous last night certainly helped!" Bobby said. "You know he could help you with this situation with Eddie Holland. Senator Tunney knows all kinds of people, and he is really tight with Senator Ted Kennedy—they're best friends."

"So, what are you getting at, Bobby?" I asked.

"This situation between you and Eddie, something's got to happen. Even if you go back to him, he's only gonna bring you down."

I believed it then and I believe it now. I said, "Yes. You know what Bobby, I'm pissed because they haven't paid me my royalties. That is the straw that broke the camel's back."

He said, "I can see you resolving the situation, but I can't see Eddie changing. If you go back to him, he will only treat you worse."

In addition to my business situation with Eddie, our personal relationship was just as bad. He had a woman in his life by the name of Jamie, and he had written a song about her years ago called "Jamie," which was released on Motown Records in 1962. Eddie, being born under the sign of Scorpio, could be secretive as well.

Not only did he have a son by Jamie, there was also an additional woman in his life as well, by the name of Vernelle. At this point I was so mad at Eddie for mistreating me. This was not the kind of relationship I wanted. At least, in the case of Berry Gordy and Diana Ross, Berry treated Diana in a way in which he made her feel like a queen. I had to put an end to this situation.

So Bobby said to me, "I'm gonna write a letter to Senator Tunney asking for help. Freda, if you don't approve of it, I won't do it. But, I can tell by the way he was looking at you, that he is going to want to help you."

I said, "Well, how do you know he can help me, Bobby?"

Bobby just happened to be a little bit psychic, and very intuitive. He used to give psychic readings for people. He said, "Freda, I know he'll help you. I can write him a letter. Do you want me to write it, and drop this bomb or not?"

"Okay," I said, "what have I got to lose?"

Bobby wrote the letter, and he got a prompt response. John Tunney wrote Bobby back, and he connected us with the law firm of O'Melveny & Myers in Century City, and they took my case on for next to nothing, all because of Senator Tunney.

At first my lawyer was Nelson Rising at the firm. At a certain point, he left the firm and then Bert Pines took over my case. These were some heavy hitters in the lawyer realm, and I was happy they took me under their wing. Later, Bert Pines went on to run politically for the office of Los Angeles City Attorney, and he won.

My lawyers told me, "We are going to sue Invictus. We are going to sue them from here in Los Angeles. We want you to register to vote in the state of California. Do you have a Michigan driver's license?"

"Yes," I replied.

"We want you to get a California driver's license as well." So, I did.

Before I rented a house of my own in the Hollywood Hills, I was living in the Bel Air home of movie star Maureen O'Hara. She was very famous for her series of Western films with John Wayne like *The Quiet Man* (1952) and *McLintock!* (1963), but she also had a varied career that included comedy, suspense, and melodramas. She first came to the screen in Alfred Hitchcock's *Jamaica Inn* (1939), and was such a sensation in it that she came to Hollywood. She was immediately signed to be the female star of *The Hunchback of Notre Dame* (1939), and she scored hit-after-hit with films like *How Green Was My Valley* (1941) and *Miracle on 34th Street* (1947). I loved her movies!

We had a movie theater just down the street from where I grew up, called The Regent Theater. We would go and see films there on Saturday afternoons. The Regent was just a block away on Woodward Boulevard. In Detroit, Woodward was the main thoroughfare, and that was back when we still had streetcars. I recall seeing Maureen up on the screen with her distinctive flame red hair.

I had always admired her acting, as she often played no-non-sense women, the kind of woman who had no problem standing up for herself. I was thrilled to be living in her house. Living there was inspiring for me, at a time when I was standing up for myself. This was the beginning of my West Coast life, and how exciting and fitting that I would start it off living in the home of a huge Hollywood star.

Not only was I staying in Maureen's bedroom, I was sleeping in her bed. And to top it off, I also had my first romantic rendezvous with John Tunney there. To make it even more coincidental, Maureen was Irish, and so was John!

How this all came about was that Bobby had been a really good and trusted friend of Maureen O'Hara's for years. And, he was also friends with her daughter, Bronwyn. When I say "Bobby was connected," I mean "really connected!"

Maureen was getting ready to sell her house, which had a swimming pool and an additional apartment located over the garage. She was married to Brigadier General Charles F. Blair Jr., so she was selling her Bel Air house, to move to the Caribbean Islands, where Charles worked as a pilot. From what I heard, it was a passionate love affair.

Sadly, in 1978 Blair was killed in a plane crash. O'Hara remained in the Caribbean and came back to Hollywood in 1991 to star opposite John Candy in the comedy film *Only The Lonely*.

When she came back to Hollywood after that, I got to know her even better. My friend David Gest was giving a birthday party for Anthony Quinn on April 21, 1995, and Maureen was one of many celebrity guests. David invited me to sing at the party. David had to fly me in from the road where I was in a production of *Jelly's Last Jam*.

Red Buttons was one of the guests there. Red was the M.C. of the show and he made a joke about Anthony Quinn and his reputation for fathering several children. From the stage Red said to Anthony, "You are the only actor in Hollywood who never wore a condom." Everyone just cracked up at that.

I sat down next to Maureen to catch up with her and we spoke about our dear friend Bobby, who had passed away in October of 1994. At that party was the last time I saw Maureen O'Hara.

When her Bel Air house was up for sale in 1972, and Maureen was preparing to move to the Caribbean, she said to Bobby, "I would like you to come and stay in the house, and even though the realtor will come to the house to show it, I want you to stay there until we can sell it, so that it doesn't look unoccupied." Maureen was also perfectly happy to have me stay there along with Bobby and his friend "Slim." Although her first name was Roberta, we always called her "Slim." Slim was a tall Caucasian girl who had natural blonde hair, and she had a five-year-old daughter by the name of Caroline who lived there also. She and Bobby were very close. Bronwyn had a child too, who was about six months old at the time.

I lived there in that house, with Maureen's permission, for three or four months. During my stay in the master bedroom, John Tunney and I made love. I had several of our rendezvous at that house. After that, I thought I was in love with him.

There were rumors that he was being considered as a presidential candidate at the time. And, I used to imagine him running for President, and me becoming the First Lady.

One day I said to Bobby, "I'm in love with John Tunney."

He said to me, "Freda, you are crazy! I've got a friend who is a psychiatrist. I am gonna pay for him to analyze you in a session." And, he did!

Afterwards, the doctor's prognosis was: "There is nothing wrong with her. She's got all her faculties; she's got good sense." Marry John Tunny and become First Lady? I wasn't crazy, I was just ahead of my time!

It was something like The Temptations song "Just My Imagination" running away with me! I suppose the notion of me being First Lady could never have happened. Can you imagine an interracial couple in the White House, especially in the 1970s? That would never have flown!

I did get a big laugh out of those illusions of grandeur. I would daydream about me as First Lady being followed wherever I go by the Secret Service. Oh well, it was a great daydream while it lasted!

John Tunney was married at the time to a woman by the name of Mieke Sprengers, but Bobby, with his psychic abilities, claimed, "His marriage is breaking up." Bobby was correct in that prediction. Tunney later remarried, but not to me. His second wife was a woman by the name of Kathinka Osborne.

Bobby used to read the Tarot cards. In one of his readings for me he saw the "Flaming Tower" card, and he said, "That represents the break up of John Tunney and his wife."

While I was involved with John Tunney, I was booked for an engagement in Washington D.C., so John made arrangements for Bobby and me to have lunch with him in the Senate dining room. As we sat there, I looked around, and at another table I spotted someone I recognized.

I said to Bobby, "Look, there's Warren Beatty sitting over there."

Bobby responded, "It sure is!"

Apparently Warren was having lunch with another Senator, while we were dining with Tunney.

Meanwhile, back at the Maureen O'Hara house, Bobby told me, "The guy from the realtor's office complained to Maureen, 'Why are there black people living in the house while I am showing it?'"

In reality, I was the only one who was actually black. The way Bobby looked, he could pass for Jewish, or Italian, because he was very fair-skinned. He was balding on top, and occasionally he wore a toupee. I was definitely the only person of color in that house.

Meanwhile, there was Slim, who was white, thin, beautiful, and tall as a glass of champagne. Who knows, maybe the realtor was just bitching to Maureen, "Who are these people living in your house?" He probably wanted the house to be empty when he showed it to potential buyers. Regardless, I ended up staying at Maureen's house for several months, and Slim ended up becoming my personal assistant and secretary.

In 1970 Mae West had starred in a campy and controversial movie called *Myra Breckenridge*, and in it she had an innuendo-filled musical number called "Hard To Handle." As she performed the song, her back-up performers were a sexy group of all-black tuxedo-clad male dancers. Robert Johnson wanted to do an interview with Mae West for *Jet* magazine, to talk about her amusing musical number, and her life as a trailblazer.

Known for her overt sexuality, Mae was also known for her battles with film industry censors in the 1930s and 1940s. In films like *I'm No Angel* (1933) and *Klondike Annie* (1936), she illustrated how a clever woman could be the master of her own destiny in a man's world. She was also something of a gay icon.

It just so happened that my friend Bobby Lucas seemed to know everyone in show business, and he even knew Mae West. So he simply phoned her and set up the interview and photo session. Ike Sutton was set to do the photographs, and Robert invited me to join them at Miss West's apartment. She lived in an apartment building in Los Angeles, called Ravenswood.

We all had a great time listening to her colorful stories. Originally Mae promised to give us only 45 minutes of her time, but we were so entertained, and Mae was having such fun that we ended up staying for two hours. I loved being in Hollywood, and meeting so many of the stars who made it so glamorous, like the legendary Mae West no less!

One night, during this era in which I was having my affair with

John Tunney, and living in Maureen O'Hara's house, I decided to stop in at The Bel Air Hotel for an event that was there. I was invited, and I had to pass right by there, so I decided to stop in. It wasn't like a big party, but it was several Hollywood celebrities hanging out, including Tom Jones.

When I got ready to leave the party, Tom walked me to the door, grabbed me, and laid the biggest "low down" kiss on me! And let me tell you, he could kiss!

He said to me, "I want you to stay."

"I can't," I replied.

"Why?"

"Because I'm in love with someone, and I don't believe in cheating."

And I left.

The funny thing is that Tom has always remembered that evening. I am the one who turned him down!

I am that kind a person. When I am in love with someone, that is "it." I was so in love with John Tunney, I wasn't going to be unfaithful to him.

I was in love with Quincy Jones too. I was so in love with him. Those were my three big love affairs: Quincy Jones, Eddie Holland, and John Tunney.

After that I rented a house up in the Hollywood Hills, right around Sunset Plaza Drive. That way I had a permanent California residence to my name. The address was 8818 Hollywood Boulevard. I remember it well. I continued to see John Tunney even after I rented the place on Hollywood Boulevard. The last time I saw him was at that house.

One day Slim told me that she had received a phone call, and on the other end of the line was someone questioning her: "What Senator has called this number from the Senatorial Cloakroom?"

Slim was shocked to receive that call, but she was able to diffuse it by saying, "I think this is a mistake, and they received a wrong number."

Whenever Bobby and I had a telephone conversation, we used a nickname for Tunney. We didn't even mention his real name, especially on the phone. Our nickname for him was "Willard."

It was starting to unravel at that point. When this happened, Tunney and I had to take a break from seeing each other. After that, our affair just started to fizzle and dissolve. I assumed he had been approached about the knowledge of our love affair, and he figured the relationship was way too risky, and could destroy his political career.

Later on he had an affair with the actress Elizabeth Ashley, and I became insanely jealous.

I remember thinking to myself, "What does he want with that old bitch? She's six years older than me!" Ah, to be 30 again!

Years later, when John Tunney's re-election came up, he lost. So, he didn't stay in office too long as a Senator.

Meanwhile, my lawsuit against Invictus Records certainly stirred things up with the Holland-Dozier-Holland camp. If I had to fight for what was mine, I was ready to do battle. I had to get that resolved and figure out what was next for me.

CHAPTER SEVEN

"Regaining Control"

Once everything was in order, my new Century City law firm, O'Melveny & Myers, sued Invictus like they promised. They made an offer for a settlement to Eddie and his lawyer, Fred Patman. I would have loved to have seen the look on Eddie Holland's face when he received this lawsuit on his desk. He and Fred Patman must have wondered, "How in the world did she get these high-powered lawyers?"

Well, eventually, within the next few months they would find out. Bobby Lucas found out that a letter had been delivered to Invictus by accident. It was addressed to me, but they sent it to Invictus.

Ultimately, it took two years of wrangling for us to fully settle the lawsuit. To hold up my part of the contract, I recorded one more album for Invictus Records called *Reaching Out*, which was released in 1973. I flew back to Detroit to record that. The album was comprised of newly recorded songs. "Two Wrongs Don't Make a Right" became a hit on the R&B charts. The two standards I recorded for this album were the songs "If You Go Away" by Rod McKuen and Jacques Brel, and "Rainy Days and Mondays," which was written by Paul Williams, and had been a hit for The Carpenters.

The photo on the cover of the *Reaching Out* album was of me in a sexy pink form-fitting two-piece bikini, thigh deep in the water of a deserted tropical bay in Puerto Rico. On the back cover, I was shown in the same bathing suit and same setting, from behind. These photos were done by photographer Anthony Barboza, and they were really great looking. I guess you could say this was the beginning of my "bathing suit model" phase.

My original concept was for us to go into the rain forest of Puerto Rico. I wanted to find a waterfall, and my idea was to have me standing under the waterfall, with the water dripping down in front of me over my face and body. However, there wasn't time for us to scout out the right location. So we settled for a photo of me in the ocean, playfully posing for the camera in my bikini.

On the subject of photo shoots, in the early 1970s I was photographed by a man who was with actress Ursula Andress at the time. He was a professional photographer, and one of my publicists arranged for this to happen.

It sounded like a lot of fun, and it was. For this solo photo shoot I was wearing a two piece playsuit in a shade of coral, with loose pants and a tunic with the sides cut out. It was slit on the right and left sides.

"Would you mind taking off the pants, and just posing in the tunic?" the photographer asked.

I thought about it for a moment. "Why not?" I replied, and then I removed the pants to the suit. Underneath I wore sheer pantyhose, but it gave the illusion I was nude. You could see my bare thighs, as my sides were exposed, all the way up to my breasts. It made for a very sexy image.

I have to tell you, that was the best sexy "pin-up" photo that I have taken in my entire career. It was such a great photo, it was used time-and-time-again as a promotional shot, and it became infamous for being a bit *risqué*. I got so much use out of it. It even ran in *Jet* magazine, and it was used in countless newspaper stories about me.

The fads and fashions of the 1970s was certainly a whole new ball game as well. It was the era of bell-bottomed pants, chunky platform shoes, and new hairstyles too. I have a photo of myself that was taken in Hawaii from this era. It was clearly the '70s, as I am wearing my stylish new Afro hair-do.

Another thing that became very fashionable in the early 1970s was an all-out homage to 1930s styles. Ruby Keeler, who had starred in movie musicals in the 1930s, was suddenly the toast of Broadway in *No, No, Nanette*. And, The Pointer Sisters really brought back 1930s styles of dresses cut on the bias, chic hats, and platform shoes.

I got to have my big 1930s moment on the movie screen in 1973, when I was cast in the film production of *The Book of Numbers*. How this came about was through Raymond St. Jacques. He was the star of the film, and he was also the director.

The executive producer of the film was George Barrie, who owned the Fabergé cosmetics company. The film was set in El Dorado, Arkansas, and it was about two black waiters who get into a "numbers running" gambling game. Set in the 1930s, it was based on a 1969 novel by Robert Deane Pharr. At the time, Raymond St. Jacques was famous for his acting in such films as *Black Like Me*, *Mister Buddwing*, *The Comedians*, *The Green Berets*, and *Cotton Comes to Harlem*. This was to be his directorial debut.

One day, out of the blue, Raymond St. Jacques phoned me, and asked me if I wanted to be in the film. The role was mine if I wanted it. I didn't have to read for it, or audition or anything. I guess he figured since I had done Broadway, that was obviously an indication that I could hold my own as an actress. It was also due to the fact that I had two *Gold* records, and my name would be a draw on theater marquees. It wasn't like I was a totally unknown actress.

Raymond hired me, and my co-star in the film was a young and handsome Phillip Michael Thomas. He was an actor on the rise at that point. It wasn't until ten years later that he became an international sensation in the hit TV show *Miami Vice*, alongside Don Johnson. That was when his career blew-up, and really blew-up big. *Miami Vice* ran from 1984 to 1989, and it was a huge smash. Phillip and Don were on the "cover of *Time* magazine," which was as highly prestigious then as it is now.

When we were on the set of *The Book of Numbers*, Phillip Michael Thomas and I instantly hit it off, and we had quite the little affair there during that period. However, Phillip turned out to be one of those kind of guys who was a real womanizer, and something of a playboy. He was like a little bee, flying from flower-to-flower, distributing his pollen.

I thought he was absolutely adorable, and he was tremendously talented as an actor. I looked upon him as being like a little cherry tart—something good to eat! He was such a great looking guy, but our romance only lasted for the run of the film's production. Phillip still tried to pursue me afterwards, but that didn't work. I had by then realized that he fancied himself as a Hollywood playboy. And, come to find out, he was married at the time, and had a child. Nothing serious was possible with him.

Playing "the numbers," and the whole "numbers" business, was a big illegal gambling racket. I remember that my grandmother used to play "the numbers" game back in Detroit, and was involved in that business at one time. It seemed that everybody was playing "the numbers" back then, and now. I never did it, but a lot of people sure did and do.

I recall that people would keep "dream books," and they would place their bets based on things that they had dreamed. You would have a certain dream, and you would look up what number was associated with that kind of dream. They had all kinds of crazy associations. According to legend, if you dream about feces—or dog poop—the number that would be associated with that is "3-6-9." If you dream about the dead or someone dying, there is a number for that. This didn't just happen in Detroit, it was very prevalent all over the U.S. It was—and is—also very illegal.

The Book of Numbers was a very stylish film, and several of the reviews commented on its artful portrait of the South in that era. Although the story took place in Arkansas, we actually filmed it in Dallas, Texas. They used several vintage cars in the film, and the art direction and the fashions were very authentically 1930s looking.

It was hot and very steamy that summer, but it was a great experience. Part of my wardrobe was a wool skirt, and a little wool cardigan sweater, and I remember being so hot and uncomfortable. They didn't have me wearing any wigs in the film. Each day a hairdresser would do my own hair, so what you see on camera is all me.

The name of my character was "Kelly Simms." Raymond St. Jacques was the boss of this numbers racket in the plot of the film, and he was playing the role older than he actually was at the time. I was playing his niece. Phillip portrayed one of the guys working with him in this numbers business. In the film we played sweethearts. A perfect example of art imitating life!

One of the other actors in it was a man by the name of D'Urville Martin. He played the role of Bill Bowlegs. Also, Hope Clark was in it, in the role of Pigmeat Goins. I first worked with Hope in *Hallelujah Baby!* She is a really good actress, and a great dancer.

This movie came out during the whole "Blaxploitation" movement, with films like *Superfly* and *Cleopatra Jones* and a whole slew of them. By contrast, *The Book of Numbers* was looked at as being a much more prestigious film.

Although *The Book of Numbers* didn't become a huge box-office success, it did get the attention of several critics, and even *Time* magazine wrote, "*The Book of Numbers* has a raucous, picaresque, raunchy kind of charm…two black con men (Raymond St. Jacques and Philip [Michael] Thomas) descended on an Arkansas town called El Dorado during the '30s to start a numbers band. Thomas has a rather meandering love affair with a 'high yellow' woman (Freda Payne), leaving him little time to help St. Jacques." (10) In film terms, my character was what they call "the love interest," and—according to the press—I made quite a seductive one!

I was booked to perform in Chicago at Mister Kelly's in 1973. This time—thanks to "Band of Gold" and my recent hit singles—I was the headliner and my opening act, was an up-and-coming comedian by the name of Jay Leno. He wrote about this booking in his 1996 memoir, *Leading With My Chin*. It was his first time working at Mister Kelly's. There was a marquee out front, and my name was on top, and his name was underneath mine, and it was spelled: "Jay Lno."

When he questioned the club manager about this, he was told, "Well, Freda Payne is the star, and we needed to use two 'E's' to spell her name, and we didn't have an extra 'E' for 'Leno.'" When he became a big TV star, and was the host of *The Tonight Show,* Jay even told this story to Bill Cosby on the air. The two of them were discussing stories about their careers when they were just starting out. And this is the story that Jay told.

Years later, I became Jay's opening act, working in Atlantic City, in Lake Tahoe, and at Caesar's Palace in Las Vegas. Jay is so personable and an absolute pleasure to be around. I recently was on a program with him, where he was the host and I performed. It was at The Bel Air Country Club, and I had been invited to perform by the late Hal David's widow, Eunice David. Hal was the lyricist for all of those great hits written with Burt Bacharach. Together, they literally launched Dionne Warwick's career with their music. That evening I sang Hal and Burt's composition "A House Is Not a Home."

I had become acquainted with Dick Gregory back in New York. In fact, when I opened at Mister Kelly's, he had sent me a bouquet of flowers to congratulate me. The flowers he sent me were anthuriums, which I love. These red tropical flowers are not cheap as they are grown in Hawaii; they are much more expensive than roses, and I was quite impressed.

I had lots of interviews and TV performances booked by the club, and my schedule was very full, in addition to performing two shows every night. I was already tired, and I was worried that the strain could harm my voice. I certainly didn't want to end up getting hoarse, or coming down with laryngitis.

I had a lot of press interviews while I was in the Windy City. One famed columnist in Chicago was Irv Kupcinet, who wrote for *The Chicago Tribune*. He also had his own TV show. He had taken a great liking to me, and I admired him as well. I always looked forward to appearing on his show.

While I was in Chicago for this engagement, Rev. Jesse Jackson heard that I was performing in town. Since "Band of Gold" and "Bring The Boys Home" were still popular on the radio, it seemed I was everywhere in Chicago at that time. Operation Breadbasket was Rev. Jackson's political movement based in Chicago to inspire people of color. His catch phrase was "I may be poor, I may be black, but I am somebody," and he had his crowds repeat that chant. While I was at my hotel Jesse Jackson called me, and he said, "I want you to come down to Operation Breadbasket. We meet every Saturday morning at 9:00 a.m."

I said to him, "I would love to do that, but I am doing two shows a night during this engagement. It's hard on me. And then they are having me do radio broadcasts and TV shows here and there. I am afraid that I will be too tired and lose my voice if I fit in any more activities, let alone getting up that early. Maybe next time I come back in Chicago we can do something."

But he argued, "Freda, you can take a nap in the afternoon."

"That is not the point," I explained. "It's still gonna be hard on me to do that."

Instead of being sympathetic to my pleas, Jesse instead became bullying and said, "Well if you don't do it, I'm gonna send some people down to Mister Kelly's to boycott your shows!"

I was in shock! The nerve of him!

So, after I got off the phone with Jesse Jackson, I called Dick Gregory up and told him what had just happened.

"What do you think I should do?" I asked him.

He said to me, "Well, I think you should do it Freda. Go to Jesse's meeting. You don't need that kind of trouble, with Jesse Jackson putting out a bad word about you."

I was being railroaded into this, and I was absolutely pissed-off this had happened. However, I did go to the meeting just to avoid trouble. I never trusted Jesse Jackson after that. And, to top it off, I did get a bit hoarse because of this event I had to attend. But I was able to make it through and do my shows.

Then, to add insult to injury, Jesse had the nerve to "hit" on me. I wasn't surprised, because he was known for being a womanizer. I couldn't believe that he blackmailed me into coming to his meeting, and then thought he could come on to me romantically. Now I was really pissed-off at him.

I later found out that Rev. Jesse Jackson has a long line of female entertainers that he has been involved with, including Roberta Flack, and Nancy Wilson. Roberta had a song she recorded on one of her biggest albums called "Jesse," and that was supposedly about him.

Although one superstar female diva hinted at an affair with Jesse in her own autobiography, she never mentions his name. Obviously she did it that way out of respect for his often cheated upon wife. And that female star whom I know had an affair with him was: Aretha Franklin.

In her book, when she got to the part where she started writing about her romantic involvement with a powerful politician, or some sort of powerful person, she did everything but reveal the fact that it was Jesse Jackson, I surmise.

Before Aretha passed away in August of 2018, and her health was failing, Jesse was her constant companion as a friend. He was there in Detroit close to the end, so he did prove to be a good friend to Aretha.

I remember seeing Aretha Franklin singing in downtown Detroit within a year before she passed. It was an outdoor concert in downtown Detroit, it was a free concert, and the crowds flocked to see "The Queen of Soul." I was in the audience, and Mary Wilson was also there. Aretha graciously announced both of us from the stage, and Jesse Jackson was there as well. He was standing on-stage, off to the side. I could see that he was still close to Aretha, and he obviously knew that she was very ill. It crossed my mind that he was there in case she needed him, due to her health situation.

During this era in the early '70s, for a while I was going out with actor Richard Roundtree. He had become a big star in his series of movies where he played fictional detective John Shaft. They included: *Shaft* (1971), *Shaft's Big Score* (1972), and *Shaft In Africa* (1973). I was in New York City, and I was booked to be the opening act for Bill Cosby, at Westchester Premier Theater, about an hour outside Manhattan. I decided to drive a Hertz rental car to get there. Along the way, my road manager Bobby Lucas and I had not one, but two flat tires which caused us to be late for the curtain. I was wringing my hands, hating to be late for an engagement. Finally we got there—later than expected. Richard Roundtree was there waiting to meet me. Instead of me being Bill's warm-up act, I followed him on-stage. What I remember the most was that Bill Cosby was so pissed-off at me. I was wondering if he believed me that I had two flat tires, but this time it was true! That was the last time I rented a car from Hertz.

In 1973, Motown and The Supremes once again crossed my path. This time around, it was in a totally unique way. That was the year my sister Scherrie joined The Supremes. Florence Ballard was fired from the trio in 1967, Diana Ross went solo in 1970, and Mary continued the group with Cindy Birdsong and Jean Terrell. They scored a nice string of hits including "Up The Ladder To The Roof," "Everybody's Got The Right To Love," "Nathan Jones," and "Stoned Love." Then Cindy left the group when she became pregnant in 1972, and she was replaced by Lynda Laurence. The following year, when both Jean and Lynda suddenly announced they were quitting The Supremes, they left Mary in the lurch. There were already contracts and bookings for The Supremes, and Mary was left without two other members. What she ended up doing was asking Cindy to rejoin the group, leaving her to find one more member. When she asked Lamont Dozier if he knew any great singers who had lead singer "chops" and could replace Jean Terrell, Mary was introduced to Scherrie.

The reason Holland-Dozier-Holland knew about Scherrie's vocal talent was because she was the lead singer for a group called The Glass House. The quartet had been signed to Invictus Records as well, and they scored a hit with the song "Crumbs Off The Table." Scherrie also wrote that song. At this point she had written scores of songs, but this was the first one that was recorded. Thanks to Lamont, Mary called Scherrie, heard her sing, and suddenly my baby sister was a Supreme! Scherrie and Mary shared the lead vocal on the hit single "He's My Man," and they also had a big disco hit with "I'm Gonna Let My Heart Do The Walking" with Scherrie singing the lead.

It was also in the 1970s when I first became close friends with Mary Wilson. Although we were both from Detroit, and I had certainly met her several times, our long-running friendship basically started when we were both living in Los Angeles. Then, when Scherrie joined The Supremes in 1973, I got to see and be around Mary even more. At the time she had a house on Rising Glen in the Hollywood Hills. While she had more of a working relationship with

Scherrie, Mary saw that Scherrie and I had totally different interests, and Mary and I found we had a lot in common.

This was before Mary married Pedro Ferrer. We were all hoping that she *wouldn't* marry Pedro, and that her relationship *wouldn't* get to where it got, because everybody else could see what Pedro was. Then when Mary not only married him, but made him the manager of The Supremes, that was when Berry Gordy washed his hands of The Supremes. Pedro and all of his nonsense proved to be the last straw for Berry. I heard it all first hand from Scherrie.

People who were around Mary, and were close to her were telling her, "Don't marry this guy!" But she was in love, and there was no talking her out of it. With all the men Mary had dated—like Steve McQueen, Tom Jones, and Flip Wilson—to end up with Pedro was a shocker to all of us who were close to her.

The fact of the matter is that I met Pedro Ferrer before Mary met him. I was booked to be the headliner at The El San Juan Hotel in Puerto Rico. I was in the lobby of the hotel and I was on one of the house phones. He walked up to me and in his thick accent he said, "I'm Pedro. My uncle owns this hotel, and my father is the Governor of Puerto Rico," or some sort of made-up bullshit, in his vain attempt to impress me.

I looked at him and I thought, "Who is this guy?"

"Maybe we can have dinner or something," he said aggressively.

It never happened. He so instantly turned me off. I could see through him and his false claims about who he was. I wanted nothing to do with him, and I made it crystal clear.

When I got back to Los Angeles, I talked to Scherrie, and I found out that Pedro was going out with one of the members of the group The Three Degrees: Fayette Pinkney.

Several weeks later, Scherrie said to me, "Oh, Mary is going out with this guy, Pedro Ferrer."

"Mary's going out with HIM?" I replied with disdain.

"Yeah, she likes him a lot."

"Yes, but isn't he going out with Fayette from The Three Degrees?"

"Well, he is, but he is also dating Mary," Scherrie confirmed.

He was definitely one of those guys who dates more than one woman at a time, so this didn't surprise me one bit.

I said to Scherrie, "That guy introduced himself to me, and tried to come on to me in Puerto Rico. I wasn't attracted to him at all."

There was something about him that immediately said to me, "Warning! Danger!"

The next thing I knew, Scherrie was giving me a report, "Oh Mary is really into him!" Then he started to go out on the road, and traveling with The Supremes.

My mother was still alive then. Between my mother, Scherrie, me, and all of Mary's girlfriends, we were all praying that Mary wouldn't marry Pedro. He was a friendly guy, but we just didn't feel that he was the right guy for her to marry. As friends, who were we to interfere with her personal life?

And then, Mary married him. A lot of negative things happened because of Pedro. He caused problems between Mary and The Supremes, and Motown. He was abusive and horrible to Mary, and she wrote all about it in her book *Supreme Faith*.

But, some good comes out of every situation. Mary had three lovely children with Pedro, and although their marriage didn't last long, those kids are a really positive thing. Mary's daughter Turkessa is her first born and she is especially lovely, bright, and wonderful. She is a gem. Mary also had two boys: Pedro Jr. and Rafael.

In November of 1973 I was the "toast of the town" when I appeared at The Maisonette Room in Manhattan, at The St. Regis Hotel. The Maisonette Room was a very prestigious room to play, and it regularly booked members of show business royalty, like Sarah

Vaughn. Lenny Bleecher had written a new act for me, and I loved the feeling that I was performing and staying "in the middle of everything" in New York City.

I remember venturing out to all of the chic shops in the area, like Gucci and Sak's Fifth Avenue. At Gucci I was shopping for shoes and a bag, and I even met Mr. Gucci. Another designer I met was Halston, who had his own shop on Madison Avenue in the East 60s. When I opened at The Maisonette Room, I received a huge bouquet of red roses with a card signed by Halston himself.

During this booking Lenny Bleecher took me into Cartier's on Fifth Avenue. At the time they were promoting their ultra-chic piece of gold jewelry: "The Love Bracelet." It was gold with little screws to fasten two halves together. While we were in the store Lenny and I got friendly with the owner, whose name was Michael Thomas. We invited Michael and his wife to come to the St. Regis Hotel to see my show as my guest. In return for that kindness, he put a 14 carat solid gold "Love Bracelet" on my wrist as a gift, and gave me a Cartier belt as well. At the time the bracelets were selling for about $375.00. I still have that bracelet—in my safe deposit box—as it is now worth well over ten times that amount.

Throughout the 1970s I kept busy appearing in nightclubs and in concert, drawing crowds, and getting rave reviews. When I appeared in Chicago, at The Blue Max in The Hyatt Regency Hotel, *The Chicago Tribune* covered my show, Will Leonard's flattering review was entitled "Freda Payne: More Vocal—And Impressive—Than Ever." In it he proclaimed, "Anything that Freda does, she does all the way...When she sings blues you're convinced that is the role meant for her. When she shifts to rock you see another facet of a star—and she is the only rock singer who lets you hear the words. On the rare occasions when Freda moves in the standard path with...'Feelings' or 'Send In The Clowns,' they still have some of that element of wantonness that belongs in the rock product." (11)

"Wantonness," hmmm? I guess you could say I always have been able to get an audience excited!

In 1973 one of the television shows I was featured on was the network variety program: *The Bobby Darin Show*. Bobby Darin was so talented, and such a nice guy. In fact, we got along so well together that I was booked on the program a second time during in the first half of 1973. I performed my hits, and Bobby and I also sang duets together. He was so lively and energetic on the first show when I was a guest star. Although Bobby was just as charming the second time I was on his show, I noticed that he had less energy, and he wasn't looking quite as healthy as he did before. Unfortunately, amongst other health issues—including childhood rheumatic fever—Bobby had a weak heart, and he tragically died in December of that very same year, at the age of 37.

Michael Viner was someone I became involved with in the 1970s in Los Angeles. He started a company called Dove Audio, and he began producing books-on-tape, which became all the rage. He would employ one of his celebrity friends to read the books of other authors aloud, and Michael made a fortune selling these audio books. After Dove, he went on to establish New Star Media. And after that, he started another company called Phoenix Publishing. Michael was very creative, but what he was really good at was starting up companies, declaring bankruptcy, and then starting anew again. A lot of people have very negative feelings towards Michael, but he was very good to me.

I met Michael back around 1973. We dated, and he would take me out to dinner, and he would take my mother along with us. My mother had been diagnosed with breast cancer at the time, and he told me that he had cancer too. My mother liked Michael. She felt that he was a "nice Jewish boy."

She said, "Any man who would take his girlfriend's mother out, too, is a very nice man."

Hanging out with Michael Viner was always an interesting experience, as he seemed to know everyone, including the members of The Beatles. It was Michael who introduced me to John Lennon. Michael was having a private party in the small banquet room of Chasen's, which was a very famous Beverly Hills restaurant on Beverly Boulevard and Doheny Drive. Chasen's eventually went out of business, and in that location today is a gourmet grocery store called Bristol Farms.

Michael had me sitting right next to John Lennon, and Ringo Starr was on the opposite side of the table. Ringo was quite friendly, but John Lennon was acting very strange towards me. Some people are really friendly when they talk to you, and John was not. He would just kind of stare at me in a very cynical fashion, like he was examining me. Ringo I liked a lot.

Although Michael was fun to be with, I was nowhere near in love with him, nor was I personally attracted to him. But I am the type of person who, if a guy was catering to me, or wining and dining me and treating me like a queen, I would go out with him. I figured, "Hey, it is better than going out with some jerk!"

Michael would invite me to Las Vegas. While there he would buy me little presents and things. He would also take me out to several headliners' shows at the casinos, and to all of the gourmet restaurants. At one point he announced that he wanted to marry me.

Then suddenly, everything changed. One day Michael said to me, "I went to see a psychic by the name of Peter Hurkos."

I wasn't sure where this was going.

At the time, Peter Hurkos was highly revered in celebrity circles. He was Dutch, and he was known for his accurate psychic abilities. He was on a par with Jeane Dixon, another famous psychic. I remember that I used to read about Peter in *The National Enquirer*. He was world-renowned during this era.

What I didn't know was that Michael was dating another girl at the time. The other girl was Deborah Raffin. She was an actress, and she starred in the movie version of Jacqueline Susann's book *The Love Machine*. Finally he told me about Deborah.

Then Michael announced to me, "I went to see Peter Hurkos for a reading, and I asked him which woman should I marry: you, or Deborah Raffin? So Peter said to me, 'Well, they're both okay, they're both nice, but in the long run you are going to be happier with Deborah Raffin.'"

I would have to say, the psychic was absolutely right! And, I was actually relieved. When I look back on this whole situation, I can see that Deborah would be a better fit for him as a mate. So, that is what happened.

When Michael Viner started Dove Audio, he always looked out for me, and he always called me to get me involved in projects at his company. Once he married Deborah, he never once tried to court me, or get fresh with me. I had to respect that. So, we remained good friends.

Ever since "Band of Gold" became a hit, I found that I had acquired a huge new fan base. Unbeknownst to me, I also had developed a large and devoted gay male following. I was about to become aware of this when I was booked to play at The Continental Baths in New York City.

I was talking with Lenny Bleecher one day, and he said to me, "Freda, do you realize that you have a whole new set of gay fans?"

"Really?" I said. "Well, I am sure that both gay and straight people like my music. Is that what you mean?"

"Not exactly. There is an all-male gay bathhouse on the Upper West Side of Manhattan called The Continental Baths that is regularly booking top talent, and I bet they would love to have you there. I hear it is filled on the weekends with half-undressed men in towels cheering for singing stars. It's like a crazy sort of underground part-bathhouse / part-nightclub."

I was fascinated to hear all of this. Not long afterward, Lenny introduced me to Steve Ostrow, the owner of The Continental Baths. Steve was a tall and dashing looking gay man, and when I met him he was quite charming and enthusiastic. He immediately wanted to book me to perform at his unique club, and I gladly accepted.

The Continental Baths was actually located in the basement of The Ansonia Hotel, on West 74th Street in New York City. It was a bathhouse, it was a nightclub, it had a dance floor, and there were—reportedly—all sorts of sexual exploits taking place in private rooms as well. I was quite curious to see all of this in action.

At the time, The Continental Baths was booking lots of top acts, including LaBelle, Melba Moore, Lou Christie, Leslie Gore, Gladys Knight & The Pips, The Andrews Sisters, The Pointer Sisters, and even Sarah Vaughn. One of the reasons that The Continental Baths later became so legendary, is that Bette Midler and her piano player, Barry Manilow, were frequently the star entertainers there. Not long afterward, they each landed recording deals, and both of their careers exploded.

Well, I played at The Continental Baths on February 20, 1974, and Lenny was 100% correct in his assessment of the situation: I had a legion of devoted gay fans and followers I had no idea where there. Let me tell you, "the boys" loved me at The Continental Baths, and they were very demonstrative. I was presented with all sorts of gifts from my openly-gay fans who I met there. One of them gave me a huge painting of me, which was a beautiful portrait. And another fan presented me with a pen and ink drawing he had done of me that was really stunning. In fact I still have it on one of the walls of my house. The Continental Baths only lasted as a nightclub venue for a couple of years, primarily from 1968 to 1974, but it was sure fun while it lasted!

For a while during this period I went out with singer / song-writer Bill Withers. In the early 1970s Bill had become a big star with his hits including: "Ain't No Sunshine" (1971), "Use Me" (1972), "Lean On Me" (1972), and many more. I wasn't in love with him, but I was definitely "in like" with him. However, he came with an alarming reputation attached.

In 1973 he had married actress Denise Nichols who was one of the stars of the popular TV series *Room 222*. This ended abruptly amidst tabloid headlines, when Denise suddenly divorced Bill in 1974. Reportedly, Bill had physically abused her on several occasions and she walked out on him.

There had been a private screening of a movie starring Denise and Fred Williamson. When they came to the intimate love-making scene, Bill became emotionally upset and angry, and he shouted at the screen, "She doesn't act like that with me in bed!" I got this story from Bob Johnson, Executive Editor of *Jet* magazine, who was sitting right next to Bill in the audience.

When I met Bill, he was so nice and charming. However, I was fully aware of Bill's abusive reputation.

The one time the topic of his divorce came up, I asked if the rumors were true. His reply was, "What can I say? I'm just a country boy."

A voice inside me said, "And I'm just a city girl who wasn't about to put up with that kind of nonsense!"

Although I had a good time with him when we went out, I was cautious not to get too involved with him before I knew him better. He even met my mother, and Mom liked him. Bill once said to me, "Your mother is the only mother who genuinely likes me."

I went out on several dates with Bill. At the time he had a house in Benedict Canyon. On one occasion I was there with Bill, and we were alone together and in a warm embrace. When he pulled back he said to me, "Now Freda, I want to know if you are serious about me or not? I don't want to risk falling in love with you if you are not serious about me. If your answer is 'no,' we can still be friends."

This little voice inside my head said, "If you get involved with him, he is gonna kick your ass!"

So, I said to him, "I am really absorbed with my career at the moment, and I am really not someone who moves fast in a relationship."

I used his ultimatum as the perfect opportunity to ease my way out of getting involved with Bill Withers. That was when our relationship just remained platonic.

Meanwhile, Lenny and Baba Bleecher had become involved in a royal Maltese organization, because of their charity work. Lenny had been knighted, and Baba had been dubbed a Dame. They wanted to have me involved in their organization. So I gladly complied.

Lenny and Baba were very social, and Baba was a great cook. Often they would have dinner parties for eight people at the table in their dining room. One of their elite friends they would invite over for dinner was Prince Hassan Durrani, the Prince of Afghanistan. They had been deposed, and his father and family now lived in New York City. The Prince was not greatly wealthy, but he retained his title. Having this royal title helped open doors for him in some ways.

The Prince was both charming and cute, and he told me he wanted to marry me. The romance never really happened, but the Prince certainly liked me. I was surprised and flattered when he said to me, "I would really like to marry you, and make you Princess Freda."

But that wasn't in the cards. What did happen was that the Prince offered to sponsor me to be dubbed a Dame of Malta. Malta is a little island off the coast of Italy just south of Sicily, and this was a great honor. Since the 1600s, the Maltese Cross has been considered a badge of honor and it represents service to others.

His Serene Highness Prince Robert Michael Nicholas George Bassaraba von Brancovan from Romania and his wife, Princess Audrey von Brancovan, were friends of Lenny and Baba's. Because of their friendship with all of these "titled" people, my show business buddy Lenny Bleecher was now Sir Leonard Bleecher, Baba was now Lady Bleecher, and I officially became Lady Freda Payne.

In the two hour ceremony held at The Fifth Avenue Presbyterian Church in New York City, it was proclaimed that the honor was bestowed upon me because of my "acts of compassion and charity to the less fortunate in our society." It was further proclaimed, "She has quietly performed and conducted rap sessions in prisons without recording an album or calling a press conference." (12)

The night I was dubbed a "Dame," it was a gala affair. I have a plaque that has my scroll from the ceremony, and *Jet* magazine ran a cover story of me as "Dame Freda Payne." I had always felt somewhat like show business royalty, now it was crossing over into my personal life!

"I must honestly say, in all due respect to the honor I received tonight, I just didn't feel as though I was worthy of receiving such an honor," I said that evening, as reported in *Jet* magazine. "I just got chills all through my body. I felt I just had a glorious feeling at that moment and my heart was beating wildly." (12)

Meanwhile, back at the ranch: Otis Smith started seeing that things were changing at Invictus Records, and not for the better. By 1973 he had left Invictus and went to ABC / Dunhill Records in Los Angeles. Otis began to lure Lamont Dozier away from Invictus as well. Lamont was not seeing his career unfold the way he had wanted it to, so he returned to his own singing career, and proceeded to record two of his own albums for ABC / Dunhill called *Out Here On My Own* (1973) and *Black Bach* (1974).

After recording my *Reaching Out* album for Invictus Records, Otis Smith wanted me on ABC / Dunhill with him, and Lamont was also instrumental in this transition as well. Ultimately, ABC / Dunhill paid Invictus to buy my contract for $150,000. Unfortunately, I ended up with none of it, as it was all paid to Invictus. Now I was on

ABC / Dunhill Records.

Lamont has often had an "on-again / off-again" relationship with Eddie and Brian Holland. They still come together as Holland-Dozier-Holland when it is convenient for everyone. They did that when they were working on a Broadway-bound version of the movie *First Wives Club*, in 2009. But often Lamont goes off and does his own thing. Eddie does his thing, and Brian is always along with whatever Eddie does.

After he broke away from Invictus, Lamont continued to work and produce music, and he took various pseudonyms to work under. My first album at ABC Records was produced by Lamont; McKinley Jackson also worked on the album as well. To get around Lamont being legally bound to the Hollands, McKinley Jackson was credited as the sole producer of the album under the name of Lamont's "3G's Productions." However, it was actually Lamont Dozier who produced my first ABC / Dunhill album for me.

This seemed to be a great deal for me. Otis Smith was always a big champion of mine, and ABC had some great people on the label back then. They had just signed The Fifth Dimension, and they were having luck on the charts with Chaka Khan & Rufus, The Pointer Sisters, and Steely Dan. The Four Tops were there as well for their first post-Motown albums. Otis was an excellent record executive, and he gave me some great advice.

The first album I did for ABC Records was called *Payne and Pleasure*. Since LP record albums have two sides to them, creatively you can have one side set one mood, and have the songs on the second side present a different mood. That is what we did with *Payne and Pleasure*. Side One was more contemporary sounding songs, and Side Two was comprised of lush ballads.

I had worked with Lamont, Otis and everyone else before, so this was an easy and pleasant album to record. I trusted their artistic judgment and ability. Lamont wanted my album to be accessible to everyone—not just R&B audiences. I felt it would be an advantage to do quality work with people I knew who could still give me my trademark sound. Several songs were presented to me by Lamont, and I think he came up with some really great ones.

They gave me pre-recorded tracks to work with and rehearse with at home, then we would go into the studio and record them. I was filled with optimism, and I felt like I was moving upward, and away from the Invictus debacle.

The first single that was released from the album, "It's Yours To Have," was selected to be entered into The Tokyo Music Festival. I went over there to perform the song in Japan and won the Third Prize Bronze trophy. In addition to that, I also won the top prize of Best Performance By An Artist. The Three Degrees took the second place prize for their song "When Will I See You Again." And, McKinley Jackson ended up winning as Best Producer.

One of my favorite songs on this album was a ballad called "I Get Carried Away." I always loved that song. The lyrics are beautiful and I really like how my voice sounds on that track. I wanted it to be the first single off the album. As it ended up, the song "It's Yours to Have" was selected instead. It became a minor hit on the R&B charts, only making it to Number 81. Unfortunately, that was the highest charting song off either of my two ABC Records albums.

One of the most beautiful ballads on the album was my cover of Paul Williams' "I Won't Last a Day Without You." I love Paul Williams, and I did a couple of TV shows with him. One of them was a Sammy Davis Jr. TV special that was taped down in Acapulco in 1976. Betty White was also on that program, and I recall her being so funny and nice to everyone. I know Paul was happy that I have covered two of his best songs. It is like the mutual respect that singers and songwriters have for each other.

To this day, every time I see Paul, he is actually the same towards me. He is always a nice, friendly, gracious, and engaging guy.

The *Payne and Pleasure* album concluded with a pair of very popular contemporary ballads: "The Way We Were"—written by Marvin Hamlisch and Alan & Marilyn Bergman—and Leon Russell's "A Song For You." The album also featured some great musicians on it as well, including Ray Parker Jr. on guitar and Joe Sample of The Jazz Crusaders on piano. Edna Wright of the trio Honeycone was one of the background vocalists.

For the cover art, photographer Harry Langdon was behind the camera. Harry was the "number one" Los Angeles photographer for album covers and publicity photos in the '70s and '80s. He was paid top dollar by record labels, and he was worth it. He had his own studio on Melrose between La Cienega and Crescent Heights. The gown I wore in the photo on the front of the album was made by the French designer Elaine Nicholas. She was the wife of Harold Nicholas of the dancing duo, The Nicholas Brothers.

The outfit I wore on the back cover was a gown designed and made by my friend Roxanne Spino of New York. The top of the gown I wore on the front cover was low cut, and showed ample cleavage. People have asked me over the years if that was the product of implants? No, honey. That is all Freda. To quote Flip Wilson, "What you see is what you get!"

Actually, that effect of my bulging breasts is a result of one of my little tricks. I use surgical tape; I pull my breasts together, tape them, and that makes me appear more endowed than I really am.

While I was at ABC Records, I ended up recording two albums: *Payne and Pleasure* and *Out of Payne Comes Love.* For the second album, I went into the studio with producer Bob Monaco. He was most known for his work with Chaka Khan & Rufus. For this album I had several great tracks including an upbeat song called "Look What I Found." I also liked the one called "You Brought The Woman Out of Me." And, I recorded my versions of Nicholas Ashford & Valerie Simpson's "Keep It Coming," and Stevie Wonder's "Seems So Long."

The album was released in 1975, and it instantly went nowhere on the charts. I have to say that after two years with ABC Records, I began to feel that I hadn't been getting the kind of promotion I needed. I felt lost in the shuffle there, and I was absolutely frustrated.

Here I had two huge hits with "Band of Gold" and "Bring The Boys Home" on Invictus, which were certified *Gold* million-sellers, yet when ABC bought my contract, they didn't know what to do with me. It's like some companies just let the ball roll and others take the ball and run with it. If a record is a hit: "Great!" If it isn't: "Oh, well." What were they thinking? I felt that ABC just let the dice roll and hoped for the best, instead of launching a big publicity campaign to support one of their star performers. Again, it was time for me to move on. If they had taken that $150,000.00 and put it into production, instead of giving it to Invictus, we might have had better results!

Fortunately, my performing schedule continued to keep me busy. However I longed for a continuation of the winning streak I had attained at Invictus. As fate would have it, I now had two very different record labels—Capitol and Philadelphia International—who wanted me to sign with them. How wonderful to be fought over!

Since—as Invictus' distributor—Capitol had turned my "Bring The Boys Home" into a huge hit, I had a track record with them. When I was offered my 1976 contract with Capitol Records, they were busy scoring hits with Natalie Cole, The Steve Miller Band, Glen Campbell, Paul McCartney & Wings, and even Frank Sinatra. That was the kind of company I needed to find myself with. I had high hopes that the hit-making staff at Capitol would know exactly what to do with me and my recording career.

At the same time I was being sought after by Kenny Gamble and Leon Huff at Philadelphia International Records. They were in Los Angeles to attend the BMI Awards show. They were staying at The Beverly Wilshire Hotel. We had a couple of meetings at my house on Blue Jay Way.

Here I had two of the biggest hit-producing record labels offering me a deal. Who would I choose? Looking back on this era, I should have gone with Philadelphia International Records. I can now plainly see that this is another one of those instances where I was faced with two choices, and somehow I made the wrong choice. Needless to say, I was instantly impressed with the Gamble and Huff offer. At that time they were creating truly great hit records for their artists, who included: The O'Jay's, Harold Melvin & The Blue Notes, and The Three Degrees. Later, Teddy Pendergrass left Harold Melvin, and then Gamble and Huff turned him into a superstar as well. They were amazing record producers, and I knew it would work creatively. I believe that they had the expertise and power that it would take to really get my recording career back on track.

Then on the other hand, Capitol Records also had a huge roster of stars, *AND* they were offering much more money for an up-front advance. At that time I had a lawyer / business manager by the name of Stanley Handman. And, for a short time he was also my manager.

I went to Stanley and said, "I would love to work with Gamble and Huff at Philadelphia International."

"But?"

"Look what Capitol is offering me. It's a lot more money."

"So," Stanley said, "you go with the label that is offering the most money."

With that, I accepted Capitol's deal. On the "plus" side, I finally got the kind of record advance I had somehow missed at Invictus and ABC. I have always wondered what would have happened if I had the opportunity to work with Gamble and Huff. Oh well, "The Road We Didn't Take."

Around this time, I started to think about my own personal life, and where I was in the relationship department. I was in my 30s now, and I felt I was ready to have a serious relationship. It was time to set some new goals and make some changes.

This was me when I was living in New York City, as a singing star
and an actress. At the time, the premiere photographer of recording
artists was James Kriegsmann. Here is how he saw me through
the lens of his camera in 1964. (Photo: James Kriegsmann)

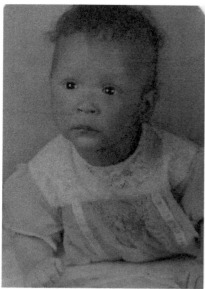

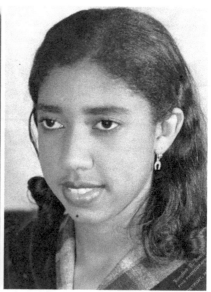

My baby photo when I was
three months old, in Detroit.

My mother, Charcle Lee Farley,
when she was 20 years old. When
I was born she was 22.

My maternal grandmother, Ada Lee
Brack, when she was in her early 40s.

My biological father, Fredrick Ezekiel
Payne. What a handsome guy he was
when he was 21 or 22 years old.

Me and Sammy Davis Jr., at WXYZ-TV, Channel 7 in Detroit, in 1955. I was 13 years old at the time, and I had just won First Prize in a Talent Contest.

Here I am holding my two First Prize trophies, as I had already won six month's earlier. Also in the photo is one of the record players I won as part of the prize.

On the radio show *Make Way For Youth*, I was part of a singing group called The Three Debs. Ursula Walker (left), me (center), and Carman Mathis (right).

This nautical photo was taken by Ike Sutton of *Jet* magazine. I was in Chicago, and the boat we were aboard was on Lake Michigan.

My very first *Jet* magazine cover, May 3, 1962, At the time I was 19 years old, and Quincy Jones' new discovery.

In the New York press photo world at the time, "Popsie" was the Number Two photographer in the business. He was much more affordable, and this sexy shot of me was taken by Popsie in 1962. (Photo: Popsie).

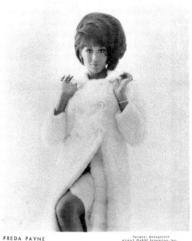

FREDA PAYNE

My family in the early '60s. My
stepdad Samuel Gene Farley
(left), my sister Scherrie (center),
my mother Charcle Lee Farley
(right), and me at the bottom.

Wrapped in a white mink coat, in
Stockholm, Sweden in 1965, on my
first European tour. At the time
my manager was Clarence Avant,
who was wonderful to work with.

My MGM pop / adult
contemporary album, *How Do
You Say I Don't Love You Anymore*,
in 1966. It included songs by The
Beatles and The Righteous Brothers.

This was me in 1968 in San Juan,
Puerto Rico. I was performing
at The San Jeronimo Hilton,
in my fringed and beaded skin-
tight jumpsuit. It was designed
and made by my dear friend
Roxanne Spino in New York.

It was the Number One song "Band of Gold" in 1970, and my Grammy-nominated 1971 *Contact* album, that changed my career, and made me a bona fide singing star.

Here I am in Paris with handsome Omar Sharif. We were—supposedly— having a mad, hot and passionate affair, in 1971.

Suddenly I was getting some very hot bookings, and none was hotter than the infamous NYC gay bathhouse: The Continental Baths. Performers who played there included: LaBelle, Melba Moore, Bette Midler, The Pointer Sisters, and Sarah Vaughn no less!

Here I am singing with Bobby Darin on his television show in 1973. I was a guest on his program twice. Tragically, he died later that very same year, at the age of 37.

Me with Lenny Bleecher (left), and our friend Jeremy Wind (right), the evening that I was dubbed a Dame of Malta in 1974. (Photo: Moneta Sleet Jr. / *Jet*)

The night I officially became a Dame, my friends at *Jet* magazine— including Executive Editor Robert Johnson—were there to "cover" me being bestowed such an honor. (Photo: Moneta Sleet Jr. / *Jet*)

Here I am with my buddy David Gest in 1973. At the time he was just leaving London Records, and starting out as an independent publicist. (Photo: Fray Zlozower)

Me and Phillip Michael Thomas in the 1973 film *The Book of Numbers*, in one of our intimate scenes. This was years before he became a star—along with Don Johnson— in the '80s TV hit *Miami Vice*.

This photo was a groundbreaker for me. I was involved in a lawsuit, against Invictus Records, and I had to do something to grab the attention of the press and the public. This photo did the trick! Sex still sells!

This is me in one of Roxanne Spino's spectacular gowns. This photo was from my first ABC Records album in 1974, *Payne and Pleasure*. (Photo: Harry Langdon)

FREDA PAYNE

This was a publicity shot for my second album release on Capitol Records, *Supernatural High,* in 1978. For the photo session I had Shirley Bassey's make-up artist, Bjorn. My hair was done by Daley Henderson. (Photo: Charles W. Bush)

Seductively sitting on a plank! I was wearing a hooded cape in this sexy pose. (Photo: Harry Langdon)

My career has encompassed jazz and pop music, theater, television,
and my love of performing for an audience. Since I was a teenager, I
have always been in love with performing. (Photos: Alan Mercer)

Starting in the '80s, I spent much of my time headlining the touring companies of hit Broadway shows. It started with *Ain't Misbehavin'* in 1981. That's Linda Hopkins (left), Della Reese (center), and me (right).

So far I have starred in eight different productions of Duke Ellington's *Sophisticated Ladies*, including two European tours. (Photo: Tony Vaughn)

Harold Nicholas and Freda Payne star in Long Beach Civic Light Opera's presentation of Duke Ellington's SOPHISTICATED LADIES, October 5 - 22 at the Terrace Theater of the Long Beach Convention Center

Here I am with Harold Nicholas in Duke Ellington's *Sophisticated Ladies,* in 1983. With his brother Fayard, he was one half of the famed dancing duo The Nicholas Brothers. Harold was a legend and a dream to work with.

Belinda Carlisle (left) and me (right) on the TV broadcast of the special *The Legendary Ladies of Rock & Roll*, in 1986. We turned our duet version of "Band of Gold" into a Top Forty hit.

Me playing the grandmother of Jelly Roll Morton, the originator of the "blues," in the touring company of the Broadway hit musical *Jelly's Last Jam*, in 1995. My character's name was Gran Mimi.

At The Post Theater in San Francisco in 2007. I was starring in *Blues In The Night* with Paulette Ivory (left) and Carol Woods (right). That's me in the center, striking a pose! Maurice Hines was also in that company.

With Teddy Pendergrass at Les Mouches disco and nightclub in New York City, in the early 1980s. We were having a brief but exciting affair at the time. (Photo: Charles Moniz)

My sister Scherrie (left), Bob Hope (center), and me (right), at one of David Gest's *American Cinema Awards* galas, at The Beverly Hilton Hotel, in the mid-1980s.

Me with the one and only Eartha Kitt (right). I was personally selected by Eartha to be her replacement in the Broadway show *Timbuktu*. Unfortunately, the show closed before that happened.

With Al Jarreau backstage at The City Center in New York City. This was one of David Gest's *Night of 100 Stars* gala's, for *The American Cinema Awards.* We sang our *Porgy & Bess* duet medley together, to a 55-piece orchestra.

Mary Wilson (left), Berry Gordy Jr. (center), and me (right) at *The B.M.I. Awards,* at The Beverly Wilshire Hotel. Both Berry and Holland-Dozier-Holland were honored that night. (Photo: Willie Tassain)

Melba Moore (left) and me (right) in Atlantic City, where we did a double bill together, in the 1990s.

Me and the legendary Lena Horne at Avery Fisher Hall at Lincoln Center in NYC, celebrating Lena's 80th birthday in 1997. Also performing that evening were Liza Minnelli, Rita Moreno, and several more movie and singing stars. We loved Lena!

215

With Eddie Murphy. I was thrilled to have a role in one of his films *The Nutty Professor II, The Klumps,* in 2000.

In NYC in 2002 at The Regency Hotel, on Park Avenue: Darlene Love (left), Michael Feinstein (center), and me (right). Michael put us together in an act called *Love & Payne*.

Here I am with The Queen of Soul: Aretha Franklin (right). We had known about each other since we were kids growing up in Detroit.

Justin Chambers of TV's *Grey's Anatomy,* and me, after one of my concerts at The Catalina Bar & Grill in Hollywood.

Me, feeling fabulous in a Linda Stokes designed gown. (Photo: Alan Mercer)

With the phenomenally talented Johnny Mathis! He and I just recently recorded a duet together, and it was heaven.

Me and Quincy Jones, in my dressing room at The Catalina Bar & Grill on Sunset Boulevard in LA.

Scherrie (left), Jon Hendricks (center), and me (right) at a pre-Grammy Awards party, where Jon was being honored.

With Ice-T on the set of a video for the film we were in together, *Rhapsody.*

At The Hotel Britannia in Liverpool, England with David Gest (center), and our friend Pearly Gates a/k/a "Vi" from the group The Flirtations (right). We were there for one of David's all-star events.

Me in another favorite Linda Stokes dress, which was created by her company, LSO Designs. (Photo by Alan Mercer)

Here I am with author Mark Bego (center) and Mary Wilson (right) at The Luxe Hotel on Sunset Boulevard in 2019. (Photo: David Salidor)

This is me today! Still feeling great, and entertaining audiences around the world. I would like to think of myself as being much *more* than just a "Band of Gold!" (Photo: Alan Mercer)

CHAPTER EIGHT

"Two Suitors, One Marriage, One Divorce"

My recent move from New York to Los Angeles had been something of an adjustment for me, but an adjustment that I made very well. I had been living on the West Coast for a couple of years at this point. I was very comfortable in the first house I bought, located on Blue Jay Way, in the Hollywood Hills of Los Angeles, which I had purchased in 1974. It was August 5 of that year that I moved in, and I loved living there.

Naturally, I kept in touch with all of my New York friends, and I often appeared in nightclubs there, so I felt very "bicoastal."

This was the period when I first met Gregory Abbott. How I met him was that he was with my friend Sandra McPherson when she came to my house in Los Angeles to visit me.

Sandy had moved up to San Francisco for a while, but she kept her apartment in New York. She was doing some singing, dancing and acting work with Oscar Brown Jr. in the Bay Area. She was a talented dancer along the lines of Judith Jamison, and she had also been a part of the George Faison dance company as well. Debbie Allen was in that dance company, too.

Well, when Sandy showed up at my house, she had this guy with her. She had come down to LA to take care of some business, and the guy she had traveling with her was Gregory Abbott.

Gregory was a nice looking African American guy, but I was not instantly attracted to him. Sometimes the timing and the chemistry just have to be right for things to work out. At that time I remember her bringing him over, meeting him, and he just sat on the couch of my living room, and that was about it. It was Sandy and me who did all the talking. Sandy and Gregory only stayed over for a brief visit, and then they left. I was so happy to see Sandy that day, I really didn't have any thoughts about Gregory one way or another.

Sandra wasn't romantically involved with Gregory. They were just hanging out together, and he simply came down to Los Angeles for the ride.

It was almost a year later, and I was invited to a birthday party in Hollywood, located not far from where I lived. It was just down the hill on Holloway Drive. It was the birthday of David Downing, an actor friend of mine I had known in New York City. He was an actor from The Negro Ensemble acting company.

I was at this birthday party, and at that time I wasn't involved with anyone. They were playing great music, people were dancing, and I was dancing with this little short guy who kept asking me questions about my life and my career. I was totally bored, and although we were having a conversation, I found my mind drifting.

I thought to myself, "Why am I dancing with this boring guy?"

As I was dancing with Mr. Dullsville, I looked across the dimly-lit room to one corner of it, and there was a sconce type of lamp on the wall, and it reflected the light in a nice way. And there in the light was standing Gregory Abbott. The way he was standing, it gave his hair a fascinating glow, and I said to myself, "Who is that cute guy? I want to talk to him."

So I excused myself from the boring guy I was dancing with, and I walked over to Gregory, and I looked at him, then I suddenly realized I had seen him before. So, I said, "Don't I know you?"

He replied, "Yes, you know me. I was at your house with Sandy."

"Oh, yes," I said. "Gregory?"

"That's me!"

So we started talking. Then we danced. Finally I said to him, "Do you want to come up to my house for a nightcap?"

Naturally, he said, "Yes."

Well, that was the beginning of it. Gregory was still in college up in Berkeley. He was attending Stanford University, and he was working on his doctor's degree in English Literature. All he had to do was complete his dissertation, and he would have gotten his doctor's degree. From that point forward, he would come back and forth from the San Francisco area, down to Los Angeles to see me.

I found out that Gregory actually grew up in the same housing complex that Motown executive and TV producer Suzanne DePasse grew up in, in Harlem. They were childhood sweethearts. Gregory had not been exposed to the show business world when I first met him, and he never verbalized any deep interest in singing, recording or performing.

Meanwhile, among my New York friends I was constantly in touch with were Lenny and Baba Bleecher. Lenny called me one day and said, "Freda, there is this guy named Edgar Bronfman Jr. His father is Edgar Bronfman Sr., and they own Seagram's Liquor, and they also own a percentage of Air Canada, as well as 40% of DuPont chemicals. They are Jewish, and his father is the head of a very powerful Jewish Alliance. They are one of the richest families in America although they were originally from Canada. Edgar Jr. mentioned to me that he is a big fan of yours, and he would love to have dinner with you. He is 20 years old."

I was 31 at the time. When Lenny told me this, I said to him, "I don't want to go out on a 'blind date' with a 20-year-old, even if he is a millionaire."

Lenny argued, "But he is so rich and handsome, and you are adorable. He is a big fan of yours. He is dying to meet you. Do it for me, Freda. Just do it for me, go to dinner with him. He wants to meet you so bad. Just dinner, that's all. Nothing else."

I said to him, "No Lenny. I don't want to go out with a 20-year-old boy."

Lenny kept trying to talk me into it, saying things like, "Freda, please do it. Even if you don't want do this, just do it for me. It will just be dinner. Just go and have dinner with him."

Finally, he wore me down. "This is the first time I have been out on a 'blind date,' ever. Okay, I will do this for you, Lenny. Just this once." To this day, I have never been on a "blind date" again.

So, Lenny set it up, and arranged it so that Edgar came to pick me up.

At the appointed time, Edgar arrived at my house on Blue Jay Way. He came up to the front door and rang my doorbell. I went to the door, and when I opened it, there he stood: a big tall handsome guy about six-foot-three-inches tall with curly reddish brown hair, and a beard. He had a nice and pleasant personality, and he walked into my living room very confidently.

So, we went out to dinner, and he took me to La Scala in Beverly Hills. We sat down, and the head of Fox Studios was also there having dinner, and he sent a bottle of wine over to our table. Suddenly, I was quite impressed. Of course, I noticed by the way Edgar talked, expressed himself, and carried himself, it was like he was a high-powered executive, and not a goofy 20-year-old.

I thought to myself, "He looks so mature. He might be 20, but he has the business brain and the mentality of a 50-year-old."

He had just produced Shirley MacLaine's latest TV special. So, Edgar announced at the restaurant, "We have to hurry up and get back to your place to see the TV special, because I produced it." This was quite impressive to hear.

Scherrie had dropped by the house to visit, and she was still there when we returned. She was in the den, watching TV. Scherrie was watching something else, and Edgar just walked up to the TV set and changed the channel, and Scherrie got pissed-off at him. She didn't say anything, but she was taken aback. She was amazed that he had been so aggressive about commandeering control of the TV. However, I was curious to see the show that Edgar had produced, as well.

The TV special that was broadcast that night was called *Gypsy In My Soul*, and in it Shirley MacLaine saluted Broadway dancers, and played host to guest star Lucille Ball. I was very excited when Edgar's name came up in the credits. The show was such a huge success that Shirley ended up winning an Emmy Award for her performance on it, which was great for Edgar. He also dabbled in films and songwriting. When Edgar was writing, he did so under a pseudonym, and it was "Junior Miles." He also used another pseudonym, "Sam Roman," for some of his other show business projects.

After we watched the Shirley MacLaine show, Edgar and I talked some more. We also kissed a little bit. Then he said, "When can I see you again?"

"Hmmm," I thought to myself, "He's a perfect gentleman, he took me for a wonderful dinner in Beverly Hills, and he is a TV producer." That left a big impression on me. I liked him, so we started dating.

At that time I was in Los Angeles for a few more days, before going out on the road for some more gigs. So, I explained, "I have another week before I have to go out of town again."

"Then let's go out together again while you are here," he replied.

So, I agreed, and he came over to pick me up for our second date. He came in, and announced, "Instead of us going out to another restaurant, why don't we stay in, and you let me cook for you?"

"You want to cook for me?" I said in awe.

"Yes, I do."

"Sure!" I replied.

So, we drove to Ralph's grocery store located on Doheny Drive and Beverly Boulevard. First we went to the liquor department, and Edgar would point to various liquor bottles, and he would say, "We own that company. We own this company. This is a Seagram's product." He would point to one bottle after another, from whiskies to vodkas to whatever there was, that were part of the Seagram's line of products.

"What do you want to have for dinner?" he asked me.

"I don't know. What would you like?"

He said, "Do you eat pork chops?"

"Sure, I eat pork chops," I replied. "I didn't know Jews ate pork." "Awww, we do," he said. "We just don't broadcast it."

So we bought everything we needed at Ralph's, and we headed back to my house. We had pork chops, mashed potatoes, and broccoli with Hollandaise sauce to cook.

I said to him, "I know you are going to ask me to cook for you."

"Oh, no I'm not," he laughed. And, he was a man of his word.

He proceeded to cook the entire dinner. Everything came out great, and the pork chops were outstanding. They were cooked perfectly, and he served them with some sort of a white sauce that was just out of this world.

I asked him, "Where did you learn how to do that?"

He said, "I learned by observation, because I used to stand in the kitchen and watch our cook."

I was highly amused envisioning this sight.

We ate, and he ended up spending the night with me at my house. After that, we went out a few more times. This was all going on during the time I had also started going out with Gregory. But I didn't feel I had to tell Gregory about any of what happened with Edgar, because he was still living up in Berkeley. And, I wasn't at all serious about him.

So, I proceeded to go out with Edgar. I really liked him, and

I thought things were going well. One day Edgar came over to my house, and sat down in my living room. And all of a sudden he announced, "I'm not ready to get married yet."

"Who said anything about marriage?" I said in disbelief, "We are just dating." I didn't understand where he was coming from; we had just started seeing each other. I wasn't at a point where I was thinking of marriage at all, but apparently he had been.

He explained, "I just wanted to tell you that I am not ready to get married, and I am leaving for Italy. Why don't we just chill out for a while?"

It was almost like he was breaking up with me. I was shocked and amazed.

"We have never discussed marriage," I said with disbelief. "Why are you bringing this up now? Marriage? Italy? Are you crazy?"

I could have definitely married Edgar, but the problem was that I thought he was just a little bit crazy. Well, I could have dealt with a little craziness. However, there was another issue to consider. I thought that he would never marry a black woman, because of his family wealth and power. His father was the head of The Jewish Alliance, so these are very rich and powerful people, who just happen to have a slightly crazy son who decided he wants to marry a black woman!

I kept telling myself, "He is never going to marry me. I'm not going to go nuts and lose my head over some guy who is crazy, and who will clearly never end up married to a black woman."

So, Edgar went off to Italy, and about a week or so later I received a letter from him. In it he wrote, "I have to think about some things. I've got stuff I've got to work out in my head....I've got to think things over...I've got to get my head together and do some self-evaluation...blah...blah...blah."

That was when I decided, "This guy's really crazy. He is taking everything way too seriously."

I think that it was one of those things where he was on the bor-
derline of deciding what he was going to do with his life, or he was
on some sort of personal spiritual quest. Was he going to get further
into show business? Was he going to get into songwriting? Or, was he
going to stay in the family liquor business?

This gave me a lot to think about. I could see that I needed to
concentrate on my own life. Here I was, I had just recently gotten
settled in my house in Los Angeles, and I realized that Edgar was
stationed in New York City. I was enjoying living on the West Coast,
and I didn't want to turn around and move back there.

I also knew that Edgar was hanging out with Bruce Roberts, the
songwriter. They were the best of friends, and Edgar was trying his
hand at songwriting as well. He absolutely loved show business, so I
had no idea what he was going to do. And, apparently neither did he.

"Maybe he is going to go off with Bruce Roberts and become a
songwriting team?" I thought to myself. "Maybe he is going to stay
in Italy? Whatever it is, I can't wait around until he figures out what
he wants to do with his life. Besides that, he's 20 years old!"

Edgar is a Taurus, so his birthday was in May. He had just
turned 21. To make a long story short, after he sent that letter to
me, I didn't hear from Edgar for a while. I figured this was the end of
that. A month went by and still no word. I certainly wasn't going to
sit around and wait until Edgar made up his mind about what he was
going to do with his life. While this was going on, I had put Gregory
"on hold." Gregory called me, and I invited him to come down from
Berkeley to Los Angeles, and for us to start seeing each other again.

I started dating Gregory, and it became the way to get me over
the strange relationship I had just experienced with Edgar.

"Well, at least I've got this guy Gregory I can rely on," I figured.

I certainly liked Gregory, and here I was on the rebound from
dating Edgar. Although I was not in love with Gregory, I was comfortable with him. So, the next thing I did was to invite him to live

with me at my place in Los Angeles.

So, he said, "Okay" He had been working on his doctorate degree, but he explained that he had his fill with the educational system for a while. So he moved to LA and started living with me.

He lived with me in April and May of 1976, and then in June I had a booking at The Rainbow Grill which was located on the 65th floor of The Rockefeller Center building in New York City. That is the same building where the NBC network is located. The Rainbow Grill was a really nice and chic supper club room, in the middle of Manhattan, and I was booked to headline there for two weeks.

I had performed there more than once, and they continued to invite me back. Gregory did not come with me to New York. But he was going to join me afterward in Bermuda, because I was booked to perform there next, at The South Hampton Princess Hotel. While I was in New York, he remained at my house in Los Angeles.

While I was booked at The Rainbow Grill, Edgar—who was back from Italy—came to see me perform. As a matter of fact, he brought his father with him to see the show and to meet me. And then he came back another night to see me again.

After my last song was over and I left the stage, Edgar came to my dressing room and said to me, "What are you doing after the show?"

"I don't have any plans tonight," I told him. "I guess I will just go back to where I am staying." I was staying at Lenny and Baba's apartment during my New York engagement.

"Do you want to go get a little bite at a private club?" Edgar asked.

I said, "Why sure. I would love to."

The place Edgar took me to was a private little "after hours" kind of place. It was very nice, and it stayed open late.

We sat at this club and we ordered some drinks and something to eat. While we sat there Edgar asked me, "Freda, are you happy?"

"I'm Okay. I am alright. Are you happy?"

He said, "Yeah. I'm Okay. Are you involved with anybody?"

"Yes, actually I am."

"What's his name?"

"Gregory." And, I proceeded to tell Edgar all about him. I also told Edgar about Gregory living in my house with me.

Edgar was astonished. "He is living with you?" he asked in disbelief. "Now Freda, are you actually in love with Gregory?"

"No, I am not in love with him. I like him a lot," I said. "But I'm not in love with him."

Since I had broken up with Edgar, I had heard it through the grapevine about his dating Sherry "Peaches" Brewer. I had met her before she met Edgar. She was a chorine, and she had also been part of the cast of *Hello Dolly!* when Pearl Bailey and Cab Calloway starred in it on Broadway. I saw her in that production. This was back in 1968.

Actually, I had met Sherry before that, back in 1963. She must have been no more than 14 or 15 years old at that time, and she was a local Chicago girl, who was studying to be a professional dancer. The way I met her was that I was in Chicago then, working with *Larry Steele's Smart Affairs*. It was at The McCormick Place. At the same time, in that building, Duke Ellington and His Orchestra were appearing in their theater space, The Arie Crown Theater. He was doing his ballet called *Come Sunday*, which he wrote. It was The Alvin Ailey Dance Company who were performing the dance numbers while Duke and His Orchestra played the musical accompaniment. The McCormick Place has several performing spaces.

After I stopped dating Edgar, Dionne Warwick had introduced Sherry to Edgar, as Dionne was one of Edgar's friends.

So I turned the tables on Edgar and I said to him, "Are you dating or involved with anyone?"

"Well, yeah," he replied.

Well, naturally it was Sherry "Peaches" Brewer.

So I asked him, "Are you in love with Sherry?"

He answered, "No, I'm not in love with Sherry. I just like her a lot. Why don't you and I try to get back together again? Since you're not in love with Gregory, and I'm not really in love with Sherry, why don't we get back together? I would like to try it again."

"Well," I said, thinking out loud.

"Where are you going when you leave New York?" Edgar asked.

I said, "After I close here at The Rainbow Grill, I'm going to Bermuda for my next engagement. I am going to be at The South Hampton Princess Hotel in Bermuda. I am booked there for two weeks, and I will be going there directly from here. Why don't *you* come to Bermuda, Edgar?"

He said, "Is Gregory going to be coming to Bermuda?"

"Yes, Gregory's going to join me there," I told him. "Why don't you come to Bermuda anyway?"

He thought about it for a moment, and said, "Okay."

It was like me saying to him, "If you really want me, come and get me, like a real man!"

We did not make specific plans, but I assumed that he would come to Bermuda if he was serious. I thought to myself, "This is going to be interesting: me in Bermuda with not one, but two boyfriends! Now who is crazy?" Maybe I was the crazy one?

However, Edgar didn't come to Bermuda at all. I guess he got cold feet!

Later on, and a couple of years after that incident, when I talked to him I asked him, "Why didn't you come to meet me in Bermuda?"

He said to me, "Are you kidding? Are you crazy? Do you think I wanted to get my head blown off by Gregory?"

Gregory didn't want a confrontation or anything like that. Had Edgar come and swept me off my feet, I might have married Edgar. You see how silly I was? A year later, after dating Sherry, Edgar ended up marrying her. Ironically, Gregory came to Bermuda, and that is where he proposed marriage to me.

He gave me such a small diamond engagement ring that I eventually took it off and put it away, and I've never worn it since. Imagine the kind of diamond that Edgar would have given me? If I wanted to pursue marrying a millionaire, that was my big chance. I guess this is living proof that I was not a "gold digger!"

I have been exposed to the finer things in life, and I fully appreciate them. Some people can be exposed to the finer things in life, and they still cling to their self-perception of being less-than-well-off. Another way of putting it is to say: "They have tasted caviar and champagne, but they have never left the ghetto."

It's kind of like that old song, "How you gonna keep them down on the farm, after they've seen *Par-ee?*" I am one of those. I know what quality is, and I know what cheap things are, too. I know fabrics and fashions, and especially cuisine. I consider myself a gourmet, and I know a superior wine from a substandard one. I much prefer being in Paris than I do being down on the farm! (Being down on the farm is okay for a couple of weeks, but not permanently, like a summer home!)

Then on the flip side of that, I can also appreciate the simpler things in life as well. It's just that I know that by having higher standards it makes you want to achieve more.

I guess you could say that I lost my "gold digger" reputation when I married Gregory, and not Edgar. But at the time I was looking for someone who was dependable, and would be there for me. I thought I had made the right decision about Gregory.

Actually, getting married wasn't my idea. Gregory is the one who wanted me as his wife. When he moved in with me he kept saying, "I want to marry you. I don't want to just be your boyfriend. I want to be your husband."

I should have known, that was a red-flag right there! I should have heeded that warning!

I was happy just living together with Gregory. He was in my house, and I was the one paying all of the bills.

The Bermuda incident happened in June of 1976, and I married Gregory on December 1, 1976. The ceremony was held in Chicago, at the home of my uncle, the Reverend Bishop Elgin Little. He was married to my Aunt Velma, who was a Payne. She was one of my father's six sisters. As a matter of a fact, it was Uncle Elgin who kept encouraging me to get married. This was because Gregory had been living with me in Los Angeles, and he had been living with me for ten months prior to our wedding.

We all make our own decisions. There comes a point where we can go left or we can go right. Both paths look like they have the biggest potential, but you finally have to make a decision and take one direction or another.

At the time, I thought I was making a sane, level-headed decision. It was actually "fear" that made me choose the path I did at that time. I was afraid. I had just recently purchased my lovely house on Blue Jay Way in the Hollywood Hills. And, I was thinking, "If I would go with Edgar I might have to move back to Manhattan." I wasn't quite ready for that. It wasn't that I didn't like New York. I had already lived there eight years of my life, and I was enjoying my new life in Los Angeles.

It was in February of 1977 that I found out I was pregnant. As odd as it seems, I think that I became pregnant on my honeymoon with Gregory, in Acapulco, Mexico. Gregory and I had been flown to Acapulco to participate and perform on a Sammy Davis Jr. TV special, so we turned this trip into our honeymoon.

At first I didn't realize that I was pregnant. What happened was that I wanted to start taking birth control pills, because Gregory didn't want a baby. He had already been married once and divorced, and he had fathered a child whom he saw rarely. His first wife's name was Ruth Burks. They met in college, they went through school together, and she later became a college professor. They had a son, and his name is Gyaci, and he is four years older than my son.

When I told him I was pregnant, Gregory wanted me to have an abortion. His logic was: he had one child, whom he could barely support.

Since I had a very active career, and since it was me paying for all of the bills for both of us, this was not a valid consideration. I was the bread winner, and I decided I wanted this baby. It was time for me to have a child. I was 34 years old at the time, and my biological clock was ticking!

While all of this was going on, my mother was continuing her battle with breast cancer. Her many doctor's visits didn't seem to help. We had sent her to stay in Chicago with Uncle Elgin and Aunt Velma. Mother Botto was the mother of Uncle Elgin, and she was the head of her church, and she was also a spiritual healer. They called her "the mother of the church." Many important people would come to her for her famed healing powers. When you are faced with a loved one battling cancer, you try everything you can to help them, and we certainly thought this couldn't hurt.

(NOTE: Today, the pastor of Uncle Elgin's church, God's House of All Nations Pentecostal Church, is Lavel Hardy, who is my first cousin, and Uncle Elgin and Aunt Velma's daughter.)

Unfortunately, Mother Botto's powers did not work, and Mom showed no further signs of improvement. At one point she was admitted to The Chicago University Hospital. Finally, I brought her out to Los Angeles to stay with me and Gregory. We set up a hospital bed for her, and she had hospice care. Scherrie would come over and take care of her, too. On March 20, 1977, my mother passed away in my house.

She had been staying at my house. I had flown to San Juan, Puerto Rico, where I had a two week engagement at The Caribe

Hilton. I had an act that consisted of me and two male dancers. They had flown us to Puerto Rico, and my musical director and drummer as well. I was there for approximately three nights before I received the phone call that my mother had passed. So, I immediately cancelled the rest of the engagement, and flew to Detroit, because that's where her body had been shipped.

Mom had two funeral services. She passed away in LA, and we had her shipped back to Detroit, because that's where all of her family and friends were living. Her service was held at Bethel AME Church in Detroit. That was the church she belonged to, and the church Scherrie and I attended as children, up into our teen years.

The day after that service, her body was flown back to Los Angeles for a final service, Gregory was with me, and he and I flew back to LA as well. Mother was interred at Forest Lawn in Burbank, California. Several of my friends came to the service including Bill Withers, and he was one of the official pall bearers.

Right after that, I had an engagement in Las Vegas, at The Tropicana Hotel & Casino, with The Four Tops. Although I was pregnant at the time, I was still able to dance and perform as well.

When Mom passed away, I was four months pregnant. I had so wished that she had lived long enough to see her grandson.

It just so happened that Mary Wilson and I became pregnant at the same time. I was pregnant with Gregory Jr., and Mary with her son Pedro Jr. She came to my baby shower, and so did Natalie Cole. Pam Grier was at the shower as well. We took a great photo of the three of us: Mary, Natalie, and me. It ran in *Jet* magazine. We looked glowingly happy, three pregnant divas of song. I was a very happy mother-to-be at this time.

Also, ironically at the same time, Melba Moore was pregnant and gave birth the same year. She had a daughter who was born in June of 1977. I gave birth in September, and Mary and Natalie both gave birth that October.

While I was pregnant I was still thinking that I could make this marriage to Gregory work, if I wanted it to continue. Gregory was helping me, semi-managing me, but he didn't have a real job with a paycheck. He had certain traits where he could be very haughty and very arrogant, and sometimes he could be downright nasty. Not 'nasty' in a dirty way, but just an arrogant attitude.

He never was violent or anything like that, but he was not at all on the same wavelength as me. In spite of his occasionally negative attitude, he was very smart and very bright, and well educated. I thought those traits were part of being a good husband. On the other hand, he was strikingly handsome, so we looked like a "Barbie doll" perfect couple from the outside.

In fact, *After Dark* magazine did an article about me during my time with Gregory, and photographer Kenn Duncan took a beautiful photo of Gregory and me bare-chested together. Gregory was standing behind me with his arms around me, so it was sexy, yet it was still a very tasteful photo. It made us look like the perfect couple. If only the photo could have become reality.

Along the way there were some good things that Gregory did for me during our short marriage. He identified and isolated an additional money source, where I could earn more by writing one or more of the songs on my albums. Gregory was the one who not only encouraged that, but he directed me into it.

"There were even more royalties to be made for every album sold by being one of the songwriters, as well as being the recording artist," he would say. In other words, he had a good business mind. If there were ten tracks on an album, and I, as the artist, recorded one or two of my own compositions on my albums, it meant more money in my pocket. That way I could be paid twice: as the singer, *and* as the songwriter.

Gregory was smart, and he was into the business end of it. Probably if we had stayed married, I would have written more songs.

As it was, one of the songs that Gregory and I wrote together, "Bring Back the Joy," appeared on my 1977 *Stares And Whispers* album.

By the mid- to late-1970s the record business was changing. Suddenly danceable "disco" music was all the rage. In 1974, when The Hues Corporation released "Rock The Boat," a whole tidal wave of disco began. Then in 1975 Donna Summer released "Love to Love You Baby." Discotheques began opening in every city across America and suddenly the whole R&B / Soul music market dramatically changed. If you wanted to stay in the marketplace, you had to do disco. In 1978, when Gloria Gaynor released "I Will Survive," disco officially ruled the airwaves.

When I got signed to Capitol Records in 1976, it was Larkin Arnold who was the head of A&R, and he championed getting me on the label. At the time the whole disco wave was coming on strong. It was the year of "Don't Leave Me This Way" by Thelma Houston, "You Should Be Dancing" by The Bee Gees, "Turn the Beat Around" by Vicki Sue Robinson, and "Heaven Must Be Missing An Angel" by Tavares. This is why a lot of the songs on my three Capitol albums were also disco oriented.

The first of three albums I did at Capitol Records was called *Stares And Whispers*. I was really happy when I recorded it, as it was a beautiful album, and I loved all of the songs. I can truly say that *Stares And Whispers* was a labor of love for me, as it was recorded during a special time in my life. I had just gotten married, and I was pregnant with my son, Gregory Abbott Jr., so it seemed like I had it all.

I was actually eight months pregnant when the photo on the cover was taken. The doctor originally told me that the expected birth date of my baby was to be October 6. Back then the technology had yet to be developed to be able to determine the sex of an unborn child, so I didn't know whether I would be having a boy or a girl. Because of this, when I had my baby shower, the designated color was a neutral yellow, rather than pink for a girl, or blue if it's a boy. As it turned out, my son was born two weeks early, and as a further bond, his birth date was September 19, exactly the same as my birthday!

When I gave birth on September 19, 1977, my OBGYN doctor, Marshall Kadner, said to me, "Congratulations Mrs. Abbott, you have a baby boy, and Happy Birthday." So, my son was my birthday gift! I was feeling great! I had a new record label, my marriage was still young and fresh, and by the time the *Stares And Whispers* album was released, I was celebrating being a new mother.

In an interview I did for the September 1977 issue of Great Britain's *Blues & Soul* magazine, I proclaimed to interviewer David Nathan, "These days, you have to study more, because it's tougher than it's ever been. There are more records, more companies and the competition is really keen. It keeps you on your toes and stops you from becoming lazy! Basically over the years, I left it to other people. When I was with Holland-Dozier-Holland, I knew they were producers and it was their job. But nowadays I'm more aware of what should be happening in the studio when I record—I guess I've learned from experience. So many times I've talked about what I thought should have happened, what we could have done. Now I'm beginning to get that confidence to do it myself." (13)

I also spoke about the fact that I tried my hand at songwriting at the time. I was especially proud of myself because I had never written anything before. I had to sit down and concentrate, and I found that it was fairly easy for me to get the basic hook for a song. At the time I had Gregory encouraging me to come up with song ideas. Gregory was the one who really pushed and gave me the incentive to write my own songs. He encouraged me to come up with lyrics and titles from my own experiences.

After I came up with the song titles, Gregory came up with lyrics based on my titles and my ideas. Try as I might, I couldn't seem to get involved in writing the verses. The fact that Gregory had studied to be a professor of English Literature, helped greatly. I found that the basis of a good song was being able to express the thoughts of the song in the simplest way possible. I certainly didn't imagine myself to be the next Stevie Wonder or Carole King, but I did come up with some good songs.

On my first Capitol Records album I was really happy with "Bring Back The Joy" which Gregory and I wrote together. And Gregory co-wrote the song "Loving You Means So Much to Me" with another writer. "Bring Back The Joy" was produced by Tony Camillo.

The main producer of the album was Frank Wilson, who was a Motown alumnus. He is famous for his work with Eddie Kendricks ("Keep On Truckin'"), The Supremes ("Stoned Love"), and The Four Tops ("All In The Game"). It was Larkin Arnold's idea to have Frank as the key producer. Although I knew of him, I had never worked with him before. I think Frank did a wonderful job.

Years later, Frank Wilson became the pastor of his own church. He used to have Bible studies in his home located in the Hollywood Hills. It would be Frank and his wife, Bunny, and their two girls. Gregory and I used to attend those Bible studies when we were together.

Four singles were released from the *Stares And Whispers* album: "I Get High (On Your Memory)," "Bring Back The Joy," "Love Magnet," and "Feed Me Your Love." The song "Love Magnet" became the biggest hit, reaching Number 85 on the R&B charts, and Number 18 on the Disco charts.

Since the disco era had come on so strong on the charts, there was a concentrated effort to come up with songs that could be "remixed" into hot disco numbers. During this same era I recorded a duet song with the Capitol Records group Tavares. They were in the studio recording their *Love Storm* album for the label, and I ended up recording the song "I Wanna See You Soon" with them.

It was Larkin Arnold and producer Freddie Perren who came up the idea of doing that duet, so I figured, "Why not?" After all, it seemed to work for Dionne Warwick and The Spinners when they recorded "Then Came You." Our duet song was available on Tavares' *Love Storm* album, and it was later part of the 2011 deluxe CD release of my *Stares And Whispers* album as well. We sounded great together and the song became a popular hit on the radio in the U.K.

I had great expectations for the *Stares And Whispers* album. It was beautifully recorded and packaged, but it didn't seem to accomplish the kind of success we had hoped it would have. I was happy with the enthusiasm Capitol Records had for me, but I was disappointed that this album didn't become a big hit.

Meanwhile, I was adjusting to my new roles: wife and mother. When our son Gregory Abbott Jr. was born, I thought that I was going to give the marriage a try. Maybe the dynamics of our marriage would change now that we were parents. I had a baby now, and I still needed Gregory to help.

There were definitely some challenges along the way. My son Gregory Jr., when he was two months old, was diagnosed with eczema.

It was something that I had to suffer through as a mother. I was constantly taking him to doctors, to dermatologists, and to allergists. Nothing seemed to totally clear it up. Gregory suffered so much with that eczema. As his mother, it was painful to watch and to feel helpless at finding a solution. In addition, Gregory also had allergies, which only magnified the situation.

Nothing the doctors prescribed seemed to improve his condition. It only remedied it for a while, but then it came back. Finally, I took him to Chinese herbalists to see if they could help. One of them I took Gregory to see was an acupuncturist / herbalist / doctor. She said to me, "Take him off all meats, except pork."

I said to her, "I thought pork is supposed to be so bad for you. Even in certain religions, they don't eat pork."

She said, "It's the cleanest meat. Chicken has too much 'heat.' And beef: 'no.'"

Then on the other end, the American doctor / allergist I took him to see said, "Take him off all red meat except turkey. Feed him the 'tom' turkey. The 'tom' turkey is much better to eat. The female turkey has too much bacteria in the skin."

I would try again-and-again to find a solution for Gregory Jr. Each of these specialists were able to do him some good, and others seemed to clear it up. However, it would just come right back again.

It has caused him to become angry and upset that he has to deal with this in his life. But he deals with it now. The only solution he has found involves using steroids, which can have side effects. However, nowadays he has found certain herbs and supplements that help him, but he still has to take steroids to keep it under control.

My second Capitol Records album was called *Supernatural High* and it was produced by Skip Scarborough. Released in 1978, it was my idea to record the 1929 hit "Happy Days Are Here Again" as a disco song. It was so upbeat and so uplifting a song, I thought it would be perfect with a danceable beat. It turned out I was right. It became the album's lead single, and there was a 12" dance single of it as well. That was the sign you were truly a disco star.

One of the songs on this album, "Just The Thought of You," I really liked. It was a ballad written by Thom Bell and Linda Bell. I never performed it live, but I should have. Another of the songs on the album was written by the singer Deniece Williams, called "Falling In Love." I was at Skip's house and Deniece came over to the house, and she brought the song over for me to hear. As soon as I heard it, I loved it. I was especially happy to sing a song by another singer, and fans have told me through the years that this is their favorite song on the album.

Another song that I sang on the album was the song "Storybook Romance," written by my sister Scherrie Payne. Nepotism at it's finest! It was a really good song, and we all thought it was a great idea to add a song Scherrie wrote on the album. It stood up to be as good as all of the other songs on the album, and I was happy to do it.

The cover was a beautiful close-up photo of me by Charles W. Bush. In this photo I have my head tilted back, my eyes closed, and a big smile on my face, as though I was thinking of something joyful. However, if my lips look like I just had a collagen injection, that isn't true. I legitimately had a "fat lip." What happened was that my son Gregory, who was about eight months old at the time, was in bed with me, he was resting on my chest, and he had lifted his head up and accidentally came down on my face, and his forehead hit me in the lips. Unfortunately, that was earlier in the day of the photo shoot for my album cover, and here I was with a swollen lip. When I went to the photo shoot, I told the photographer what had happened, and he gave me one of those looks of quizzical disbelief.

"My eight-month-old son did this to me," I explained.

"Yeah, right," was his reply.

I said to the make-up artist, "How are we going to deal with this?"

Somehow we made it work. Even though my lip is fatter than usual, it's still a great album cover photo!

Throughout my marriage to Gregory I continued to travel around the globe with my nightclub show. In June of 1978 I was back in New York City performing at The Rainbow Grill. I was able to fit my new disco hits in my act easily to make for a show that appealed to a wide audience, and they loved it. By now I had several new hit records to perform in my stage act, and I continued to be in high demand.

When Manhattan's *CUE* magazine reviewed my show they claimed, "With the allure of a lodestone, luscious singer / actress

Freda Payne's show at The Rainbow Grill finds the stylish songbird off in a colorful multitude of vocal shades. Opening with slightly 'middle-of-the-roadized' versions of her searing disco numbers 'Love Magnet' and 'Master of Love,' Freda embarks on a tastefully elegant flight. Whether plaintively cooing 'I've Never Been To Me,' or demanding to know where love went on 'Band of Gold,' Payne seductively entices. In a clever impersonation segment, she pays tribute to other singers with a catty Eartha Kitt and a nasally 'vibratoed' Judy Garland, each distinctively executed. The sultry singer proves especially powerful on the ballads 'Stares & Whispers' and 'Evergreen.'…a most pleasurable Payne." (14)

Back in the era of Studio 54, that was when I was married to Gregory Abbott. Without a doubt, Studio 54 was the Number One discotheque in the world. It was open to the public, but it was operated like a private disco, in that the doorman chose who was allowed into the club, and who was not. Whenever we showed up there, they always let us in. It was so much fun. I remember the owners, Steve Rubell and Ian Schrager, and how welcoming they were whenever I went there. Everything that you heard about Studio 54 was accurate: the drugs, the pot, the wildly colorful outfits, the pulsing music, and the notorious balcony where all sorts of nefarious things were going on in the shadows.

I remember being at Studio 54 and meeting the famed designer Diane Von Fürstenberg, and her bisexual husband, Prince Egon Von Fürstenberg. I remember Diane saying to me, "Egon really likes you! And he usually doesn't like women!"

I said something like, "Okay. Thank you for the compliment." How do you take a backhanded compliment like that?

Oh well, that's the way things were back then at wild and crazy Studio 54: it was truly *la disco magnifique!*

In 1979 I joined the cast of a Broadway-bound musical called *Daddy Goodness*. It starred me along with Ted Ross from the original Broadway production of *The Wiz*, and Clifton Davis. Also in the show was actor Rod Perry. Motown Records had something to do with putting money up for this production. We started out in Philadelphia rehearsing, and then we opened at The Forest Theater there. Next we went to Washington D.C., and we were at The National Theater. And from there we were supposed to go to The Winter Garden Theater in Manhattan, but we just didn't make it to Broadway.

It featured the songs of Ron Miller and Ken Hirsch. The book was by Ron Miller and Shauneille Perry. Ron was known for writing such Motown hits as "For Once In My Life" by Stevie Wonder (which Tony Bennett later recorded), "I've Never Been To Me" by Charlene (later Nancy Wilson recorded it too), and "Touch Me In The Morning" by Diana Ross. I had high hopes for *Daddy Goodness* reaching Broadway, but it was apparently not meant to be.

The story *Daddy Goodness* told was about a homeless man who wandered into a cemetery, where he drunkenly passed out. When he woke up, people mistakenly thought he had come back from the dead as a prophet. My role was that of a "wayward woman."

Although the plot had some holes in it, I had a good part and some great songs. I was the female lead, and it was fun to work with Ted Ross and Clifton Davis. Clifton has been a popular movie and TV actor for years. In fact, Clifton is still out there on the acting scene where he is very active in the business. He has recently had a major role in TV's *Madame Secretary*, and in Broadway's *Aladdin*. Clifton is also a songwriter as well. He wrote one of The Jackson Five's biggest hits: "Never Can Say Goodbye."

In 1979, I released my third and final album for Capitol, entitled *Hot*. It was meant to really capitalize on the disco phenomenon. It was produced by John Florez and Dr. Cecil Hale. The singles on it included "I'll Do Anything For You," "Red Hot," and "Can't Wait." Also on the *Hot* album was the song "Hungry" from *Daddy Goodness*.

Unfortunately, that is one of the few remnants of that show that exists.

Also unfortunate was the fact that my *Hot* album totally failed to find an audience. My big gamble of signing with Capitol Records came to an end after that. Several things seemed to be falling apart for me in 1979.

By this time I knew that being married to Gregory wasn't going to work, and I decided to divorce him. Looking back on my marriage to him, part of the reason that I think I married him was because of my mother. At the time I married Gregory, Mom was going through fighting breast cancer. I think that I needed someone to lean on to get me through this sad and trying experience and Gregory was there. He gave me emotional support.

That was why Gregory was such a great support through this ordeal. When I think of this period, I felt that Gregory was "acting" like a great supportive spouse, as though it was one of his many acting roles. Before we got married he was the perfect partner.

After Gregory Jr. was born, our marriage was basically okay. It wasn't great, or overflowing with love and happiness. It wasn't bad either; it was just okay. It was right before Gregory Jr. had turned two years old, in 1979, that Gregory and I officially separated.

It simply wasn't working, and I wasn't happy at all. I looked at it this way: "If it is going to be like this, I can't see continuing it." I now knew it was a mistake.

Gregory's mother made an effort to keep Gregory and me together. She suggested that we go to a marriage counselor, but I knew this relationship was too far "gone" to even want to salvage it. I thought at one point that maybe I was the one who was unfair to him, and that made it worse. It was just one of those things where it was not meant to be.

I had a housekeeper who came in five days a week. Her name was Lydia, and she was an older woman from Guatemala. I remember one day she came into my bedroom, and she was going through one of my drawers and she showed me a pair of women's panties, and they were large. She knew these were not mine.

"Mrs. Freda," she said as she held them up for me to see, "these are not your size. Are these yours?"

I said to her, "They are not mine. Just throw them out."

Immediately the gears started turning in my head, and I found myself thinking, "Who could these possibly belong to?" Now the suspicions began. Was Gregory having an affair? I surmised that it was someone who was close to Gregory and me.

Whoever those panties belonged to, I am certain they were left there on purpose. This is a little trick that some women use to let another woman know that her man had cheated on her. But that was never proven.

Gregory had this intellectual thing going at the time, where he would be befriending different people. Because he was married to me, he suddenly had this social circle that included the "who's who" of the entertainment world. He had befriended one of Natalie Cole's sisters, Carol. They had some sort of intellectual friendship together. He would spend a lot of time talking on the phone to her. Gregory also became friendly with Marvin Gaye. They would get together to play basketball.

He was into all sorts of things. Gregory also wrote articles for a magazine which was edited and owned by Michael St. John, and he was into celebrity gossip. Because Gregory was married to me, Michael gave him his own gossip column. Being my husband instantly opened doors for Gregory.

I had received something like $50,000.00 as a signing advance from Capitol, and Gregory said to me, "Why is it that Stanley Handman hasn't advised you to invest some of this money, instead of just letting it sit there?"

Gregory was smart. When we dated, and when we got married,

he didn't have a real job. I even had to lease him a car. I was driving a four door Mercedes Benz sedan at the time, and I had to lease him a car so he had mobility. I wanted him to be able to get around town, doing things for me and himself, so he had to have transportation. He was pursuing starting his own career as a writer and a business man, as well as helping me with my career.

When I was dating Gregory, my mother would say to me, "Freda, why are you marrying him?"

I said, "Well, Mom, I think it's finally time for me to get married. I like him a lot."

"Do you love him?"

"It's not like I am head-over-heels in love with him. I love him somewhat, but mainly I like him a lot," I said.

"I don't see why you would even consider marrying him. He doesn't even have a job."

"He's educated, he is good looking. He is devoted to me."

Mom said, "Freda, you've had good looking boyfriends before, even better looking than him."

"He is very pleasant to be with, and I think I need to settle down, Mom."

"Why does he want to marry you, if he doesn't have a job?"

"Well, I don't think he is looking for a handout."

"Freda," Mom said, "he wants what you've got. And by marrying you, it will set him up for what he really wants."

She was trying to tell me how she saw things, but I was stubborn and hardheaded. I had made up my mind that I was marrying Gregory, and I didn't want to listen to her advice, even though she turned out to be 100% correct in her premonition as to what was really happening.

She also suggested that I make him sign a "pre-nuptial agreement," which I neglected to do.

Mom would always say to Scherrie and me, "Don't marry a man

who doesn't have a job. Look for a man with a job."

Well, my mother turned out to be correct again. She was right for not letting me sign a ten year contract with Duke Ellington. She was right for not letting me sign my career away to Berry Gordy Jr. and Motown Records. And she was right about her perceptions of Gregory. But this time around, I was too stubborn to listen to her. And, after she was gone, I finally realized it.

She was very bright, and very sharp. A lot of my friends who had met my mother remember that about her. She was a very smart woman, and she could "read" people instantly. She knew who she trusted, and she knew who she didn't like.

Looking back on this era, there are a lot of situations or opportunities that I just let pass me by. I certainly could have married a lot better. Had I really been more brave, and had I been more of an opportunist, I could have married Edgar Bronfman Jr., the heir to the Seagram's liquor empire. But I chose another path.

None of my friends could understand why I would choose to marry Gregory. Yes, he was handsome, but he didn't have a job, and he was someone who was definitely unsure of what he was going to do with his life. Still, for a couple of years we looked like we were a perfect pair when we were together in public. Gregory had a lot of great attributes, he just didn't have the finances. He was good looking, young, very highly educated. I called him a "professional student." I decided to take a chance on love. Big mistake!

As smart as Gregory was intellectually, he was not that clever a cook. I had a grill in my backyard, and one day we were going to barbecue ribs on it. There stood Gregory with the lighter fluid and charcoal. He squirted the lighter fluid on the charcoal, and threw a lit match on it, and he started to put the meat immediately on the grill to cook it.

I said to him, "Gregory, you don't know how to barbecue? You have to let the lighter fluid burn off the coals first. You don't want the flame leaping everywhere, you want to get the coals hot first." He knew a little bit about a lot of things, but barbecuing wasn't one of them. I'm sure he is better at it now.

Women in show business are often faced with such dilemmas. I certainly wasn't the only female singing star who made the wrong choice when it came to affairs of the heart.

As I mentioned before, it was because of Pedro Ferrer, that Berry Gordy Jr. lost interest in promoting The Supremes. Pedro was a bully who insisted that he was right in his decisions about Mary, and Scherrie, and Cindy Birdsong—and later Susaye Greene who replaced Cindy in The Supremes in 1976. When Mary made Pedro her manager, that was the end of Berry's interest in The Supremes all-together. No question: it was Pedro Ferrer who brought about the end to The Supremes.

After the 1976 album, *Mary, Scherrie & Susaye*, the trio disbanded. Scherrie wasn't certain what was going to happen to her career. It ended up being a "two acts out of one" kind of situation. In 1979 Mary recorded a solo album for Motown, and Scherrie and Susaye remained together as a duet, recording their own Motown album, *Partners*. I was really happy for Scherrie's success with The Supremes. It was a great opportunity for her to show off her singing and performing talent.

I guess we ladies in the music business are determined to love and marry whomever we choose, and there is no talking us out of it! It's funny when you think about it, I recorded the song on my *Contact* album called "The Road We Didn't Take." That song means even more to me when I think about my relationship with Eddie Holland, and how things could have been taken care of so much better, had he been more mature at that time in his decision making. When it comes to matters of the heart, it is easy to take the wrong path. Look at what I did! I could have had so much more.

It is funny to think about how some things in life are somehow predestined. It was like I was predestined to accomplish certain things. Years ago, when I was starting out in the business, I knew I was meant to go far. I somehow knew that I was going to live a life where I would reach "diamond box" status. I knew I had the talent for that. There was just no question where my life was going to take me.

Then, on the other side of the coin, I did make some wrong choices along the way. Marrying Gregory was one of those wrong turns. Maybe I went down that path because I had a lesson to learn in doing that. I have a wonderful son, and I love him dearly, although his life has been plagued with some minor physical ailments—like his eczema, asthma, and food allergies.

It is hard to believe that I almost lost my son, at the age of 13 months, due to an asthma attack. This incident all happened when I was on a flight back to Los Angeles from Atlanta, Georgia. It took place when my housekeeper, Lydia, was watching Gregory Jr. At 9:30 am when Lydia looked in on him in his crib, she noticed that his breathing was quite erratic. At the time, Gregory Sr. was out running errands, and had no idea this was happening.

By coincidence, Scherrie decided on a whim to just stop over to the house to check on little Gregory, because she loved him so much. She came into the house, and went to his room, and there was Lydia in a panic yelling in broken English, "Baby sick! Not breathe right!"

Scherrie was horrified by what she witnessed, because she had asthma herself, and she recognized the signs. She recognized the wheezing sound that she heard while little Gregory was breathing. Scherrie instantly swept Gregory Jr. up, and drove him straight to Dr. Carter Wright, his pediatrician. She raced into the doctor's waiting room, and insisted she see Dr. Wright immediately.

When he saw Gregory he instantly said to Scherrie, "You've got to get him to the hospital RIGHT NOW."

"We need an ambulance!" Scherrie exclaimed.

"You don't have time for an ambulance, drive him there as fast as you can!"

So she did, and pulled right up to the Emergency entrance at Cedars Sinai Hospital. Meanwhile, Gregory Sr. had arrived back at the house, encountered Lydia, called the doctor, and then raced to Cedars as well.

When Gregory Sr. arrived at the hospital, the doctors told he and Scherrie that they were shocked that a baby of this age, with no other signs, could suddenly be breathing so shallowly and irregularly.

When one of the doctors announced that he wanted consent to perform a tracheotomy on Gregory Jr., Gregory Sr. protested.

It just so happened that Gregory Sr. had once been a surgical nurse at U.C. Berkeley. According to him, he had seen too many "rush judgments" in the operating room, and he insisted, "Check him again, he has asthma."

"That's impossible for a child of this age to have asthma," the doctor argued. "We have never had a patient this young with asthma." At this point, little Gregory was nearly to the stage where his lips were turning blue, from lack of oxygen.

The argument continued, and the doctor was on the verge of calling Security to escort Gregory Sr. out of the hospital. Finally, they realized that these were the classic signs of asthma, treated him for that, and saw him show improvement.

In the meantime, I had no idea that all of this drama was taking place in Los Angeles, as I was on a plane flying home. Fortunately, Scherrie drove to LAX airport to meet me when my flight arrived. She explained what had happened to me, and then she drove me to Cedars Sinai.

When we got to the hospital, I was escorted the Intensive Care Unit where I saw my baby with tubes and wires attached to him, I broke down crying. What ended up happening was that Gregory Jr. spent four days in the ICU. Once they determined that it was indeed asthma, and treated him for it, he fully recovered.

There was one more asthma episode that occurred when Gregory Jr. was three years old. He had another asthma attack, and he had to spend two days in the hospital this time around. After that, we were able to control the asthma with prescription drugs, and with the use of inhalers.

Fortunately, as an adult, things are much better for Gregory Jr. He has become something of a late bloomer, who has now found his way in life. He outgrew the asthma by the time he was in his teens, and the food allergies are far less prevalent.

Although I found out that marrying Gregory was a mistake, marrying Edgar would have been a different kind of mistake. When Edgar married Sherry, he was ostracized by his family. I was right. By marrying a black girl, the family distanced themselves from him. He ended up having to move to Europe, because they didn't want to have much to do with him. They were disappointed.

Had I married Edgar, that could have been me, exiled to Europe with him. In fact Edgar and Sherry lived in Spain for five years. However, that situation lasted only until his brother, Sam Bronfman, pulled a "fast one" and turned out to be a real loser. Sam faked his own kidnapping in an effort to bilk ransom money out of his family. It was all over the news. They had helicopters flying around New York City looking for him, and all of that drama. The police were out searching for him. Then it all came to light that it was one big hoax.

After Sam turned out to be such a scam artist, his father, Edgar Bronfman Sr., took Edgar back into the fold, and patched things up. His father ended up putting Edgar in charge of Seagram's International in London. Then shortly after that, he brought Edgar back to New York and put him in charge of the whole family business.

Ironically, Edgar's mother and I have the same birthday, September 19. It was almost like marriage to Edgar was meant to be, yet it was not.

Unfortunately, these are things that never happened because of decisions that I made. We never get to go back in time and see what would have happened if the other path had been chosen. I could have been the wife to a handsome millionaire, or I could have been the shining star of Motown Records, but that is not what happened. Those were simply roads I didn't take. You cannot rewrite history, so I will never know what would have happened had I married Edgar.

To complete the Edgar Bronfman story, I have to jump ahead ten years for a moment. In the late 1980s, I moved out of my house on Blue Jay Way, and Gregory Jr. and I moved to an apartment on Elm Drive in Beverly Hills.

The idea of renting out my house came through Amy Hoban. Amy was the mother of Gregory's schoolmate Cassidy. They were both attending The Center For Early Education, which is a private school. Amy and I had become friends, and our kids would even have "sleepovers" now and again. At the time, Amy had been leasing her home out during the summer months while she and Cassidy vacationed in Europe. She advised me that maybe I should try leasing my house as well, for extra cash. Amy explained that was why she had the money for the European vacation.

Until this time, I had never entertained that thought, but Amy recommended her real estate lady, and I met with her to discuss this idea. She told me that I could get as much as $6,500.00 a month renting out my house. My eyes popped open to hear this. Although I was skeptical, I told her to see what she could do, and I would consider it. I wasn't desperate to rent my house out, but I was open to the idea. I figured that I could pay a lot of my bills by doing this.

A week later, I was in New York City performing, and I heard from the real estate lady, and she said, "Freda, where do I deposit or send your check?"

"What check?" I said with astonishment.

"The check to rent your house out."

"What? How much is the check?"

"It is for $18,000.00. It is for the first and last month's rent, and the security deposit."

I slightly panicked, but I was happy that she was able to work so fast to get me a rental client. My brain started buzzing, thinking about all of the preparations I had to make to vacate the house. Fortunately, I was going to rent out the house "furnished," so all I had to pack were my personal belongings.

Another reason that I was happy with this move was because I wanted Gregory Jr. to attend Beverly Vista Elementary school in Beverly Hills. For that to happen I had to live in that school district, and I had to have a Beverly Hills address. As a matter of fact, the apartment building we lived in on Elm Drive was right across the street from the school.

The first person who rented out my house on Blue Jay Way was comedy writer Alan Zweibel and his wife. Alan is best known for being a writer on *Saturday Night Live*, and several other shows. When he wrote his memoir Alan recalled that he played host to the majority of the *Saturday Night Live* cast while he lived there. He also recalled that he received several surprise visits from people looking for me. According to Zweibel, "I lived by myself in a home [off] Doheny Drive above Sunset Boulevard that I rented from singer Freda Payne…And, though I am loath to make any assumptions, on occasion my loneliness was interrupted by late-night knocks on the front door by an assortment of singers like Tom Jones and Luther Vandross who looked incredibly disappointed when I told them that Freda wasn't home." (15)

During this era, around 1987 or 1988, while I was living on Elm Drive in Beverly Hills, Edgar called me out-of-the-blue one day. At this point in time he was still married to Sherry, and together they had two children. I was completely startled to receive his phone call.

Edgar said to me, "I just want a 'yes' or 'no' answer. I'm going to

Barbados for a long weekend, and I'm renting a private house, with a cook and a maid. Would you be interested in coming and spending the weekend with me?"

I thought for a moment, and then I said, "Yes."

He flew me First Class from LA to Miami, from Miami to Trinidad, Trinidad to Barbados. When I arrived at my destination, he was there to meet me.

I was thinking inside, "This is it. We are finally going to end up married to each other." So I went for the weekend. His Uncle Louie was there. It was like the ten years hadn't passed, and we instantly hit it off together. It was almost like a honeymoon.

I had a great time, but I wasn't sure where this was all leading. After a wonderful weekend together I returned to LA. When I got home Edgar telephoned and told me, "I am getting a divorce from Sherry."

Then he told me he was also dating a woman from Venezuela at that time. This was his way of letting me know our revived love affair was not going to continue. I was disappointed and hurt. I felt like I had just failed my audition! I simply wasn't meant to be with Edgar. It wasn't in the cards!

So, he ended up marrying this woman from Venezuela. I never met her, but I was told she was tall and blonde. Oh well! He was definitely enamored with me for a time. A guy like that, he has to be into you and pursuing you, you can't be pursuing him. That just won't fly.

When I look back on the whole Edgar Bronfman Jr. episode, I have to admit, plain and simple: "I really fucked that up!" When my marital choices had been between Edgar and Gregory, I made the wrong decision.

When Edgar married Sherry "Peaches" Brewer, and made her Sherry Bronfman, they ostracized him for five years. Had I married him, this would have totally changed my life for the better, even if I had to move to Spain for five years. He was producing TV specials for Shirley MacLaine. He was writing songs. I would have been his wife, doing things like dedicating The Freda Bronfman Cancer Center at Cedars Sinai Hospital and things like that. What was I thinking at the time?

I think that a lot of my ideas and attitudes about relationships were subsequently filtered into my psyche from my mother. My parents were married, had me and my sister, and then very shortly thereafter divorced. The reason my parents' marriage didn't work was because my mother discovered my dad's infidelities, and she found that unforgivable. I know that when some people split up, it is over something they find to be unforgivable in their partner or spouse.

After he was gone, my mother always vilified my dad. She always talked about him bad. She'd be so happy, and we'd be talking about something else, and then all of a sudden my grandmother would say, "Fred called," and Mom's whole expression would suddenly show displeasure at the mere mention of his name.

However, this did not stop me from loving my dad. Mom also made sure that my sister and I always had a relationship with him and his family. That was a good thing. Mom's theories about men and relationships were very complicated, and I think she passed that down to me, because when I get into a relationship with someone, I always become suspicious.

When I was married to Gregory Abbott in 1976, I thought he was the perfect mate, and that our relationship could last forever. However, our marriage only lasted two years. I don't know what it is, but when a person goes through the ceremony, signs that marriage license, and everything settles down, then the real personality comes out.

If I could go back and change things around, who knows what would have happened. It is like the 2019 Quentin Tarantino film *Once Upon a Time in Hollywood*, where the notorious Manson murders were given a new twist, and in this fantasy version of the facts, it was the killers who died and not Sharon Tate and her friends. But we never get the chance to go back and take the other path. Like I said in the song "The Road We Didn't Take," I guess I will never know.

When, I married Gregory, by the time the wedding photos arrived at my house from Chicago two weeks later, I already knew this marriage was over. Oh well, that was my one marital misadventure, and when it was over, it was time for me to move on.

CHAPTER NINE

"A Legendary Lady of The '80s"

I n 1981 and 1982, I was the star and hostess of a TV talk show called *Today's Black Woman*. It was an ABC-TV syndicated show, which I did for two years, broadcast out of New York City. We also did some location filming of the show at my Blue Jay Way house in the Hollywood Hills.

The episodes of *Today's Black Woman* were thematic. On one episode of the show the theme was "Black Women in Politics," and among the guests was Congresswoman Shirley Chisholm, who was the first African American woman to seek the nomination for President of the United States. I did a show called "The Rape Crisis Intervention Handbook," and another one on "Careers Behind The Modeling Industry" which featured several of the top models of the day. I did a whole episode on poet laureate Maya Angelou. Other episodes included: "Art Treasures of Ancient Nigeria," and "Miracle Therapy." On the episode called "The Difficulties of Bringing Black Theater to Broadway" my guests where: Douglas Turner Ward, director of The Negro Ensemble Company, Joe Crone, producer of the Broadway show *Home,* and Sam Art Williams, author of *Home.* My guests on various shows included the Reverend Jesse Jackson, and Vernon Jordan who was the president of The National Urban League, on the political side of things.

I still hadn't quite forgiven Jesse Jackson for how he acted towards me in Chicago when I was booked at Mister Kelly's in the early '70s. However, I knew he would make an interesting TV show guest, and he did.

I went to an industry party in Los Angeles in the early 1980s, and it was there that I met Teddy Pendergrass for the first time. Since Teddy had left Harold Melvin & The Blue Notes in 1976, he had become a major star on Gamble & Huff's famed Philadelphia International Records.

At that time, Teddy had rented a house on Doheny Drive in the Hollywood Hills, very close to where I lived. It was very temporary; he had the house maybe a month or two.

He started pursuing me, and he started showing up at some of my performance engagements. I was always happy to see him, and I eventually started going out with him.

I remember the time when my sister Scherrie had a lovely home in Laurel Canyon, and Teddy and I attended a barbecue there together. He brought his five-year-old son, and my son Gregory was around four or five at the time as well. We had some wonderful barbecue, and a lot of great soul food.

As Scherrie's barbecue ended, we left to go back to my house. While I was driving us in my car down Sunset Boulevard, Teddy suddenly said to me, "Pull over for a minute, I want to look at some of these sports cars."

We came to a stop in front of a sports car dealership, and there were all of these sharp looking classic, expensive sports cars on display in the window. Teddy absolutely loved sports cars, and there was a particular one in the window he wanted to see.

So I pulled over and parked, so he could have a closer look through the plate glass window. However, before Teddy could get out of my car, there were lights flashing in the rear view mirror behind us. It was unmistakably a police car.

My first thought was, "I wonder what they could stop us for? I haven't done anything wrong. And I am not in a No Parking zone."

Immediately, Teddy pulled out a little glass vial which contained some white powder. Naturally it was cocaine.

Teddy passed it to me and he said, "Here, put this in your bra."

So, I did. Seconds later the police officer came up to the window and asked for my driver's license and registration. After that was cleared, they said, "Okay, you can go on."

I don't know if they recognized who we were, or what was going on, but they let me go after checking my driver's license and car registration. I couldn't exactly figure out why we were pulled over, but I thought that maybe the police had recognized Teddy. I knew that Teddy had a history of problems with the police in Philadelphia, and I suspected that had something to do with it. That incident made me rethink my logic about dating Teddy Pendergrass. After that our relationship cooled off, but we did remain friends. Sadly, in March of 1982 Teddy had a major car accident which left him paralyzed from the waist down for the rest of his life. This occurred when he was driving his Rolls Royce, with a transvestite in the car, and he lost control of the car and crashed. It was horribly tragic.

During this same time period, I started going out with Edmond Sylvers, who was the lead singer of the family recording group, The Sylvers. They were kind of like The Jackson Five, or DeBarge, or those other family singing groups. At one point The Sylvers were rated as a top group, right behind The Jackson Five. Their biggest song was the Number One hit, "Boogie Fever" (1976). I had worked with The Sylvers before. It was at The Ambassador Hotel in Los Angeles, in their prestigious nightclub, The Coconut Grove. The Sylvers were my opening act, and I was the headliner. It was a New Year's Eve show, 1970 going into 1971.

Edmond and I started dating in 1981, into 1982. He lived with me for those couple of years. I found him exciting, and we got along great, because we are both performers. It was refreshing to be dating someone who was also in the same business. We shared many of the same tastes.

When I was married to Gregory Abbott, he would always complain to me about, "All you ever talk about is show business all day. Show business!"

After Gregory and I divorced, I finally ended up with a boyfriend who was in the same business, so that was all we did talk about! So, on that level, Edmond and I had a lot more in common than Gregory and I ever had.

While I was still with Edmond, he produced a song for me called "In Motion." It was in "heavy rotation" on WBLS in New York, and D.J. Frankie Crocker was playing it all the time. As it was, it made it to Number 63 on the R&B chart in the U.S.

It was a very good record, and it should have succeeded. "In Motion" was released on a division of Buddha Records, called Kama Sutra Records. Art Kass was the head of Buddha Records, and he wanted a full album from me, but he didn't want Edmond to produce it. The fact of the matter was that Edmond didn't produce "In Motion" in its entirety. It was actually Leon Sylvers who gave his brother Edmond the pre-recorded track for me to record to, which I did.

Art Kass said to me, "Freda, I love you, and I believe in you. You have one of the most distinctive voices in the music business."

"Thank you, Art," I replied.

"I really want to do an album with you on my label."

"I would love that!" I said.

"However, I do not want Edmond to be the producer. I would rather have Leon Sylvers produce it. And, if you don't want him to do it, I would be willing to contact Quincy Jones, and have him produce an album for you."

"But, Art," I argued, "I really want Edmond to produce it. I am very devoted to him. He is my boyfriend at the moment, and I would like him to be the producer."

"So, you are insisting that Edmond produce the album?"

"I am, Art."

"Then I am rescinding the album offer."

"But Art…" I began to argue.

"I can't get in the middle of 'pillow talk,'" he said. "I did it once with Gladys Knight and her husband, Barry Hankerson, and I am not going there again. Gladys insisted that Barry produce her album on Buddha, and it was a disaster. I am not getting involved in 'pillow talk.' I wish you well."

That was it. When I decided to be loyal with Edmond as the producer, Art Kass dropped the whole thing. That was the end of that. Looking back on this mistake I made, I realize in retrospect, that I was a fool for making this decision. Instead of looking at the bigger picture, I did like the Tammy Wynette song and decided to "Stand By Your Man." What was I thinking?

Several of my friends were not supportive of my relationship with Edmond. Dick Griffey, who was the president of Solar Records in Los Angeles was one of them. He used to say to me, "Freda, you are dating the wrong Sylver!"

David Gest was another one who questioned my being with Edmond. He said to me, "I don't get it Freda. I don't think Edmond has a lot of brains."

I simply explained it to him, "Trust me, David, it's not his brain I'm in love with!"

I guess you could say, "It was a lust and love thing." It was fun while it was going on. Then, at a certain point, I came to the realization that my relationship with Edmond wasn't ever going to grow into anything positive and long-lasting. I realized that Edmond was not the marrying type, and I had already gone through that routine. At least Gregory was smarter, and not as much of a playboy as Edmond was. Gregory did try hard to fit in, and did try to learn more about show business in our relationship. Eventually, I decided to walk away from my relationship with Edmond. It wasn't destined to last. That ended in 1982.

For the majority of the rest of the decade, I suddenly became involved in theater again. In the early part of 1982, I went on tour in a production of the Broadway hit musical *Ain't Misbehavin'*. The line-up for that show was Della Reese, Linda Hopkins, myself, Ted Ross, and Lonnie McNeil. We did theaters in the round, like Painter's Mill in Baltimore, Valley Forge in Pennsylvania, and The Westbury Music Fair in New York. This was just before I broke up with Edmond, and he came to visit me on the road for a week.

After that tour ended, I was approached to play a starring role in the Las Vegas company of a Broadway musical, and away I went. And whose music would I be singing? Why, Duke Ellington's of course! And the show? Duke Ellington's *Sophisticated Ladies*.

My first time starring in a company of Duke Ellington's *Sophisticated Ladies* was in Vegas, at The Desert Inn. It was an eight-month run, along with Paula Kelly and Harold Nicholas of the famed Hollywood dancing act, The Nicholas Brothers. That was in 1982-1983. Two years later, in 1985, I was asked to star in a road company of Duke Ellington's *Sophisticated Ladies*. I did eight months on the road with this national touring company. We started rehearsals in Los Angeles, and then we worked our way all around the East Coast, and then back, via: Detroit, Michigan; Austin, Texas; San Antonio, Texas; Phoenix, Arizona; Palm Springs, California, and everywhere in between.

I was also in a company of Duke Ellington's *Sophisticated Ladies* which was performed at The Sacramento Civic Light Opera. Paula Kelly was not in that touring company, but Harold Nicholas was with us. Theresa Hayes was in that production as well, in the "lead dancer" role.

When I was booked for my first run with *Sophisticated Ladies*, I would stand there on-stage during the opening of the second act and there was a sense of *déjà vu*. This was when I was about to enter the stage singing "In a Sentimental Mood." My gown was a wrap-around sort of robe in white satin, and it had a long train I had to lift up to walk, and it had long sleeves. The sleeves were trimmed in white ostrich plumes.

I also wore a long beautiful wig that had waves in it, in a Hedy Lamarr style. I remember going on-stage, and on the backdrop was a staircase going up, with a huge silhouette of Duke Ellington wearing a top hat. As I was about to sing, I would look up at his image and think to myself, "Duke, you finally got me!"

It was in Las Vegas, when I was 17 years old, where I once sang with Duke Ellington himself, and now here I am in the same town in this production that salutes Duke! If this wasn't *déjà vu*, I don't know what is!

So far, I have starred in eight different companies of Duke Ellington's *Sophisticated Ladies*, both in the United States, and in Europe as well. In Italy I was part of a European touring company. I also did it in Oslo, Norway. Then there was also a run of the show at The Long Beach Civic Light Opera at The Terrace Theater in Long Beach, California. And, then I did it again at the Sacramento Civic Light Opera company in Sacramento, California.

Actually, I have quite a history with the show Duke Ellington's *Sophisticated Ladies*. Donald McKayle, who was the original choreographer and creator for the show, had contacted me in 1974. He was the man who conceived the idea of doing a Duke Ellington show all together.

I was living in an apartment in Los Angeles, and he called me on the phone. He said to me, "We are putting together a tribute show using the music of Duke Ellington. We are trying to decide if it is going to be a 'revue,' or if it is going to be a 'book show' with dialogue. Right now we have Gregory Hines, and Judith Jameson committed to be in it. I am calling you, because I heard that before 'Band of Gold' you were also a jazz singer. Do you have any interest in doing a show like this?"

I said, "Yes! Absolutely."

He also told me that Nancy Wilson was contacted to star in the show. She was managed by John Levy at the time. John told them that they were not offering enough money to book and pay Nancy. She was a huge star, and she was especially known to be a great jazz singer.

Since Nancy couldn't do it, they were looking for someone with a "name" who can sing jazz. I would have loved to do the show at that time, but I never heard back from him.

Flash forward to 1981, that's when I found out that Duke Ellington's *Sophisticated Ladies* was opening on Broadway, with Phyllis Hyman in the show. It was a huge success, and Phyllis ended up with a Tony Award Nomination. The show ran on Broadway until January of 1983.

I received a phone call asking me if I would like to audition for the Los Angeles company of Duke Ellington's *Sophisticated Ladies*. I went to it, and I blew the producers away with my singing. After the audition, one of the producers, Manheim "Manny" Fox, ran out after me, and told me how impressed he was with me.

"I didn't know you could sing jazz so well!" Manny exclaimed.

I thought to myself: "I got this!"

As impressed as they were, it was my friend Dee Dee Bridgewater who was cast in the LA company of the show. Almost a year later I received a call from Oscar Cohen of ABC Booking and he made me an offer to do the upcoming Las Vegas company.

From all of the touring companies of Duke Ellington's *Sophisticated Ladies* I appeared in, I garnered several glowing reviews. *The Los Angeles Times* especially loved me in the show, proclaiming,

"Freda Payne, a simmering delight as the torch singer, sets fire to 'In a Sentimental Mood' and the electric 'Take the "A" Train'…Payne sang with Ellington early in her career and carries the memory in her silken voice, which glides easily into an entrancing growl for lyric punctuation." (16)

I appeared in the show for so many years, it got to the point where those costumes were getting really old and funky. In one of the later productions I did of Duke Ellington's *Sophisticated Ladies*, when I went to put on the "Take The 'A' Train" suit, my name was still written inside of the skirt on a label, because they were still using the original costumes years later. Who knows how many times they had been let-out, or taken-in, to accommodate different singers. The gown which had been decorated with the ostrich feathers was looking decidedly "ratty" instead of "wispy" at this point. But on-stage under the lights the audience couldn't tell. It was nowhere near as cute as it had once been! It was like I was wearing my own hand-me-downs. They were fabulous costumes, and they were designed by Willa Kim, who won the Tony Award for them.

I especially remember my first run with *Sophisticated Ladies* in Las Vegas. The Desert Inn, was quite a popular spot back then. We started rehearsals in '82 and then we opened that November. Our ten month "sit-down" run took us into the following September of 1983.

With two shows an evening, I found that I had a lot of spare time on my hands during the day. I had to find something to occupy myself. If you are not into gambling, you have to be creative in finding ways to keep yourself busy when you are booked for several months at a time. I am not someone who is all that fascinated with gambling.

For example, my friend Ike Sutton was in Las Vegas to see the show, and he was crazy about me. Ike was still one of the main photographers for *Jet* magazine. I had known him for so long, that he was a friend of the family by then. We would even invite him over for

Thanksgiving, or Christmas dinner. Most of the pictures that were taken of me for *Jet*, where taken by him.

Ike came to Las Vegas to see me in Duke Ellington's *Sophisticated Ladies*, and after the show he said to me, "Let's go to the casino and do the slot machines. Let's gamble!"

I said, "Ike, you know I don't gamble."

He bought a stack of $100.00 chips and he said to me, "Here, gamble with these!"

So I told him, "Ike, if I win, I'm keeping it!"

Well, that didn't happen. I didn't win. When the chips were gone, I said, "Ike, I'm done."

As a non-gambler I certainly was not going to be hanging out in the casino during my off time. Back then there weren't any really good gyms to work out in, so I had to find something else to occupy my time, that I could enjoy. That was back when you could buy Jane Fonda's workout tapes, and do exercise routines at home in front of your own television screen. It wasn't until later that big, sleek, and appealing gyms really came into fashion in Vegas, so that was not an option.

Speaking of Jane Fonda, in the early 1980s she used to have an exercise studio in Los Angeles on Robertson Boulevard, in Beverly Hills. I used to go there to work out and be an active participant in the classes. I don't remember her teaching any of the classes, but I would see her there from time-to-time.

This Las Vegas company of Duke Ellington's *Sophisticated Ladies* starred Harold Nicholas of The Nicholas Brothers, Paula Kelly, and me. We all had a great time working together.

Paula was a superb dancer, actress, and singer. She had an extensive resume, and she was not only one of the stars of the film *Sweet Charity* (1969), she had an impressive career on TV and in the movies, as well as Broadway. Her films included *The Andromeda Strain* (1971), *Soylent Green* (1973), and *Jo Jo Dancer, Your Life Is Calling* with Richard Pryor (1986). Paula Kelly's understudy / stand-in, when she missed shows, was a singer / dancer by the name of Lorraine Fields.

The Nicholas Brothers were a dance duo consisting of Harold and his brother Fayard. Together they were featured in so many great Hollywood films of the 1930s and 1940s. Usually they would show up in a nightclub scene of a film, where they would do their inventive dance and tap routines. Some of their best routines were featured in films like *Down Argentine Way* (1940), *Sun Valley Serenade* (1941), and *Stormy Weather* (1943). They also did a great song and dance number with Gene Kelly in *The Pirate* (1948), and with Donald O'Connor in *Song and Dance Man*, a TV show where Donald and The Nicholas Brothers did a "challenge dance" (1966). They were considered big stars back then.

On my "off days," I would fly back to Los Angeles. That would have been Monday. There was a Sunday afternoon performance, so I would fly back to Los Angeles on Sunday evening, and return to Vegas on Tuesday morning. It is only a one hour flight, and I would leave my leased car parked in Vegas at the McCarran International Airport. I would land, go home, and be back in Vegas in time for the Tuesday night shows.

Gregory Abbott Jr. was five years old at the time. I had a live-in housekeeper, who was also the nanny, and she would stay with him in Los Angeles, as he was going to pre-school. He was at The Center For Early Education, which is a private school on Melrose Avenue in LA. I didn't want to take him out of school, so he stayed along with the nanny while I was performing in the show.

Sometimes my sister Scherrie would come over and pick him up and take him to her house as well. She would frequently help out with little Gregory, especially on weekends when she wasn't working. That way the nanny, whose name was Lorraina, would have a break, and Scherrie would return him home on Sunday night. On some occasions I would fly Gregory and Lorraina to Las Vegas to be with me, during spring break and during the summertime.

As one of the stars of the show I was provided with my own apartment at The Country Club Towers. Since I was going to be living in Vegas for nearly a year, I figured that I had to do something to pass that time away, so I became a fisherwoman.

Sometimes, on our day off, I would go fishing at Lake Mead. I wound up buying all of the equipment, including one of those gas lanterns that people use for night fishing. I really got into this! You could say: "I was into it, hook, line, and sinker!"

I had a friend, Pete Peterson. Pete had once worked for Motown, as an administrator, and was now living in Vegas at the time, and he loved to fish. He was hooked on it even more than me! Sometimes he would invite me to go fishing with him. Even when I got back to LA, he and I would go fishing together. He would come to pick me up and drive outside of Los Angeles to fish. Sometimes we would go up to Lake Pyramid, just north of Magic Mountain, and we would go to some of the other surrounding lakes as well.

I remember once that Pete and I went to another spot, away from Lake Mead, to fish and we were on a fishing marathon! I would get up at 4:00 or 5:00 in the morning. By the time we got to the lake it would be about 6:00 am, and we would fish all day on my day off from the show.

Our favorite bait was frozen anchovies, and our other choice was blood worms. We didn't use any artificial tackle. You had to know exactly how to get those anchovies on the hook, and you had to get it on perfectly. We would bring a large cooler with ice, for cold drinks, to keep the anchovies frozen, and later in the day—to put the fish we had caught into it.

What you have to do is to weave the anchovy onto the hook, so that the fish can't get to the anchovy without biting onto the hook. Otherwise, the fish can steal your bait. They can be really slick when they want to be! The same would go for the bloodworms. You think that you have your bait on the hook, then you feel a little tug, then the next thing you know, you pull up the line and your bait is gone. Those fish aren't as dumb as you think!

One day I was fishing, and a few yards from me there was a lady and her husband, within shouting distance from me. I shouted over to them, "I think I have something on the line!"

And she shouted back, "It's not what you have on *the line*, honey, it's what you have on *the hook*!"

To immerse myself into the whole fishing genre, I bought a book called *Freshwater Fishing*. I read that whole book, and I learned a lot about the subject, like what "test" of line to use for catching what fish. You just don't use any kind of fishing line. You go by the weight and the kind of fish you are after. You would use a different kind of "test" line for five to ten pounds, and another "test" line for ten to twenty pounds, and so on. It goes up-and-up with relationship to what kind of fish you are going to go after. Actually that pertains to the poles you use as well.

I learned all about the swivels—the little metal things that turn on the line, and the sinkers to use. And of course there is the importance of getting the right hook. They go by numbers and they go by size. For instance, if you are going for large-mouthed bass, that is like a Number Two. If you are going after a catfish there is a special hook. And a trout requires a smaller hook, because they have a smaller mouth.

When it comes to bait, you can use either live bait, or you can use artificial bait. Sometimes the artificial bait works better than the real thing. What they were using out at Lake Mead, where I was fishing while in Las Vegas, was mainly the frozen anchovies, or bloodworms. Those bloodworms certainly live up to their name. It is literally a worm that has blood if you break it open. If you use those, you have to be prepared to get dirty.

I did all of this stuff. If I didn't go to Los Angeles to see my son Gregory, I would go to Lake Mead on my days off from Duke Ellington's *Sophisticated Ladies*. Sometimes I would even stay there into the evening. If I did that, I would bring my little propane gas lantern. I had my cooler, tackle box, and two fishing poles. One of them is nicknamed The Ugly Stick. It is made out of fiberglass, and it is a very sturdy fishing pole. The Ugly Stick is actually the brand name of that fishing pole, and it is still sold in sporting stores today.

During this stay in Vegas, 80% of the time I would go fishing by myself. I had a car that I rented. I would have all of my supplies and the cooler. I would stop on the way to the lake, at a little fishing and tackle store. You could stop there to get your bait, ice, and whatever else you needed.

I would catch one or two, maybe three fish, and on a good day I might catch four, five, or six fish. They would mainly be large mouthed bass, catfish, or there were also blue fish. More than a couple of times I caught catfish, but I didn't like them. Catfish is a nasty fish to clean. The bass is the better fish. However, the cleanest and easiest fish to clean is trout. I would go back to my apartment, scale, clean, and filet the fish and put it in the refrigerator.

At The Desert Inn we had almost a two hour break between the first show of the evening and the second show. We all had to be backstage at the theater at least half an hour before the show started each night. In fact, it is a requirement by Actor's Equity that you had to be at the theater and signed in by "half hour" before the show. I would sign in, and put my make-up on, and then my "dresser" would come in, and she would be there to help me put on my costume. She would help me with everything from the dresses, to the shoes. Then there was a separate person who would help me put the wig on.

My first appearance in the show was the song "It Don't Mean a Thing If It Ain't Got That Swing." For this song I wore a corset that was encrusted with rhinestones and beads. I had ostrich feather plumes that flowed above my head as part of the costume. Then I had cuffs which were bejeweled. Ostrich feathers were coming down the back of the dress. It was absolutely beautiful.

The first show would end, and I would get dressed, go to my car, and drive just a few blocks to my apartment. I would take my fish *filets* out of the refrigerator, bread them in a combination of cornmeal and flour, and I would season the fish with salt, pepper, and touch of garlic powder. I would fry it up, or sauté it, and I would have a vegetable or a salad, and that would be my dinner.

I used to think to myself, "This fish is fresh, I just caught it today!" Then I would go back to The Desert Inn, touch up my make-up, and do the second show. Then after the second show I would be a little tired, and I would go back to my apartment, unless I had friends in the audience who wanted to come backstage and hang out or go out for a drink.

One evening Jerry Lewis came to see the show, with his buddy, Sammy Davis Jr. At that point I had worked with both of them, so they were very happy to see that I was back in Vegas and working on the strip. Gregory Hines came to see me in the show, as well as Sarah Vaughn. I was especially on edge when Gregory came to see the show because he had been in the Broadway run. And, his brother, Maurice Hines was currently starring in the show in New York on Broadway. Maurice had taken over when Gregory left the show. And, my dear friend David Gest came to see me as well.

I will never forget the night Sarah Vaughn came to see the show, because she was considered to be one of the finest voices in jazz, on par with Ella Fitzgerald. Some critics have even said that Sarah was a better singer than Ella. One of them was Frank Sinatra, who later changed his mind.

That evening when Sarah came to see the show, afterwards I was in my apartment at The Country Club Towers. I had my patio doors open, and I heard some nice jazz music that somebody was playing.

It just so happened that Paula Kelly lived in the apartment about two floors above mine, and my phone rang. It was Paula.

She said to me, "Sarah Vaughn is here with me. We are just having a glass of champagne, why don't you come and join us?" And, so I did. I was so delighted, because I had always admired Sarah Vaughn. I had met her on several occasions back in New York, but this was one of the first times I got to actually hang out with her. It is amazing how some big established entertainers can harbor their own personal feelings about other entertainers. I think she was slightly intimidated by the fact that people would constantly ponder: "Who is the best singer, Ella or Sarah?"

Sarah told us about a little riff she had with Mel Tormé. I think it had something to do with billing on a show, as to who was going to get the top billing, Mel or Sarah? If it was done alphabetically, Mel on top, followed by Sarah, as the "T" in Tormé comes before the "V" in Vaughn. Whatever the logic was, she didn't want to play "second fiddle" to Mel Tormé.

Sarah had a fun sense of humor. We had a great time laughing together. Then she made a reference to me, to the effect of: "Look at Freda, men love her because she has nice big titties, and a nice little ass. That's what they are looking at."

So Paula said in my defense, "But Sarah, Freda's a really good singer, too."

All this was done while drinking champagne and sharing a joint. Yes, it's true, I got high with Sarah Vaughn! I left Paula's apartment feeling very nice.

I looked at Sarah as being a giant in the music business and the jazz world. It was interesting to see that even someone like Sarah had insecurities, too.

Another evening in Vegas, Berry Gordy Jr. came to the see the show. At that time his lady friend's name was Grace. He came to the show with her, along with Roger Campbell. Roger Campbell was

Berry's driver and security man. After the show, they came back-stage, and they went in Paula Kelly's dressing room on the first floor. (When Roger Campbell passed away in the 2010s, he insisted that I sing at his funeral service. In fact, he had that request in his will, and I gladly complied.)

Berry, Grace, and Roger came backstage and went to Paula's dressing room on the first floor. I was invited to join them.

I came into the room, and Paula said, "Freda, this is Berry Gordy."

"I know Berry!" I replied.

"How do you know Berry?" Paula asked.

"Well, I know him from Detroit."

"She knows me *quite* well," Berry laughed.

So Paula said, "Well, Berry, how do you know Freda so well?"

Then Berry explained, "I have known Freda since she was a teenager. She was my first female protégée. I saw in her what I needed to do."

This is something I thought I would never hear coming out of his mouth. Looking back on it now, I think that the reason he rejected me so coldly when I questioned his Motown contract in 1965, was that he already saw what he wanted to do with Diana Ross. He has a very strong intuition, and is a brilliant man.

I think he also saw that Diana, Florence and Mary were click-ing with the public, and that Diana was more marketable, and more commercial. I think he also knew that if I came to Motown Records, and took some of the spotlight, there would be a problem between Diana and me.

Diana and I are the same "type," except that I don't have the nasal sounding, more commercial voice, and she has it. He must have already seen that there could be a conflict of interests between me and Diana, and he was right.

At the time, Diana was more determined and could handle

more pressure. There would have been too much backstabbing and jealousy. All that happened to Diana, but she could take it, and she fought back. Then again, Berry was there taking care of her. And the rest, is history!

When The Supremes and The Temptations did their *TCB* TV special in 1968, Diana Ross did a solo Afro-Cuban dance number in the middle of the show. Imagine my surprise!? It was rather eerie for me to watch that. When I saw it I thought to myself, "Gee, where did he get that idea from?" I instantly flashed back to the time when Berry used to watch me while I was in my Afro-Cuban dance class back in Detroit. Obviously he was making mental notes.

I remember Berry watching me as I was being instructed by the man who called himself Taboo, back in Detroit. I am certain that watching my dancing, is where Berry got the idea to have Diana do that number. End of story.

The second company of Duke Ellington's *Sophisticated Ladies* that I headlined was in 1985. We rehearsed it in Los Angeles, then we went back east, to New York State: Buffalo, and Niagara Falls. From there we went all the way down to Florida, and all places in between. For that run, I had my name over the title on the marquee, as I was the draw. A lot of the chorus people who had been in the Vegas company with me, were on this tour as well.

When we played Fort Lauderdale, Florida, we were at The Broward County Performing Arts Center. I remember we stayed at this Marriott Hotel right on the beach, and that was so nice. It was like being on a vacation. That was also one of the times I sent for my son Gregory, to come join me. He flew from Los Angeles, unaccompanied. I had to get special clearance, and an adult had to take him to the airport. It is called "flying unaccompanied by a specified adult." In that instance someone would take the child to the gate and the stewardess would be the responsible party during the flight, and an adult had to pick him up and present identification. When he landed in Fort Lauderdale, I was unable to pick him up at the airport. So I arranged for a lady, who had formerly worked for me as my secretary, to pick him up. Her name is Florence Young, and she and her husband George were permanent residents of Fort Lauderdale, Florida. Gregory was six years old then.

Florence brought Gregory Jr. to the hotel, where I was waiting for them in the lobby. It was such a joy to have him with me at the time. We had so much fun. We drove up to Orlando to Disney World, on one of my days off. We spent the whole day going through Disney World, and The Epcot Center. That day it was me, Gregory, and my friend Cysco Drayton. Cysco was one of the dancers in Duke Ellington's *Sophisticated Ladies*, and we became great friends during the run of the show. Those were some really good times.

The next company of Duke Ellington's *Sophisticated Ladies* I did was in 1987 also in the U.S. Then in the 1990s I did a company in Europe, and we were in Italy for six weeks. Mercer Ellington, was the conductor of the orchestra for the first two weeks, then he was replaced by Billy McDaniels, who was a New Yorker. It was so fascinating how Mercer and I crossed paths again at that time. It was Mercer who originally came to my home in Detroit on Glenn Court and 14th Street to listen to me sing, and took me to meet his dad. All these years later, here we were working together on a show to honor his father: "The Duke of Ellington!"

In the 1980s my ex-husband Gregory Abbott Sr. went through a phenomenal change of luck. He landed a recording deal with Columbia Records, and he had a huge Number One hit record. How this happened was that he had a job on Wall Street, where he got someone to back him, and to finance him into going into the recording studio and eventually landing a record deal. Then he took his tapes to Columbia Records, to a guy by the name of Charles Koppelman. That was how he got his deal at Columbia. Gregory had an uncle, Mike Abbott. I knew Mike when I first came to New York

City when I was 18 in the 1960s, and he told me that he also had a hand in getting Gregory that record deal, but that is his side of the story. (Gregory is not to be confused with the current "Greg Abbott" who is the Governor of Texas.

I was following all of Gregory's success in *Jet*. The first time I heard anything about it, I was reading the magazine one day and it said in print: "Gregory Abbott lands a record deal on Columbia Records."

I thought to myself, "Well, good for Gregory! So, he wasn't wasting his time after all. He really got a record deal for himself." I was happy for him.

The next thing I know, the 1986 single, "Shake You Down" comes out, and it hits Number One! Gregory was Number One in *Billboard* on the Pop Chart, and Number One on the R&B Chart at the same time. Now that's phenomenal. Not only did he sing the song, he was the artist and the songwriter, and he was one of the producers. It is like hitting the trifecta at a horse race: get paid to write it, produce it, and sing it.

The second single off his debut album *Shake You Down*, was called "I've Got The Feelin' (It's Over)," and it hit Number Five on the R&B chart. Although he recorded several more albums, he was never able to replicate the success of that first single. He had a short-lived recording career, but he earned a *Platinum* album out of it, and his own spot in music history.

He won many awards including a BMI Award as "Best New Artist" and several more distinctions. With a last name like "Abbott," I guess it was a case of "luck of the Irish!" Ha, ha!

Although our marriage didn't work out, I never felt any animosity towards him. I never wished him any bad luck whatsoever. I was not jealous of his success with "Shake You Down." I was happy for him. This was all because he was Gregory Jr.'s father. I wanted my son to have someone to look up to as his father, with pride.

On the other hand, I have always felt that Gregory held a grudge against me. After we divorced we did not have a good or friendly relationship with each other. I think he felt betrayed or something, because I was the one who wanted out of the marriage.

But you know what? I did him a favor. If we hadn't divorced, his successful record career never would have happened. After we parted, it drove him to want to achieve something on his own, and he did it, all the way to the top of the record charts. He would have never had his own recording career, if he hadn't spent those two years helping me with my career.

It was like it was predestined that we should marry, have a child, and then divorce. That was somehow meant to happen. And if he hadn't seen how the whole music business worked, via watching me in my career, he would have never accomplished his own dreams of having a Number One record. It's funny how fate works. God works in mysterious ways.

Meanwhile, I recorded very little new music in the 1980s. Then in 1986, I suddenly scored a hit by recording a new version of my song "Band of Gold" with Belinda Carlisle of The Go-Go's. It hit Number 26 on *Billboard* magazine's Hot Dance / Disco chart in the U.S., and it became a Pop hit in Canada. The success of the song brought with it several notable television appearances for Belinda and I together. And it also put the spotlight on me as a recording artist, and made me contemporary in a new and updated 1980s way.

How this came about was that I received a phone call from Belinda's management company. Her manager's name at the time was Ron Stone.

He said to me, "I know that 'Band of Gold' is your song, and Belinda wants to record it with you involved."

I thought about it for a minute, and then I agreed.

I was flattered, and we ended up recording and releasing it as a single billed as "Belinda Carlisle featuring Freda Payne." Belinda had become a huge sensation as the main lead singer of the all-girl rock band The Go-Go's, and she was just launching her solo career. I thought the whole project sounded like a fun idea, and it was! There was even a special 12-inch vinyl single with an extended re-mix of the song that lasted almost seven minutes in length. A special "collectors edition" of the 12-inch single was pressed on gold-colored vinyl.

Someone else who also recorded "Band of Gold" was the disco singer Sylvester. And Bonnie Tyler recorded it too, during this era.

As a result of my new recording, Belinda and I ended up performing it together in 1987 on the hit TV show *Solid Gold*. I loved watching *Solid Gold*. It was one of the last great all-star all-music TV variety shows, and it ran from 1980 to 1988. For anyone who doesn't remember, it was originally hosted by Dionne Warwick. When she left it, they replaced her with Marilyn McCoo of The Fifth Dimension. The other hosts and co-hosts included Andy Gibb, Rex Smith, Rick Dees, Nina Blackwood, and Arsenio Hall. The guests on the show included new and classic stars, and it was a lot of fun to do.

On the episode that Belinda and I performed in, it was Marilyn McCoo who introduced us. It was the height of the "shoulder pads and glitz" '80s fashion. Marilyn wore a silver lamé outfit, I was dressed in a deep purple low-cut top with huge puffy sleeves, and a mini skirt. Belinda was dressed in an all-white suit with squared off shoulder pads. I loved '80s fashion. It was so unique and over-the-top. Belinda and I had a wonderful time taping that show.

But the big payoff came when we sang the song on the 1987 TV special: *The Legendary Ladies of Rock & Roll*. The program was part of the HBO / Cinemax TV network's series, *Super Sessions*. The way it was set up, Grace Slick of The Jefferson Airplane and Belinda were the show's hosts, and their guest stars included Martha Reeves, Leslie Gore, Mary Wells, Ronnie Spector of The Ronettes, Brenda Lee, Shirley Alston Reeves of The Shirelles, and me. Naturally, Belinda and I did our duet version of "Band of Gold" in the middle of the show.

The TV taping was so much fun to do with all of these rock legends. Clarence Clemons, who is famous for being the flamboyant saxophone player of Bruce Springsteen's E Street Band, had a guest spot in the show. Chubby Checker got up on-stage and danced with us in the group numbers, and Carly Simon was shown on camera singing and dancing in the audience. Naturally everyone did their own hits on the show, and then there were a couple of ensemble numbers where we were all up on-stage singing The Crystals' "Da Doo Ron Ron" and Martha & The Vandellas' "Dancing In The Street." It was a wonderful experience to be a part of this girl group spectacular. And, I loved being considered a "Legendary Lady!"

In 1987 I met a man by the name of John Phillips—not to be confused with the head of The Mamas & The Papas. This John Phillips organized several celebrity tennis and golf tournaments. His family also owned the grocery store chain Food For Less. I was contacted to perform at a gala tennis weekend in Bentonville, Arkansas. It was my pianist and musical director at the time, Jim Vukovich, who got me involved in being booked for this particular event. He has since moved to Houston, Texas, where he teaches at a college as a music professor.

The all-star celebrity guest list included champion tennis players, golfers, and football players, as well as actresses, actors, and singing stars. They wanted me to perform, and I also played in the celebrity tennis tournament as well.

Among the many celebrities were exercise guru Jack LaLanne, and baseball stars Mickey Mantle and Ernie Banks. The show business VIP's included Pat Boone, Fess Parker, Leslie Nielsen, Hal Linden, Hugh O'Brien, Patrick Duffy of *Dallas* fame, and actor Spanky McFarland who played Spanky in the *Our Gang* movies in the 1930s. My friends Billy Davis Jr. and Marilyn McCoo from The Fifth Dimension were there, too. Songwriter Carol Connors, who wrote the theme from the *Rocky* movies was there, as well as country singing star Charlie Pride.

Speaking of Charlie Pride, at the time he was the most famous black country singer around, dating back to the 1960s, and he was a great guy. Once when I was performing with Sammy Davis Jr. at Harrah's in Lake Tahoe, Charlie came to see the show, and afterward we had a drink together in the lounge. He was quite complimentary about my singing, and he especially loved the jazz songs I performed that night. As Charlie and I sat there together, he said to me, "If I was tied to a gate, and someone threatened to beat me to death until I sang a jazz song, I would be in big trouble. I certainly couldn't sing jazz music like that."

Leslie Nielsen was a funny guy, and all weekend he carried around a "whoopee cushion" to make "fart" noises. His original reputation was as a straight actor in the 1950s and 1960s, then he started doing comedy films later, including *Airplane!* That weekend he was a real comedian. I met the wife of celebrity hair stylist Vidal Sassoon, Beverly Sassoon, who was there. Astronaut Neil Armstrong was also with us, and I got to talk with him again.

There were several politicians in attendance too, in fact I met future-President Bill Clinton at John Phillips' house, and it was his father, John Phillips Sr., who introduced me to him. At the time Clinton was the Governor of the state of Arkansas.

That weekend I also met multi-millionaire Sam Walton, who founded Walmart stores. We were on the sidelines after playing a set of tennis. It was one of those hot Arkansas days, and he went and got a Gatorade, and came back and sat next to me. He opened the bottle, and offered me a drink. I was hot and thirsty myself, so I obliged. He then drank out of the bottle himself.

Then he handed it back to me to take another drink. At first I was hesitant to drink again for sanitary reasons, but I did so, and Sam and I shared the rest of his Gatorade. That's how friendly he was with me.

Something else notable happened that weekend as well. Tournament organizer John Phillips and I had an affair that began almost instantly upon my arrival. Jim and I had just arrived from New York, and there was an afternoon Meet-and-Greet cocktail party. That was when I first met John.

We started talking, and John announced to me, "I'm gonna handcuff myself to you, Freda."

I thought it was amusing at first and that he was kidding. I didn't think he was serious. Well, that was the beginning of it. John was married at the time, but that didn't seem to matter to him at all. By the time the weekend came to a close he told me that he had fallen deeply in love with me. After that we had several romantic interludes. He would fly out to where I was booked to perform, and we also had a rendezvous at The Fairmont Hotel in San Francisco, because he flew me up there to meet him. We also got together when I was performing at The Trump Castle in Atlantic City, and he came to several of my other shows in other cities as well.

John Phillips was in love with me, and he wanted me to come live in Arkansas. There was no question that I loved John as well, but there were several other issues that had to be taken into consideration. First of all, John was Caucasian, and I am African American. That was not a problem for me at all. However, I had to think about how this would work. After all, this was the South, and the racial issues seemed more apparent there, especially among the locals, and I had to think about that. My son, Gregory Jr. and I would have to leave Los Angeles and move to Arkansas.

Gregory was ten years old at the time, and after careful consideration, I decided that I didn't want to raise my son in Arkansas. First of all, there was the issue of his allergies which was magnified by his severe case of eczema. I was afraid that all of the trees and pollen would cause him added discomfort. Then there was the matter of racial sensitivities. There are certainly racially sensitive people every-where, but I suspected that if we moved to Arkansas at one point or another Gregory would encounter some racial prejudice living in a state in the South, as opposed to being in Los Angeles. In Arkansas it was known there were "white supremacists," and the Ku Klux Klan existed in that state.

I loved John, and I was torn as to what I should do. At this par-ticular point in 1987 came my brief reunion with Edgar Bronfman Jr. As I mentioned before, I went off and had a romantic weekend with Edgar on a Caribbean island. Well, I used that particular week-end fling with Edgar to help me break it off with John. When I told John that I had an affair with a former lover, this was something he could not accept, and we broke up. Although I was emotionally torn at that time, I feel that I made the right decision.

I heard later that John went on to divorce his wife, and ended up marrying his next door neighbor. I thought that was a real "hoot! I guess it sounds like the Stephen Stills song, 'if you are not with the one you love,' "Love The One You're With!" Her name was Marsha, and I met her that weekend. She was married at the time to a doctor, and I believe that he was one of John's doctors as well.

In my life I have been thankful for having so many great life-long friends. One of these was David Gest. I knew David Gest for 38 years. He would come in-and-out of my life for decades. I first met him in the early 1970s. At the time I was living in an apart-ment on Hollywood Boulevard. It was a high rise building called The Hollywood Versailles Towers, which was a very well-kept and nice building, with a doorman and a swimming pool. It was run as an apartment building, but it eventually became a condominium in the late '70s.

Actually, Scherrie lived there for a couple of years. I remember when she moved out, they were about to convert it into condos.

I had Apartment 1209 on the twelfth floor, which was also

the top floor. I remember David getting in touch with me, and at the time he was a publicist for London Records. He started sending me albums from some of their artists. Then he invited me to come to The Whiskey A-Go-Go, a club located on Sunset Boulevard in Hollywood, to see The Moody Blues perform there. We started what became a lifelong friendship.

Then when David Gest launched his own public relations company, he contacted me to announce its formation. He had gotten the "seed money" to start it from one of his London Records clients, soul singer Al Green. Al was actually on Hi Records, but London Records distributed that label. Ann Peebles was on the Hi Records label, too. Al Green put the money behind David, and he immediately landed some high profile clients, including Burt Bacharach, Angie Dickinson, The Doobie Brothers, Deniece Williams, and songwriter Carole Bayer Sager.

I worked with Al Green several times in the 1970s and 1980s. He and I performed together in Los Angeles at The Dorothy Chandler Pavilion in The Music Center. In Detroit we starred in a show together at The Fisher Theater. Then I worked with him in Washington D.C, at The Carter Baron outdoor theater. Also on that show were the trio known as LaBelle: Patti LaBelle, Nona Hendryx, and Sarah Dash.

David Gest and I were good friends, so we would hang out together. He would invite me out to movies and things like that. Then, in the early 1980s, David, along with actor Joseph Cotten and his wife Patricia Medina Cotten, Michael Jackson, and Michael's sister-in-law Dee Dee Jackson, got together and they formed The American Cinema Awards. There was also a man involved by the name of Peter McCrea who had something to do with the finances of that awards show. Of course, David would invite me to everything that was involved with that organization.

Joseph Cotten is best known for his roles in films like *Citizen*

Kane (1941), Alfred Hitchcock's *Shadow Of A Doubt* (1943), and *Hush...Hush, Sweet Charlotte* (1964). Cotten's participation in these awards gave David's movie awards the classic Hollywood legitimacy it needed.

The American Cinema Awards started out small in 1983, but it began to grow. Of course he would invite Michael McDonald of The Doobie Brothers to everything he was involved in, because he liked Michael a lot. David just loved him, so he would have Michael McDonald perform at all of his events whenever possible. He would also have me perform at several of them as well.

Around 1984 or 1985 The American Cinema Awards had started to gain momentum and it got bigger and more prestigious. By then David would hold the awards ceremony at The Beverly Hilton Hotel. I saw David Gest transform from being just a regular behind-the-scenes working class nice Jewish guy, to become this sort of entrepreneur kind of executive and event producer.

Then, in addition to that, he physically started to transform as well. He began to dabble in plastic surgery. It started with his nose, then it was his eyes. He started to develop a dimple in his chin that he didn't have before.

One day I said to him, "David, why are you getting all of this plastic surgery?"

He replied, "Well, it has to do with how people treat you when you look better, and you're more attractive looking."

The plastic surgeon he used was one of the best ones in the business: Dr. Steven Hoefflin, who is the same surgeon Michael Jackson went to for all of his work. He is still around. In fact I just saw him recently at a Hollywood event for The Thalians. It was at a birthday party for my friend Dr. Irwin Lehrhoff, who was a family friend of David's. He is a psychologist. He knew David's father, who had passed away while David was still a teenager. David used to go to Dr. Lehrhoff as a patient, and they were close friends as well.

David was such a devoted friend and he would always include me in whatever new event he was promoting. At one of these gala affairs, he had me singing a duet with Michael McDonald. This was when David had a collaboration with Academy Award-winning actress Sophia Loren.

This particular event was in Florida, on Williams Island. On this same show Donna Summer performed, too. I sang with Michael McDonald, and we did his Number One duet, "On My Own," that he had originally recorded with Patti LaBelle.

Michael is such a great guy. And, because of David, a few years after that, I got to do a duet with Joe Williams, and I also got to do a duet with Al Jarreau who I was most excited about, due to the fact that he was known as one of the top jazz vocalists around. He was also a six time Grammy Award-winner. Working with Al was one of my "ah-ha" moments, and it came about because David Gest made it happen. He was like my "bad" little brother, but he was a real deal-maker and a true entrepreneur.

Although some friends of mine have expressed the thought that David could have done more for me, I am on the side of being thankful for all of the things he DID do for me. It is easy for others to say that when they are on the outside looking in, but I understand their sentiment, and I know that they mean well. I will just leave it at that.

Joe Williams was a singer who I was always impressed with, and as a teenager I first heard him singing with The Count Basie Orchestra. They collaborated on the song "Everyday (I Have The Blues)," which they recorded back in 1956. When I heard that as a teenager, I became an instant fan of Joe and his music, and The Count Basie Orchestra.

For the Joe Williams duet, we sang "The Very Thought of You" by Ray Noble, accompanied by a full orchestra and strings. With Al Jarreau, we sang a medley of songs from the American opera by George & Ira Gershwin: *Porgy & Bess*. It was at an event in New York

City, at The City Center called *Night of 200 Stars*, and it was held on December 2, 1995. Al and I performed with a 55 piece orchestra, and that was heaven!

I remember David Gest calling me about this show and saying, "Freda, I want you to do a duet with Al Jarreau."

"David, I would love to do that," I said. "I think we would be perfect together!"

"I want you to call him on the phone right now," David insisted. "He is in Brussels, Belgium, and he is in his hotel room now. I just got off the phone with him. I want you to call and tell him how excited you are about singing with him, and I want the two of you to do a duet medley from *Porgy and Bess*."

"Which songs do you want to have us sing?" I asked.

"Freda, you choose the songs you want to sing with Al. I have a great guy to do the arrangements for whatever songs you pick out."

Come to find out Al was staying at the same hotel in Brussels that I had stayed at during one of the European runs of Duke Ellington's *Sophisticated Ladies*. I thought it was rather serendipitous.

So, I did as David requested and I phoned Al Jarreau in his hotel room. During our conversation, I said to him, "We should start out singing 'Summertime' as a duet, Al, then you should sing solo 'There's A Boat That's Leaving Soon For New York,' which is the character Sporting Life's song, and then we should end it with 'I Loves You Porgy.'"

He said, "I love it a lot. That sounds great Freda, let's do it exactly like that." I thought that was perfect.

So I called David Gest back and he hired an arranger by the name of Ray Charles—no relation to the singer Ray Charles—and he did a great job of arranging the music for those three songs, and the result was wonderful.

While Al and I were rehearsing for the show at The City Center, I tape recorded our rehearsal on my Sony Walkman. We sounded great together. That is the only recorded version of our duets together, and I still have it to this day as a memento. When I was later having a conversation with David Gest, he told me that he had the whole show filmed on video tape, and that one day we would sit and watch it. Sadly, it never did happen.

Present that night in New York City were several true Hollywood legends including June Allyson, Ann Miller, Anthony Quinn, Robert Goulet, Tony Bennett, Anthony Hopkins, and many more. They even honored Ginger Rogers, who attended the event in a wheelchair. It was an amazing evening. I remember that I shared a dressing room with Shirley Bassey. There were several of David Gest's favorite singers there, including Michael McDonald, and Whitney Houston. The Four Tops performed too, so it was a really great all-star show.

I have such fond memories of Joe Williams. The last time I performed with him, it was at The Fairmont Hotel in Santa Monica, California, located on Ocean Drive. We sang together, and it was only three weeks later that he died. He was living in Las Vegas, and he became ill. He was in the hospital, when he became delirious. He had wandered out onto the street, collapsed and died.

About a year later, at another one of David Gest's events, he had Al Jarreau and me repeat our *Porgy & Bess* medley. This time it was at The Beverly Hilton, in The International Ballroom.

In the 1980s I had recorded only two songs: "In Motion" and the duet version of "Band of Gold" with Belinda Carlisle. However, I successfully transformed myself into a TV hostess, and a lead Broadway touring company star. This all made perfect sense, since my career has always encompassed acting, singing, and dancing. I was already considered to be a lady of jazz, and a lady of the theater, and now I was honored to be considered a "Legendary Lady of Rock & Roll."

CHAPTER TEN

"Ready For The '90s"

When the new decade started, I found myself drawn into several theatrical productions that would take me all over the world. It began in 1990 when I was cast as one of the stars of a production of the Broadway show *Blues In The Night*.

This show was based on such a clever and highly appealing premise. It was a musical comprised of all classic blues music and standards, and it followed the lives of three women all living in the same hotel. And, that particular trio of women had reasons to sing the blues. Also in the hotel was a man whose songs showed off the blues from a different perspective.

As opposed to being a "book show" with a detailed plot, this was more of a revue, where any character development is strictly defined by the songs the woman and one man sing. In that way, it was quite similar to Duke Ellington's *Sophisticated Ladies*. My co-stars in this first production of *Blues In The Night* were Obba Babatundé, Leilani Jones, and Joann Jackson. It was so popular that it was staged again-and-again.

Obba was in the original cast of *Dreamgirls* on Broadway, and since then he has had an extensive career in movie and television roles. Leilani Jones, who was also a Broadway performer, won a Tony Award for the musical, *Grind*. She was married to the comedian and screenplay writer, Larry Wilmore, who had his own cable TV show. They had two children, one boy and a girl. They have since divorced.

To date I have toured in six different companies of *Blues In The Night*. The first company I was part of was presented in the downtown Los Angeles Theater Center. It was staged in The Tom Bradley Theater, which is a 500 seat theater. Our production of the show had a solid eight-week run. The original show itself was such a hit it was nominated for a Tony Award when it was on Broadway. Our production ended up winning several distinctions and theater awards too, including the NAACP Theater Award, and a Drama-Logue Award.

After that production closed I went on to do five more companies. One of them was at The Seattle Repertory Theater, in Washington state. Then I did it at The Pasadena Playhouse in California. I was even one of the stars of a run of *Blues In The Night* in Japan! We were in Kyoto, Tokyo, and several other cities in Japan. The cast members for that production were Roz Ryan, Jennifer Warren, and Alan Weeks. I knew Alan from *Hallelujah Baby!*, as he was in that Broadway production, too. He was a wonderful and talented guy.

The last time I did *Blues In The Night* was in 2007. It starred Maurice Hines, me, Carol Woods—who is known as a Broadway diva herself—and a lady by the name of Paulette Ivory as the ingénue. Paulette is an excellent performer, and a wonderful singer. The show was presented in San Francisco at The Post Theater in Union Square. We were there for about two and a half months.

My role in the show was called The Woman Of The World. I was down on my luck and I was looking back at my life. Carol Woods' part was The Blues Lady. And, Paulette Ivory was the ingénue, billed as A Girl Waiting For A Date. Paulette is originally from the U.K., but she is an American citizen by now. Then Maurice Hines' role was The Man In The Saloon, who observes and critiques all of these women. There was one set that we performed on—all four of us are living in a rundown hotel, and the sections of the set are our little rooms.

On the far right was my room, with me sitting at my dressing table with my perfumes and my mirror. In the show I am reminiscing about the days when I was really "the toast of the town." My character was someone who once had rich boyfriends, and was very sophisticated and really doing well. But her present day situation, is less-than-glamorous.

At center stage is The Blues Lady. Her demeanor is that of hopeless dreams, and thinking, "I'm going to get it together and really do it all again, better than ever. I am going to get booked in shows again, and they are gonna call me any minute. The agency is called T.O.B.A. That means Tough On Black Asses." That is an actual line in the script. She has more dialogue, and she has her own featured songs.

Then there is A Girl Waiting For A Date, and her songs show her off as being all young and fresh. She is a young woman who is aspiring to do great things, or meet a guy who is going to take her out and show her the world. The part of The Man In The Tavern is kind of cynical, and he looks down at the ladies and makes judgments about them. He is in a way, something of a streetwise pimp. His songs included Bessie Smith's "Baby Doll" and Duke Ellington's "I'm Just A Lucky So-And-So."

It was a great show to do, and it always received wonderful reviews. Five of the companies I performed in were directed by Sheldon Epps. His title in the program credited him as having "conceived and directed" the show, and he is the one who came up with the idea for the show concept to begin with. He was also the artistic director of The Pasadena Playhouse for several years.

Maurice Hines had performed since he was a toddler, and he performed in an act with his brother Gregory Hines, and their dad Maurice Hines Sr. They were very well known as "Hines, Hines &

Dad" in the 1960s and were even featured on *The Ed Sullivan Show*. Gregory and Maurice were also featured in Martin Scorsese's movie *The Cotton Club*, and on Broadway they performed together in the show *Eubie*, which saluted the music of Eubie Blake.

One production of *Blues In The Night* I did was a summer stock run of the play in Mt. Gretna, Pennsylvania, and I was the headliner of the show. That was in 1999, and it was a three-week run. There I was out in the woods in a resort area. They provided me with a car, and I would go out exploring. It was fun to be out in the wilderness. The show was presented in an outdoor amphitheater.

Sheldon Epps didn't do the choreography for this one, nor did he direct it. So, according to theater union rules, the choreography had to be redone for this production.

I also ended up doing another production of *Blues In The Night* for The Black Theater Festival, in Winston-Salem, North Carolina in the late 1990s. We only performed the show two nights, but it was easy for me to fall right back into my role. That show was directed by Obba Babatundé. The choreography was done by Kiki Sheppard.

I loved being one of the stars of all of these companies of this fantastic show. The musical numbers that were used in the show were blues songs composed by such famous writers as Bessie Smith, Duke Ellington, Johnny Mercer, Harold Arlen, Alberta Hunter and several other notable songwriters.

My featured songs included: "Nobody Knows You When You're Down And Out," "Lush Life," "Rough And Ready Man," and "Stompin' At The Savoy." "Rough And Ready Man" was my stellar number in the show, and my favorite ballad was "Lush Life" that was written by Billy Strayhorn. Then, there were certain songs where all three of the ladies would harmonize together. It took a lot of work to do that show. The Blues Lady has the standing-ovation number of the whole show: "Wasted Life Blues." She is sitting on the edge of her bed singing about having a broken heart, and it brought down the house every performance. This is a song meant for a real belter. Then The Girl Waiting For A Date has lighter songs like "Willow Weep For Me" and "Taking A Chance On Love."

When I sang "Stompin' At The Savoy," I started the song sitting at my dressing room table, and then at one point I stand up and have a whole dance number. When I finished doing that number, then I go back into: "I love the Savoy, Savvvvoooooyyyy," sustaining that last note for so long that I collapsed onto the chaise lounge in my room with exhaustion.

Signing on for *Blues In The Night* is one of those instances where I made the opposite choice, and found that sometimes taking less money is the way to go, if you feel strongly enough about a project. Case in point: the first production of *Blues In The Night* at The Los Angeles Theater Center in 1990. I really loved that show, so I accepted the salary of only $485.00 a week including three weeks of rehearsal, and a performance schedule of six evenings a week and two matinees.

In the subsequent companies I went from $485.00 a week, to $2,500.00 a week, to $3,500.00 a week. So, I guess you could say, "There is a lesson to be learned here." Sometimes choosing the path that doesn't pay the most, but offers creative possibilities, is the way to go. This is one of those instances. The last time I did *Blues In The Night* in 2007, my salary jumped to $5,000.00 a week, and that included rehearsals.

During the run of *Blues in The Night* in Japan, my co-star, Roz Ryan, and I were so popular there that we were offered starring roles in a television commercial for a Japanese Karaoke company. This turned out to be a job offer for which we were each paid $100,000.00 each. That was the era when Japan's economy was booming, and they spared no expense on this commercial. My portion of the commercial was filmed in Los Angeles. Then Roz Ryan's segment was filmed in Australia. She was on location in Sydney, where she was doing a production of *South Pacific.* The Japanese company obviously had unlimited funds.

So, I guess you could say sometimes when you take a job that doesn't pay well, eventually it can come back to you threefold and more. Needless to say, *Blues in the Night* has brought me so much good luck that I can never regret working for "Equity Scale" in the first production. Every job decision doesn't have to be based on "Oh, this is a better paying job!" Sometimes a creative gig that doesn't pay a lot, later has a lot more rewards that come out of it.

In the 1990s I turned down one offer to tour in Duke Ellington's *Sophisticated Ladies,* as I had been asked to perform in Las Vegas with Jay Leno at Caesar's Palace, and I really wanted to do that. That was a company that I could have done. It was a tour in Europe, and after I turned it down because of scheduling, Barbara McNair was hired instead of me.

I remember that while I was appearing in Las Vegas with Jay Leno, that was when Sammy Davis Jr. had died, on May 16, 1990. I was on-stage and I said during my set, "Can we please have a moment of silence to honor the passing of Sammy Davis Jr. When I was 17 and in Las Vegas with Duke Ellington, Sammy was a huge star who headlined the casinos all the time. Such a talented man! He was the greatest entertainer in the world *bar none*: singing, dancing, comedy, impressions, there was nothing he couldn't do."

In 1991 I was cast in a production of *Jelly's Last Jam,* which was a "book" type of show, this time around spotlighting the music and telling the story of jazz legend Jelly Roll Morton. I appeared in what was billed as "The World Debut of: *Jelly's Last Jam,*" at The Mark Taper Theater at The Los Angeles Music Center.

This production was starring Obba Babatundé playing Jelly Roll Morton as an adult. Savion Glover, who was one of the headliners, played Jelly Roll as a young teenager. I played the grandmother of young Jelly Roll, "Gran Mimi." In reality, "Gran Mimi" was a stern Creole woman, who was very traditional and conservative in her thinking. I am assuming that she was Catholic as well. She threw Jelly Roll out of the house after she discovered that he had been playing piano at a brothel. The show was directed by George C. Wolf, and we had a month-long run at The Mark Taper Theater.

After our successful production, it went on to Broadway, and Gregory Hines did the adult Jelly Roll Morton role. He won the Tony Award for "Best Performance by a Leading Actor in a Musical." Gregory had played the part in the "workshop" production of the show when it was in development. Then when it moved to Broadway, he returned to the role.

When *Jelly's Last Jam* played on Broadway, it was Tonya Pinkins who played the role of Anita, who was Jelly Roll Morton's love interest. Tonya ended up winning the Tony Award as "Best Performance by a Leading Actress in a Musical." She had also been in the original LA production. Keith David was in both productions as well, and was nominated for a Tony Award.

Then, after its Broadway run, I was asked to rejoin the cast, and to tour with the show, which I did. Our tour lasted a year. It was a whole year commitment including rehearsals, and it was the first and only national touring company of the show. We traveled all over the country, from the West Coast to the East Coast. That was with Savion Glover, Maurice Hines, and me. We were the three headliners. My role as "Gran Mimi" was a small one, but my name added to the draw on the marquee.

We received some great reviews. According to Markland Taylor in *Variety*, "The entire cast is a WOW, but in addition to Hines and Glover there are at least a large handful of performers who stand out, beginning with pop singer Freda Payne as a sensationally elegant Gran Mimi." (17)

In the 1990s I recorded three songs for Ian Levine's record label in England: Motorcity Records. He signed several singers who had formerly recorded for, or had some association with, Motown Records and Detroit. It was quite a clever idea. Amongst the songs I recorded for Motorcity Records are: "Memories and Souvenirs," "Only Minutes Away," and a third version of "Band of Gold." Although nothing big happened with them, it was great to be back in the recording studio.

Then, in 1993 I did a one woman concert in downtown Los Angeles, at The Tom Bradley Theater, which is a 500 seat venue—the same theater where we did *Blues In The Night*. I was booked there for four nights.

When I called Michael Viner to invite him and his wife, Deborah Raffin, to the show, Michael said, "Oh, great. How many nights will you be there?"

"Four nights," I replied.

He said, "We will come Saturday night, and I want to record the whole show." And that's what he did.

The original choreographer was set to be Lester Wilson. Lester had choreographed Liza Minnelli's stage act, and he choreographed John Travolta for his iconic dance number in the famed disco film *Saturday Night Fever*.

This particular show started out as a tribute to the music of Duke Ellington. Then Lester Wilson said to me, "You have such a rich background, Freda. You have done so much in the business. You should do a show about your life and all of the music you have done in the past."

I liked that idea, and I even added three songs from *Hallelujah Baby!* to it. But, before he even had a chance to start choreographing the show, Lester suddenly had a fatal heart attack. Lester was found by his partner, deceased on the floor in the laundry room at their house. I was devastated upon hearing the news about Lester.

Gene Jackson was the one who originally approached me with the idea of me doing a show downtown at The Los Angeles Theater

Center. Gene is an actor, and is one of my very close friends. The Theater Center approached Gene about producing a show for them. We both thought that using the talents of Lester Wilson was a great idea, but we wondered if we could even afford him, as he was in great demand. When we approached Lester, he had said, "Don't worry about the money. I will do it for 'scale.' I will work with you, for any price, don't worry about the money at all." It was coming together so nicely, then Lester was suddenly out of the picture. Now what?

When I spoke to Gene, I asked him, "What am I gonna do for a choreographer?"

He said, "Freda, you can do it yourself. You have the talent, you have the arrangements, and you know exactly what to do."

"Well, let me think about it," I told him.

So, I ended up hiring a dancer and choreographer by the name of Lorraine Fields to help me. She was Lester's assistant, so she knew about the project, and could continue what Lester started.

Lorraine Fields had also worked with me when I was performing in Duke Ellington's *Sophisticated Ladies* in Las Vegas. She was the "stand in" for Paula Kelly, and was able to do Paula's role several times.

So, Gene Jackson and I produced it together, and it became a labor of love! As far as the show itself, I ended up planning the whole thing myself, right down to the song choices, the dialogue, the musical arrangements, the gowns, everything. My costumes were done at LSO Designs, by designer Linda Stokes. I had the gowns already in my possession, so I was ready to go! I was a "one stop shop" of a singing star.

I pulled out musical arrangements dating back to my Quincy Jones big bad days when I did a couple of songs like "One Mint Julep" and "Secret Love."

I provided every element of the show, so for this show it was 100% Freda! I hired two male dancers to be part of the show, and I featured them in the *Hallelujah Baby!* production numbers. One of those dancers was Perry Moore, and he later did one of the productions of *Blues In The Night* with me at The Pasadena Playhouse. The other dancer was William Wesley.

In the show itself, I did a gospel number, and I had an all-black church choir to back me up. This particular gospel group was directed by the Reverend Ronald McGrew. This did not appear on the CD, because of the length of the show. The gospel number we performed was "When The Saints Go Marching In."

Michael Viner hired a top recording crew, they came into the theater and he had them record it professionally. That became the album, *An Evening with Freda Payne: Live in Concert*, released on Dove Audio. Both Michael Viner and I thought the album came out great.

Another album that I did for Dove Audio and Michael Viner, was based on a wild idea he had. At the time, in the early 1990s, there was a huge wave of popularity created by a children's television character: Barney the big purple dinosaur. The reason Barney became so big was that pre-school aged children worshipped him and they played episodes of *Barney & Friends* on television constantly. As a result, parents began to hate Barney, because he seemed to be all over the airwaves.

Michael had this idea to do a parody record as an adult's answer to the cloyingly irritating Barney. And so came, *Freda Payne sings "The I Hate Barney Songbook"—A Parody*. I had not recorded a new studio album since *Hot* in 1979 for Capitol Records, at the height of the disco era, so I figured, "What the hell?"

He wanted me to do that album, and he even hired me to read a couple of his books-on-tape recordings. Michael wanted to keep me working and to keep my name out there in the public, and I certainly had no problem with that plan. He always reached out to me, and I came to think of him as "one of the angels" in my life.

The following year, Michael offered me another record album deal, which became: *Christmas with Freda and Friends.* Half of the tracks were me singing solo, and the other half were recorded as duets with several friends, including: Cuba Gooding Sr., Mel Carter, O.C. Smith, and on the songs "Silver Bells" and "O Little Town Of Bethlehem," it was with my dear sister Scherrie Payne. It was executive produced by Michael Viner and Deborah Raffin, and produced and arranged by H.B. Barnum, who often worked with Aretha Franklin as her conductor and arranger. He also arranged and conducted for Donny and Marie Osmond as well. I had also worked with H.B. in the past, as a musical director and arranger, so he knew how to show me off at my best.

I was happy to have these three new albums, and it was all because of Michael Viner. He was a really good friend that way. Unfortunately, a few years later his marriage to Deborah was dissolving, and they ended up divorcing in 2005. It wasn't long afterward that he started calling me. I was happy to talk to him, as we had been friends for all those years. Then he started asking me out to dinner, and we started dating again, but there was no commitment at this point. I could see that getting physical was next on the agenda, and I wasn't at all interested.

I said to myself, "If this didn't work between us 30 years ago, why would it work out now?" I just wasn't feeling it.

He wanted me back, and I wasn't interested. He was married to Deborah for 30 years, and then he suddenly wanted to come back to me, because he still loved me? I thought to myself, "I don't think so."

It was shortly after that, I heard it through the grapevine that Michael was diagnosed with cancer, and that it was incurable. I spoke to him for the last time about five days before he died. I told him "I love you." He told me that he loved me too. It was a sad ending to a beautiful friendship. I have nothing but nice things to say about Michael Viner. He was truly one of my angels.

On January 30, 1994 something very tragic happened to my dear friend Mary Wilson. I was living in my apartment on Spaulding Drive, a half a block from Beverly Hills High School. I received a phone call from Scherrie that Mary had a horrifying car accident, near Barstow, California. She was driving with her youngest son, Ralphi, early in the morning.

Apparently Mary lost control of the car, the car rolled over, and her young son Ralphi was in critical condition and was on life support in Barstow. Mary had been flown to a hospital in Loma Linda, California.

I was so distressed, I began to pray. About 30 minutes later Scherrie called me back to tell me that she had heard from Mary's friend Alan Poe, who told her that Ralphi had passed. I felt such a deep sense of grief, not only for me but for Mary, who had to bear the weight of this incredible burden. It was so sad. Little Ralphi was her youngest child, and he was the apple of her eye. Ralphi and my son Gregory had become friends while at Beverly Hills High School, so this was especially upsetting to him.

The boys were typical boys growing up. When Ralphi passed away in that horrible car accident, it was a true tragedy. He was very charming, and he looked a lot like Mary. The last time I had seen Ralphi was when he had attended Gregory's Sweet 16 birthday party.

Ralphi could have accomplished so much in his life. But I guess God had a different plan. We can never say what "could have been." It is all conjecture. You cannot control things that happen like that.

In the 1990s, my agent at the time, Abby Hoffer, booked me along with jazz legend Jon Hendricks to do a concert at the philharmonic hall, *Kölner Philharmonie*, in Cologne, Germany, to honor the music of Duke Ellington as a tribute. Also on the show was an American performer who lived in Munich, by the name of Ron Williams. The run of this show included performances in both Cologne and Düsseldorf, in Germany. We performed with all

German musicians. The weeklong stay in Europe was financed by a German radio station, and it was such a grand experience. Here I was working with an iconic jazz singer: Jon Hendricks of the famed jazz trio Lambert, Hendricks and Ross. I loved Jon and his wife, and we had a great time. We would all go out to dinner together, and it was quite a memorable week.

I made a guest appearance in a film by the name of *Sprung* in 1997. It was a romantic comedy film about two couples and their dating habits. The stars of it included: Tisha Campbell-Martin, Rusty Cundieff, Paula Jai Parker, Joe Torry, and Clarence Williams III of *Mod Squad* fame.

There was one particular sequence in the film where there was some sort of senior gathering in a public park. There was a band performing in a gazebo, and I was the soloist who was singing. The song I was singing was the standard "Sunday Kind of Love," and it was my friend Tony Camillo who did the arrangement for the song. He also suggested to the producers to have me appear in the film, and they loved the idea.

At the time, I was in Washington state at The Seattle Repertory Company, doing a performance of *Blues In The Night*. They let me out for a day, to fly to Los Angeles to do that and then fly back. That way I only missed one show.

In 1999, I appeared in a film called *Ragdoll*. I played the role of a spiritualist who went by the name of "Gran." My character was something of a voodoo sorceress who could conjure up spirits, cast spells, and had mystic powers. It was a fun role to play.

In the plot of the film, a teenage boy who is a rapper gets into an altercation, and the thugs beat me up and put me in the hospital. He then seeks out my black magic for revenge toward those who roughed me up. It was a theatrical horror film. It didn't become a major release, but it was certainly a fun role to do.

Also, in 1999, through my own Band of Gold Records label, I

released a new CD of my music called *Freda Payne: Live in Concert.* Basically, it was a different presentation of the same live show Michael Viner had taped in 1993, but re-edited and re-packaged. Michael had given me the rights to the master tapes he had recorded. It was a CD I could sell at my shows and on the internet. The team I hired did an excellent job of repackaging it with a great photo by Alan Mercer on the cover. Duane Cramer did the additional photos for the back of the CD and the interior of the booklet. It was my agent at the time, Scott Stander, who got this repackaged for me.

I kept busy in the 1990s with theater, recording, and movies. Now I was prepared to tackle some new career challenges. It was the dawn of the new millennium, and I was ready to see what it held.

CHAPTER ELEVEN

"The 2000s"

With all of the theater work I had gotten recently, what I really needed was a role in a high budget Hollywood movie. I was thrilled when my agent called me to audition for the year 2000 film *The Nutty Professor II, The Klumps*, starring Eddie Murphy. So, I did, and I got a "call back." Then I went in and read again. After I read the second time they booked me, and I joined the cast in the role of Claudine.

The Nutty Professor II: The Klumps, also starred Janet Jackson. Everyone was so nice and friendly on the set. I saw Janet and we had a chance to talk a bit. My scene took place at the bar of a restaurant in Burbank. It was right off Barham Boulevard near The Warner Brothers lot. The film production company had booked the restaurant for the night, and we shot there.

In this film Eddie not only played the two sides of the main character—both the hefty side, and the svelte incarnation—but he also portrayed several of the main character's relatives as well. He was always really good in his roles. His performance was comic genius at its best.

I enjoyed working with Eddie Murphy so much, because he was such a professional on the set. He wasn't joking around between "cuts" and between "takes," he was quite focused on what he was doing. To see Eddie on camera, it would be a natural reaction to expect him to be comical and cracking jokes on the set. But he was nothing like that at all. Instead, he was very serene, and very introverted, like he was plotting out his next scene in his head. Eddie was very focused on his roles.

I would have loved my role to have been bigger, but I basically had a featured cameo role in it. My one scene takes place in that nightclub bar. Eddie played the role of Sherman Klump, who is quite overweight. However he has a potion which makes him into a svelte and handsome version of himself.

He walks into this club, and he walks over to me, and tries to talk to me at the bar. It was not a big role for me, but it was great to be in such a prestigious production. Like they say in acting classes: "There is no such thing as a small role." The original Eddie Murphy version of *The Nutty Professor* was a big hit when it was released in 1996, so this comic sequel was no surprise. It also co-starred several known character actors including Larry Miller, Chris Elliott, and Anna Maria Horsford. When *The Nutty Professor II: The Klumps* was released it did quite well at the box office.

One of the many roles Eddie played in the film was his character's father, Cletus. When *The New York Times* reviewed the film, Elvis Mitchell gave me a glowing write-up that proclaimed, "The rhythm-and-blues singer Freda Payne, who still looks like a hood ornament carved out of chocolate, shows up to cruise Cletus." (18) Indeed, this review made me feel like that distinctively gorgeous lady who rides atop the stylish hood of a Rolls Royce.

Being in this production put me in a good position to land more film work. Not long after that I was cast in a film called *Fire & Ice*. It was more of a 2001 cable TV production than it was a theatrical film. It wasn't a large role, but it was a good role to play. I played Glenn Turman's wife, and I had a lot of fun doing it.

In 2001 I released an album for Volt Records called *Come See*

About Me. The Volt label was based in Berkeley, California, a sub-sidiary of Fantasy Records. The irony about this project was that it was originally a deal that was put together for my dear friend Mary Wilson. This particular project dated back to 1999. Producer Preston Glass had already recorded the instrumental tracks for this album, and they were all recorded in Mary's musical keys. They just needed the vocals.

How this Mary Wilson association happened was that the president of Fantasy was Phil Jones, who was formerly the director of marketing at Motown Records. Phil knew Mary very well. He had worked in the promotions department at Motown, and he really wanted to work with Mary.

Phil is the one who called me, and convinced me to do it. The album was ready to go, but at the last minute something had gone wrong in their negotiations with Mary's manager, and they walked away from the deal. Apparently Mary and Fantasy had picked out all of the songs. They had gotten Mary's keys for each of the songs, and the tracks were already prerecorded. But Mary had never signed a contract with the label, and she decided she didn't want to do it at the last minute. This left Fantasy / Volt Records with an album of fully recorded tracks, and no singer to sing them.

So Phil called me and said, "Would you like to have this record-ing deal?"

At the time, no one was banging my door down to offer me a record deal, so I asked, "What are the songs? Let me hear them, and I will see if I can sing them in those keys."

They sent me the tracks, and I listened to them. So I called them back, and I said, "Yeah, I can do it." So they sent me an advance, I recorded my vocals in a matter of days and that was how this came about—very quickly and out of the blue I must add!

One of the songs on the album that I really like was the one that Preston Glass wrote called "Let's Make Beautiful Music." And there was also a ballad called "I'll Never Fall In Love Again," which I thought came out well. I did a cover version of Billy Vera's "At This Moment," and because it was originally planned as a Mary Wilson album, I recorded a ballad version of The Supremes' hit "Come See About Me." It was a whole different arrangement of that song.

The song "You Turned The Tables On Me," was originally sung by Ella Fitzgerald, and "I Couldn't Live Without Your Love" had been a huge international hit for Petula Clark in 1966. I also did a duet with Ali "Ollie" Woodson of The Temptations, on the song "Just Like That." It was produced by Fred Pittman and Preston Glass and executive produced by Phil Jones. We recorded the album in the year 2000 at Fantasy Studios in Berkeley, California, and it came out the following year.

Another of my memorable times with David Gest took place in September of 2001. David got this idea in his head that he wanted to celebrate Michael Jackson's 30th anniversary as a solo artist. The reasoning being that Michael's first solo single, "Got To Be There" was released in 1971. Although it was a solo recording, he was still part of The Jackson Five. This show was also billed as a reunion of Michael and his brothers.

Due to his involvement in this particular show, David ended up married to Liza Minnelli. No one could see this coming. This was without a doubt one of the most interesting things to happen so far in the new millennium!

David Gest met Liza through Michael Jackson. David and Michael were planning to turn this concert event into a huge super-star extravaganza, and it was! I remember earlier that year, I awoke from a dream I had, and in that dream, David was in one building and Michael was in another building and they were talking to each other on the phone. I had no idea what that was about. Sometimes I have these psychic moments and I have dreams that preclude coming events.

Several weeks later David told me, "Oh, I am going to be producing Michael Jackson's next concert, and we are doing this together as business partners. It is going to be an all-star event at Madison Square Garden. Michael is going to do two separate concerts. One is going to be on Friday the seventh of September, and the other one will be on Monday the tenth of September. It's going to be a TV special on CBS, and I am even going to get Elizabeth Taylor and Whitney Houston involved."

"Wow!" I said to him. "It sounds like you are going to outdo yourself."

"If I can pull this off like I've planned, you will have to be involved in it somehow."

"Okay, I am on board," I replied.

Because of my friendship with David, I heard all of the details about how this show was unfolding. Two or three months before the concert David was telling me that Michael wanted him to hire Liza Minnelli as one of the performers on the show—which he ultimately did. The plan was for the show to include several superstar opening acts leading up to Michael's segment of the show. They included 'N Sync, Usher, Monica, Al Jarreau, Jill Scott, James Ingram, Gloria Estefan, Mya, Marc Anthony, Deborah Cox, Destiny's Child, Ray Charles, guitarist Slash, Britney Spears, and Whitney Houston. To further add additional star power, there were live appearances by Marlon Brando, Samuel L. Jackson, and Elizabeth Taylor.

For the Friday concert, when Marlon Brando came out on-stage, he was supposed to do a short speech. However, he talked on-and-on about his political views for a half an hour. Finally, the audience was getting restless. Fortunately, they didn't have to "get the hook" to get him off-stage, but nearly!

David would always invite me to his events, and if I wasn't booked to perform somewhere else, I would be there. Sometimes I was actually booked on the show as one of the performers, and sometimes I would just attend as a VIP guest. For this particular engagement, he invited me to New York City for the whole week of the production.

Although David didn't book me to appear on the show in Madison Square Garden, I was booked to perform at Tavern On The Green in Central Park following the Friday night concert. That's where David threw a private "after party" for all guest stars. I performed along with Deniece Williams, Edwin Starr, James Ingram, Billy Paul, and others. Joey Melotti and Greg Phillinganes were the musical directors in charge of all the music.

At the main concert, Whitney Houston was the performer who was the most talked about by the press. She had her infamous bouts with drugs going on during this time, and that evening when she took the stage she was shockingly thin. She had lost a lot of weight, and she was obviously ravaged by the drugs. She hadn't lost her voice yet, but it was certainly moving in that direction.

The only time I ever met Whitney was at another one of David Gest's concert productions at Madison Square Garden, a couple of years prior to this one. Whitney performed on the show, and I was one of the headliners as well, along with Chaka Khan, and Patti LaBelle. David was always talking about Whitney, as he was just crazy about her. He would refer to her as "my baby."

I still have trouble trying to understand how someone can be so talented, so gifted, and yet to throw it all away for drugs. All I can think of is that she had that kind of genetic flaw that made her susceptible to substance abuse. I have read that certain people simply have the kind of chemical make-up that makes it easy for them to fall into this trap. Some people just seem to have an "addictive personality."

Poor Whitney. She had the kind of career that Diana Ross had, but it was easier for Whitney. She had it handed it to her on a silver platter. And in a way, she was standing on the shoulders of Diana Ross and others. I think that Diana had to work hard for stardom, whereas Whitney waltzed right into it. Her mother was Cissy Houston, who is a very well respected singer on her own with her own records. And Whitney's cousin was Dionne Warwick. Stardom certainly ran in Whitney's family. Everything she accomplished, she achieved by just stepping into it free and clear. What Whitney did to herself was such a senseless shame. It was almost a crime.

Since everything came to Whitney so easily, I think that was the problem. Perhaps deep down inside of her, she felt she didn't deserve it.

The second Michael Jackson concert was on a Monday night, September 10, 2001, and that was another grand performance at Madison Square Garden. The next morning I woke up, and I turned on the TV to watch *Live With Regis & Kathie Lee.* Instead of seeing Regis Philbin and Kathie Lee Gifford, I found that I was watching on the screen The World Trade Center towers, with smoke coming out of one of the buildings, towards the top of it. This was just after 9:00 in the morning. I first thought, "Oh, another private plane has hit The World Trade Center and started a fire." That had happened once before, with a small private plane.

I was thinking it was something like that. Then, three or four minutes later, all of a sudden I saw another plane fly into the second tower. That's when I instantly knew this was clearly an attack on the U.S. I realized that I was seeing something terrible happening, because that was a passenger jet. I was so horrified I thought I was going to faint. Needless to say, all of us will remember where we were when this tragic event happened.

I was stuck in New York for the next four days, because all flights were grounded in the entire United States as well as international flights from Europe. All flights coming or going anywhere ceased flying. Scherrie was with her singing group—Former Ladies Of The Supremes—and they were flying back to the states from

Amsterdam, and their flight was routed to return to the airport. It was just terrible. It seemed like we were at the start of World War III.

I had been booked on an American Airlines flight on 9/11 in the afternoon, and it was another American flight which had hit the tower that morning. I knew Barrie Berenson who was on one of the fatal flights; the one that came out of Logan airport in Boston. She was the sister of Marissa Berenson, who was one of the stars of the film *Cabaret*. Barrie was also married to actor Anthony Perkins.

My connection to Michael Jackson was completely due to David Gest. David would call me and announce, "I've got Michael on the phone, Freda." And then he would say, "Hold on, Michael just wants to say, 'Hi.'"

So I would wait, and he would put Michael on the phone with me. It was always very nice, but nothing too in-depth. It would just be something like, "Hi, how are you doing?"

"Great. What's going on?"

Then he would say, "Freda, I really like your singing."

"Thank you so much, Michael."

And then he would say, "I really like 'Band of Gold' a lot. I listen to it all the time."

That was about it. I never had a real long-lasting relationship with Michael, as far as being buddies. But over the years he would often reach out to say, "Hi."

David would have these ongoing events at The Beverly Hilton Hotel, and he would always have Michael involved. This all started back in the 1980s.

The way David became so tight with Michael Jackson, was that David grew up in Encino, California where the Jackson family lived. He met Michael when they were back in their teens. Then he cultivated a friendship with Dee Dee Jackson, who was married to Michael's brother Tito. Tito and Dee Dee had three boys, who eventually formed their own musical group, 3T. Michael was the one who funded Tito's sons' education, sending them to a private school, Buckley, located in The Valley here in LA.

Of all of Michael's brothers' wives, it was Dee Dee who became the closest to David. She was Michael's favorite sister-in-law. He was very fond of her, and they had a great relationship. Dee Dee and I became friends. She and Tito had been divorced a few years earlier. Then she started dating a guy who was a former detective and now owned his own security company. I met him with her and thought he was a very nice guy. Then they broke up and she started dating this guy by the name of Donald Bohana. I was deeply hurt when she suddenly died in 1994. Her body was found in Bohana's swimming pool, which set off a lot of suspicion. Although it was originally ruled a probable accident, it was later discovered to be a homicide.

I remember that I was in a production of *Jelly's Last Jam*, and we were in rehearsals in New York City. I was in my hotel room when David Gest called to tell me that Dee Dee had been found in Bohana's pool, drowned.

Dee Dee's sad ending was one of those cases where the guy treats you the best, and you become bored with him. So, the one who is edgy and sort of dangerous, sounds exciting on the surface. That is what happened to Dee Dee, and unfortunately that was her fatal mistake. Donald Bohana had the façade of being a successful businessman, and he was more of a challenge to her.

Also, Dee Dee had been in conversations with my sister Scherrie, because she was helping to plan Donald Bohana's daughter's wedding. Dee Dee had made plans to have Scherrie sing at the wedding. And she also had worked out a booking for the wedding couple to stay at The Kahala Hilton in Waikiki, Hawaii in a bungalow there.

Dee Dee had only gone out with Donald for about three or four months. One night she had gone over to his house, and—apparently—that fateful night Dee Dee had been drinking. They got into an argument, and he must have beat her up, or she fell into the pool and he beat her up in the pool. Either way, Donald just let her drown. In the autopsy report, the coroner found that she had over 60 bruises all over her body. And, I knew that she could not swim!

She wouldn't even have a swimming pool at her house, because of this. She only had a hot tub.

The police suspected murder, but they couldn't pin anything on Donald Bohana at the time. There were no witnesses, and they lacked the concrete evidence to arrest him. So, Michael Jackson privately paid for independent detectives to work on the case. Eventually, they cracked this case, and they were able to pin it on Bohana.

When the police went back into his past, they found that Donald had been involved in the suspicious death of another woman years before. They had gone out for a cruise in the ocean, because he had his own boat. Basically, Donald took her out for a boat ride, and when he came back, she wasn't on the boat. They were never able to pin anything on him. But finally, his karma must have come back to punish him for his deeds. He was actually a businessman, and he owned a Denny's restaurant somewhere in the city.

People who saw Scherrie and Dee Dee and I together, could have sworn that she was one of our sisters; she looked like she could have been related to us. My mother always looked very Puerto Rican, or West Indian. She had those features, and Dee Dee—who was from the Dominican Republic—looked like part of the Hickman side of my family, my mother's side. She was a dear friend, and her death was a great tragedy to me. I sang at her funeral at Forest Lawn.

David Gest and I would talk on the phone a lot. During one of our conversations in January of 2002 he said to me, "I haven't really talked about this, but I have been dating Liza Minnelli for the last four months, and I am thinking about asking her to marry me."

"You're what!?" I asked in astonishment.

"We seem to be getting along wonderfully, and I love her."

"What if she says 'no?'" I replied.

"I am just going to have to take my chances," he said.

"If this is what you want, I am all for it, David."

"And," David announced, "if she says 'yes,' I want you to be one of the bridesmaids."

"Oh, that is sweet," I replied, "but don't you think that the bride should be the one who chooses her bridesmaids? What makes you think she's gonna want me as a bridesmaid?"

"I will just have to take my chances about that as well," he said.

Well, he did ask her, and she did say "yes." I didn't know how this marriage to Liza Minnelli was going to go at all. I knew how David can "run hot and cold" with his decisions. One minute he wanted one thing, and the next minute he could totally change his mind.

A week or so later, I came home and there was a message on my answering machine. When I played it back, the person on the tape said in a delightful voice: "Hi Freda, this is Liza Minnelli. I called to ask you to be one of my bridesmaids. I know you are David's best friend, and I would really like you to be one of my bridesmaids, please Freda, please."

She was so warm and friendly on the phone, how could I not want to be one of her bridesmaids? She certainly didn't have to beg me to participate in the wedding of the century. I did return the call, and gladly said, "Yes."

Liza and David were funny when they were together. I am sure that David loved that "wow" factor that occurred whenever he went somewhere with highly-recognizable Liza on his arm. Heads turned wherever they went.

There was a restaurant called Du-Par's, in the Valley on Ventura Boulevard. It is gone now, but it was a famous place. It was just a typical coffee house, but they were especially known for their pancakes and lunches. David and Liza went to Du-Par's one evening, for pancakes or whatever. I went there with them on another occasion.

They left the restaurant on their evening together, got in the car, and drove away.

It was then, that Liza announced, "I should have gone to the restroom while we were in the restaurant."

"What do you want me to do?" David asked. "I don't want to just pull into a gas station, and have you use the facilities there."

"Well, you are going to have to pull in somewhere so I can use the toilet."

"Oh, wait a minute," David said, "Scherrie Payne lives right near here. Let me call her and see if we can run in and use her bathroom."

So he called her on his cell phone. She was home, and naturally she told David to come over with Liza immediately. Later Scherrie called me and said, "You will never guess who came over for an emergency bathroom visit?"

We had a good laugh over this wacky series of events! When a girl's gotta go, a girl's gotta go!

David told me in great detail how they started dating. Originally David didn't want to book Liza on the Michael Jackson Madison Square Garden show, because he had heard all sorts of rumors that she drank too much, and she had lost her voice. So, David got in contact with Liza, and said, "Michael is so excited about the idea of you being part of this show, I just wanted to set up a time to have my musical director, Joey Melotti, come over to see what you have in mind to sing, and what keys you like."

In other words, David wanted to use this as an excuse to find out if Liza still had "it," or if the tabloids were right for reporting that she was losing her voice. Were they trashing her voice just to make a headline? David's plan sounded like it was on the up-and-up, especially since Joey Melotti has such a great reputation in the business. I have worked with Joey in the past, and he later became musical director of Barry Manilow's residency show at The Las Vegas Hilton. Joey is truly a top notch musician.

Joey got over to Liza's, and she sang several songs for him and he reported back to David. Afterward David called me and told me, "Forget what you've heard, Liza's still got 'it.' Her singing voice is as strong and clear as ever." That was the beginning of the David and Liza story.

Well, after Liza accepted David's proposal, the parties and events started. They held a gala engagement party at Liza's Upper East Side Manhattan apartment, and it was literally a "who's who" of the celebrity world. I remember that Tony Bennett was there, Donald Trump and his wife-to-be Melania who became First Lady Trump, Kirk Douglas, Elizabeth Taylor, Diana Ross, Michael Jackson, and many more. It was like being at The Academy Awards. I had never seen anything like it!

But nothing will top the wedding of Liza and David. It was without a doubt one of the biggest, glitziest David Gest productions ever—and I am not exaggerating. The star-studded guest list made it seem like a Hollywood event in the middle of New York City! As one of the bridesmaids, I was flown into New York, and they put me up at The Plaza Athénée Hotel on the East Side.

You just never know what the outcome will be with show business marriages. David would always complain to me that he was unhappy being alone, and that one day he would find his soul mate. I sincerely hoped this union with Liza would work. David loves to produce events, and expects total professionalism from a performer. He needed someone like Liza to focus his promotional attention on, and Liza needed a man who was part husband / part manager all rolled into one. When I arrived in New York, I was hoping for the best.

It was David's first marriage, and Liza's fourth. The wedding was held on March 16, 2002, at the famed Fifth Avenue chapel, Marble Collegiate Church. There were 13 bridesmaids, 13 groomsmen, two ushers, a pair of flower girls and a pair of flower boys. The two Maids-of-Honor were Elizabeth Taylor, and Liza's *Cabaret* co-star, Marisa

Berenson. The Best Man was none other than Michael Jackson.

In true David Gest fashion, I was not only invited to be present, I was one of the 13 bridesmaids dressed in black. My fellow bridesmaids included Gina Lollobrigida, Petula Clark, Mia Farrow, Janet Leigh, newscaster Cynthia McFadden, singer Mya, and *New York Post* gossip columnist Cindy Adams among others. Naturally, Liza was married in a white Bob Mackie-designed gown. It was quite spectacular. Michael McDonald was one of the groomsmen, along with Tristan Rogers, Tito Jackson, James Ingram, and more. At the wedding, Natalie Cole sang the song that both she and her father made famous, "Unforgettable." I was there, and saw it all with my own eyes, and that was definitely the word of the evening: UNFORGETTABLE!

When we walked down the aisle, my escort and wedding partner was actor Tristan Rogers, who was one of the stars of the soap opera, *General Hospital.* He is still—to this day as I write this book—on the show. The A-List guests for this wild extravaganza included Elton John, Donald Trump, Robert Goulet, Joy Behar, Kirk Douglas, Martha Stewart, Sir Anthony Hopkins, Dame Joan Collins, Dionne Warwick, Carol Channing, Lauren Bacall, Donny Osmond, Rosie O'Donnell, Phyllis Diller, Tony Franciosa, David Hasselhoff, Barbara Walters, Diana Ross, and Mickey Rooney! Conspicuously absent was Liza's half-sister, Lorna Luft. Reportedly, Lorna and Liza were on the "outs" at that time.

The David / Liza wedding reception was held at The Regent Hotel in their ballroom. While we were there, not only did Liza perform at the wedding reception, but I did as well, singing my signature hit "Band of Gold." Gloria Gaynor sang "I Will Survive," and Andy Williams performed "Our Love Is Here To Stay." There were many other performances as well.

This was without a doubt, the most over-the-top, outrageous, star-studded, and most press-worthy David Gest-produced event ever. It even rivaled the two Michael Jackson concerts in Madison Square Garden. The Liza Minnelli / David Gest marriage only lasted a year, but it is still talked about today!

After they were married, returning Liza's career to peak form became David's number one task. He wanted the world to know that Liza still had "it," and that her voice was in great shape. On April 2, 2002 Liza headlined a concert at Royal Albert Hall in London. It was formally billed as: *David Gest Presents in Concert: Liza's Back.* The event was turned into a live album release, and it was also a true David Gest production. He got Clive Davis to sign the concert album to his J Records label; he had hit-making producer Phil Ramone aboard; and he got songwriters John Kanter and Fred Ebb to write the show's opening song. They were the duo who had written the music in the movie *Cabaret* that made Liza a star. And she won an Oscar as Best Actress in that film.

"Well, maybe this marriage could work. Maybe David and Liza are good for each other," I thought to myself.

Before their marriage got rocky, Liza and David bought a house on the island of Oahu in Hawaii. On one of his trips there he was making plans to renovate it, and I went with him. David was always in a quandary about where he wanted to live next, and he and Liza selected Hawaii.

David wanted things a certain way, and the architect had other ideas. He had a certain pattern, and he liked to be surrounded with people he felt comfortable with. For several years, Willie Green was David's security guard. Willie had been a professional NFL football player. He had played for the Denver Bronco's. Wherever David was, Willie was always in the picture. This continued throughout his marriage to Liza.

It wasn't long before he discovered that some of the gossip was true: Liza definitely had a drinking problem, and when she would drink, she wasn't always fun-loving. Instead it would apparently bring out her evil side. Because of this, David told me they would have some "knock down, drag out" fights. During one of their arguments, apparently Liza lunged at David, and was hitting him in the head. This was clearly the fight to end the whole relationship, and Willie had to step in and literally drag Liza off David as Liza continued to hit him in the head. As David's faithful friend dragged Liza off him, she bit Willie on the chest. After this, it became pretty clear that the honeymoon was over.

I remember asking Willie if this had actually happened, and he told me, "Yes, it did."

According to David, the blows that Liza delivered to him in the head made him lose some his memory. He went into the hospital in Hawaii, and when I visited him, he was displaying some very odd behavior like he was having delusions. After he left the hospital and recovered, he complained of severe pain, so he started getting Botox injections in his forehead to ease his migraine headaches. David and Liza had a wild year of crazy adventures together, but then it all began to unravel at an alarming pace. By 2003, the marriage was officially over.

One night when they were making love, Liza suddenly burst into tears, and said to him, "I can't make love tonight. I have herpes." After David told me this, he went out and got tested for it. The tests came back "negative."

David said to me, "I am going to call the tabloids, and if I get herpes I am going to sue her. She should have told me this before we got married."

I said to him, "David, please don't do this. If you do, it is going to bite you in the butt. And it is going to make you look like you are less than a man." I thought this was something very personal and private, and I told him that he should have kept it to himself.

Of course, David being David, he didn't take my advice.

As the divorce proceedings were going on, there was another

related scandal. Liza had a servant / bodyguard / former bodybuilder who had previously worked for the designer Halston. When Halston died, the man went to work for Liza. His name is M'Hammed Soumayah, and it was revealed that he even slept with Liza when he was under her employment. According to the many press reports Liza had demanded sex from him, and in doing so he ended up catching herpes from Liza. Then he subsequently sued her for having sex with him knowing she had the sexually transmitted disease. Not only did he get herpes, but he gave it to his wife too. It was a real scandal in the tabloids, and he sued Liza for $100 million and won. An out-of-court financial settlement was later reached in the case.

After their divorce, David went to Hawaii, and he lived there for a time. Then he bought a house in Memphis, Tennessee, and lived there for a while. I went to visit him at that house from time-to-time. Actress Cybill Shepherd also had a house in the exclusive community were he lived. His house was on a bluff overlooking the Mississippi River there. When I asked him why he chose Memphis to move to, he told me that he was fascinated with the city's musical history, because that's where Al Green had recorded his hits. While David was living there, naturally he staged several of his trademark shows. With all of the publicity that his marriage to Liza had generated, he was instantly recognizable wherever he went in Memphis.

Then he ended up packing his bags and moving to London. What happened was that when he and Liza divorced, David didn't handle it very well at all. He said some things to the press that angered the Hollywood community, and they turned against him. Whenever his name appeared in the tabloids, they said horrible things about him. It was like being famous for all the wrong reasons. This was because people shared the feeling of "You just don't mess with Judy Garland's daughter, and get away with it."

Everybody knows that Liza has her issues, but that is accepted as being her own eccentric behavior. But when someone bad mouths

Liza in the press, they have to stand up to Judy Garland's *and* Liza Minnelli's devoted legion of fans. You just don't treat a lady like that!

Liza is a very talented and gifted performer. She has a lot of issues, and perhaps she drinks too much, but that is another story. David didn't handle that at all well. According to him, "I'm just trying to save her from herself."

I repeatedly tried to tell David that this was not the thing to do. I said to him, "You just have to be a man about it, admit that the marriage is over, and just walk away from it."

But he was the kind of guy, who you would tell *not* to do something, and he would go ahead and do it anyway.

As a result of his stateside non-appreciation, David ended up packing his bags, selling the house in Memphis, and moving to England. Because of all of the gossipy stories that ran in the British tabloids about "The Liza and David Divorce," he was suddenly something of a recognizable name over there in his own right.

David ended up being invited to appear on a British reality show called *Help! I'm a Celebrity...Get Me Out Of Here!* as one of the celebrity contestants. He was on his way to Australia to do this TV show, and he was in Los Angeles staying at The Hollywood Roosevelt Hotel before he left. He invited me to dinner with him. That evening it was Tito Jackson and his date, actress Angie Dickenson, David and myself.

He said to me that evening, "I would really like to cancel my booking on this TV show, but they are paying me good money. We are talking *real* good money!" He told me that was the only reason he was doing it. He also took his bodyguard Willie Green along with him.

This was one of those shows where every week there are challenges and someone gets voted off the show, but David hung in there. They taped the show in the outback of Australia, and then it was broadcast in the U.K. Well, because of his staying power on the show, he became an even bigger celebrity over there. His appearance on that particular TV show made him an instant media star across the Atlantic.

One of the challenges had David getting into a tank full of water with baby alligators. He had to dive down into it, and stay there for several minutes. Even Prince Charles mentioned in the press that he admired David's bravery on the show. He became a media sensation in the U.K. overnight.

It was amazing how he truly hit the big time in the U.K. I went over there, and I witnessed it for myself. It was crazy! I would walk down the street with David, and people would recognize him and want to have a "selfie" photo with him, or get his autograph. I watched it unfold right before my very eyes. It was really something to witness first hand.

I was not performing in England at the time. The reason I went there was that David had sent for me, as one of his extravaganzas was being held in Liverpool. I was staying at the same hotel in Liverpool where David was. The hotel was called "A Hard Day's Night" named after The Beatles' hit song. It was an old hotel that had been renovated with a Beatles theme. I stayed in "The John Lennon Suite," and there was a white baby grand piano in the living room of the suite. There were framed photos of John Lennon on the walls.

That was the time when David wanted me to know how big a star he had become over there. So, he said, "Freda, let's walk to the pharmacy. It is about two or three blocks away."

So we started walking down the street and I saw for myself how people were reacting to him. They came up to him like I wasn't even there. David would have to say, "Oh, this is my friend, Freda Payne, who sang the song 'Band of Gold.'" After that, they instantly recognized who I was. But it was David who was the person they knew by sight. They had to be reminded who I was, and then they were warm and friendly to me too, and wanted my autograph.

I appeared in a movie called *Rhapsody* in 2002. It also featured actors like Ice-T, Fred Williamson, Glenn Plummer, Ali Woodson, Judge Joe Brown, and rapper M.C. Hammer. Peter Davy had put the *Rhapsody* project together with two other producers: Rick Appling and Fred Pittman, and they put their money into it. There was also another investor by the name of Patrick Miele.

The plot was basically what I call "Blaxploitation." It is described as being a film that shows the glamour of the music industry, but also shows the underside of it as rap, gangs, and organized crime collide into it. I played a woman whose son had gone astray. The film never went to mainstream theaters. It was one of those movies that went "straight to video." However, it was a fun film to do, and everyone on the crew was very impressed with me.

It was on the set of this film, where Ice-T met his future bride, Coco Austin. She was one of the extra's on the film.

Also on the film were three credited music supervisors, including Preston Glass. He did the music and the underscoring for the film *Rhapsody*. Some of you will recognize Preston's name for his work on several of Aretha Franklin's 1980s and 1990s albums. He also wrote a song for Whitney Houston called "Love Is a Contact Sport." Preston and I had previously worked on the album I did for Volt Records in 2001, *Come See About Me*. I liked his sense of professionalism, and we became friends.

In 2002 I received a phone call one day from Michael Feinstein and his manager, Allen J. Sviridoff. They were calling me to tell me they came up with this great idea of me doing a concert act with Darlene Love that would be billed as: *Love & Payne*. It was to be a unique show at Feinstein's at The Regency Hotel in New York City, and The Cinegrill in Hollywood at The Roosevelt Hotel.

I thought it was a great idea, and so did Darlene, so we both agreed to sign on for it. We all went over to Michael's house in the Los Feliz area of Los Angeles, and he and Darlene Love and I worked out what we were going to do and sing on-stage, and we rehearsed there for a couple of weeks. The show was conceived and created by Allen J. Sviridoff, and the musical arrangements were by Matt Catingub.

I had met Darlene Love, but I had never worked with her before. I certainly knew her sister, Edna Wright. Edna had been the lead vocalist of the singing trio Honeycone, who were on the Hot Wax Records division of Invictus Records when I had my hits including "Band of Gold." Honeycone's three biggest hit singles were "Want Ads," "Stick-Up" and "One Monkey Don't Stop No Show." "Want Ads" was released after I left Invictus. People would often think that was me singing that song, because her voice was so similar to mine. To tell you the truth, my sister Scherrie had recorded "Want Ads" first, but wasn't crazy about the song. Edna Wright heard it in the studio and loved it. She knew that Scherrie wasn't all that excited about "Want Ads," so Scherrie nonchalantly said to her, "I don't really like it. So, why don't you go ahead and record the song?" And that was Scherrie's big mistake. That could have been her big solo hit. Talk about "The Road We Didn't Take!" Sadly, Edna passed in 2020, and I attended her funeral.

I had always heard about Darlene from mutual friends, and I certainly knew her music. She was part of Phil Spector's famed Wall of Sound operation, and she was the voice of so many great hits in the 1960s as part of a lot of different groups including The Blossoms, The Crystals (the Number One hit "He's a Rebel"), and Bob B. Soxx & The Blue Jeans ("Zip-A-Dee-Doo-Dah"). She also had her own big solo hits as Darlene Love, like "Today I Met The Boy I'm Gonna Marry." She left the business for several years, and then had a big resurgence in the 1980s. She played the role of Danny Glover's wife in all four of the *Lethal Weapon* movies, went on tour with Cher, recorded a duet with Bette Midler, and frequently appeared on David Letterman's late night TV show. Every December she would be on the Letterman show singing her holiday hit, "Christmas (Baby Please Come Home)." Darlene's career certainly has come back in a big way. And, the Academy Award-winning documentary, *20 Feet From Stardom* from 2013, certainly put the spotlight on her.

In the structure of our show together, we were on the stage at the same time for the first two or three numbers, then we both had our solo spots, and then we came back together to close the show out. We had an opening number, and several songs we sang together, and of course we each sang our biggest hits. Among the songs we sang as a duet were Stevie Wonder's "All In Love Is Fair," Leon Russell's "A Song For You," and the Marvin Gaye hit "How Sweet It Is (To Be Loved By You)."

Darlene and I had a great time, and we drew enthusiastic audiences both in New York and Los Angeles. Even better than that, now Darlene and I are good friends. She and I share a lot in common, as both of our careers found us constantly having to reinvent ourselves. We are both actresses, singers, and survivors!

CHAPTER TWELVE

"The Beat Goes On"

In 2003 both Scherrie and I were invited to go to India for a wonderful adventure. I have been practicing yoga since 1973, and it has helped me to keep my body flexible and in good shape all of these years. A lot of the credit goes to my yoga teacher Bikram Choudhury, who is very well known in the yoga world now.

I first encountered and met Bikram Choudhury, in 1973 in Los Angeles. At that point I lived in an apartment building called The Hollywood Versailles Towers. It was located right off the corner of LaBrea on Hollywood Boulevard. There was a Pacific Security Bank right there catty-corner to where I lived, and in that building was The Holiday Spa. It was so conveniently located that I started going there regularly.

It was owned by Anne Marie Benstrom, and she had another spa that she later opened, called The Golden Door Spa in Phoenix, Arizona. I had just worked out and I was sitting in the lounge area with a couple of other ladies, and she came over to me and she said to us, "You know, there is this young man here, and he just arrived from Calcutta, India. His name is Bikram Choudhury, and he is going to be teaching a yoga class."

Anne said to a group of us, "I would like to invite you ladies to attend Bikram's yoga class that is about to start. Would you be interested?"

"Sure, why not?" I said, and we all walked in for a class.

Bikram at that time wasn't wearing Speedo's, which later became his traditional outfit. He had on a pair of cotton slacks and a short-sleeved plaid cotton shirt. That's how he was dressed for his first class there.

Upon seeing this sight I thought to myself, "Who is this guy? What kind of yoga instructor is this? He doesn't even have shorts on!" He was very naïve at that time, but he was able to instruct us in his yoga postures, and I was impressed.

He was only there two or three days, but I really liked him. When I returned to find him, he was gone. I asked someone about him, and they explained to me, "Oh, he has moved over to The Ambassador Hotel. And, he is teaching yoga classes over there."

When I went to The Ambassador Hotel, that is when I first noticed him wearing a pair of black Speedo's. I was very serious about yoga, and I really liked the way Bikram conducted his classes. Several other Hollywood celebrity ladies would be taught by him as well. He had Laine Kazan in his classes, as well as Shirley MacLaine, Raquel Welch, Juliet Prowse, and several other actresses and actors.

Bikram was only teaching his classes at The Ambassador Hotel for a couple of months, and the next thing I knew he had a new space he had leased in Beverly Hills on Wilshire Boulevard between Beverly Drive and Cañon Drive, the Sterling Plaza Building. In this office building there was a bank on the main floor, you had to go downstairs into the basement, where he had a nice space for his new yoga facility. That is were he really started to cultivate a following, and the people started flocking to his classes. As I understand, it was Shirley MacLaine who gave him the name: Bikram's Yoga College of India.

Bikram stayed in this location about six more years. He then moved to a location which was on Rexford Drive, right off the corner of Wilshire Boulevard, which was about three blocks from his former location. At this point Bikram continued to pick up celebrity clients like Quincy Jones, Herb Alpert and his wife Lani Hall, Kareem Abdul-Jabbar, and many more stars. He stayed on Rexford Drive for about five or six years, then he moved on to a facility on Robertson in Beverly Hills. So, he basically stayed in Beverly Hills for several years, and I followed his classes from place-to-place over the decades.

As Bikram's career continued to grow, he became more famous for his "hot yoga" technique. He then landed his first publishing deal, and he wrote a book called *Bikram's Beginning Yoga Class* (1978). I especially remember that book, because my son Gregory had just been born around then, in September of 1977. Bikram was shown on the cover with Juliet Prowse in one of his yoga poses. The pose she was in is called "The Standing Bow Pose." In fact, I appear in two of his books. I am shown doing "The Camel Pose" in the first one, and in the second one which came out in 1999, I appear in that one as well also doing "The Camel Pose."

Bikram is multi-talented. Although he was no Johnny Mathis, Bikram would sing *a capella* when we were in our "Resting Pose." His voice was very soothing, melodic, and comforting. His singing was very pleasant to hear during the yoga sessions. It was almost like listening to Johnny Mathis.

Then in 2003 Bikram invited Scherrie and I to go to India with him. How that came about was that Bikram had done his first album of him singing songs. The record was called *Bikram's Lounge*, and I am featured on several of the songs, singing with Bikram. I wrote some of the lyrics as well, and Scherrie was on the album and wrote lyrics too. It was an album I was very proud to have been involved with. The album was produced by Bappi Lahiri and Stephen Mehlert.

Among the songs I did were "The Om Song," "Love Is Life," and "Love Is Divine." Another one I sang was the melodic "A-O Song." They had a distinctive Hindu sound to them. They were fun listening, and some of the songs are very festive. I would sing my part in English, and Bikram would sing his in Hindi.

The album and Bikram's books would be featured for sale, and his operation had grown to the point where he had franchised branches of Bikram's Yoga in Paris and London, and other places around the globe. By now he had fallen in love and married a woman from his home town in India.

On that trip to India our party consisted of Bikram and his wife, Rajashree, Scherrie and me, a former Mr. Universe—Roland Kickinger, and another yoga instructor whose name is Leslie Christianson. She is known as a yoga champion. Bikram hosted a gala performance one night, and I did several of my songs from his album, and Scherrie performed as well. Scherrie and I both have beautiful green and red tourmaline necklaces with gold clasps that were gifts presented to us on that trip, from a wealthy and successful man we met in India who went by the name of Mr. Roy. He owned his own domestic airline in India, and he also had his own resort which he owned and operated.

Our Indian adventure lasted two weeks, and we traveled to Calcutta, New Delhi, Agra, and to Mumbai—formerly known as Bombay. When we went to Agra, we visited the Taj Mahal, which is known to be one of the Seven Wonders of the World. "Google" it and you can find out about its fascinating history. While there, I did some yoga on the terrace. I was with Rajashree, and the champion yoga instructor Leslie. It was a great and spiritual experience.

It is interesting to find out how people perceive us. We know what we look like in the mirror, but we can never truly see ourselves as others do. Case in point: a book called *Why I Love Black Women* by Michael Eric Dyson, which was published in 2003. Dyson is the *New York Times* best-selling author of several award winning books, has been a professor at Georgetown University, is currently a professor at Vanderbilt University, regularly writes opinion pieces for major newspapers, and is frequently a guest on CNN and MSNBC. *Ebony* magazine named him one of their "100 Most Influential Afro-Americans."

In this book I was surprised to find that in it, there was an amusingly elaborate six-page love-letter / Valentine written about me. It was crazy flattering to read. I am used to reviews about my music or my acting or my shows, but this seemed to be a personal review about me, and it reminded me of my younger self.

Apparently, Michael was already a fan of mine, and he had fallen even deeper in love with me from a cover story that *Ebony* magazine did on me in January of 1973. The article featured me modeling bathing suits, and apparently it made quite an impression on Mr. Dyson. He elaborately described how I looked on this partic-ular cover, and what he thought of it. In part he wrote, "Freda's regal nose was in perfect symmetry with her almost hidden ears, and her perfectly manicured and long, painted nails capped fingers on hands that were curled in a glistening, sensuous pose." (19)

Three decades had passed since that magazine issue, and I ran into Michael at a party in Hollywood. In his book he described meet-ing at that particular event. When he encountered me he found me to be: "A 55-year-old woman from whose every pore there screamed a sensuality so intense that I had to remind myself that I wasn't in a pri-vate dream where I might range freely over my imagination without censure. Freda Payne is still insanely fine, as fine as she was when I'd spot occasional clips of her on television performing her monster hit 'Band of Gold.'…I had seen her in *Sprung*, and in Eddie Murphy's *Nutty Professor II: The Klumps* and knew that she was still beautiful, but in person her form defies gravity." (19)

Michael then described asking me to dance with him at this party, and the fact that—in his eyes—I was something of a fantasy come true. He claimed he was wanting to impress me with his dance moves; however, it was I who impressed him: "The moment we hit the floor, Freda was a flurry of acrobatic activity; she twirled, gyrated, twisted, and moved her body with such electrifying sexiness that it was all I could do to watch." (19)

According to this account, Michael Eric Dyson and I danced three dances together at this party. He then wrote, "After I hugged her, I left the floor…I was floating on a cloud of sheer nostalgia that materialized into a reality that exceeded my wildest imagination." (19) Needless to say, he certainly gushed on paper! When I read this elaborate short story about this chance encounter with me, I was quite tickled and flattered to say the least.

I have always taken good care of myself, and I always want to look my best. In this particular instance, I received unmistakable validation that my beauty regimen was paying off. Apparently, Michael Eric Dyson very strongly approved of the results. "Electrifying sexiness?" Okay, I will gladly accept that compliment!

I did a movie in 2007 entitled *Cordially Invited*. In it I played the role of a bourgeois woman. It was a good comedy film, and the plot of it was about a lady whose son was getting married to a woman whom my character didn't approve of at all. His bride-to-be was someone who lived on the poor side of town. In the film, I didn't just consider her to be from "the hood," I referred to her as being from "the jungle." I had some great comic dialogue in this one.

My character, as a mother, felt that her son should marry someone equal to him. The thing about that is when somebody is in love, or if there is a chemistry there, you can't dictate what happens. Love doesn't discriminate.

In 2007 I released an album called *On The Inside*. When I recorded it, there was no record label actively involved. It was an album that was recorded in 2002, but wasn't released for five years. Among the songs I did was one called "Welcome To The Human Race," which came out really well. It was a song I wrote together with the album's producer, Preston Glass, and I was really pleased with the production. When I was unable to land a record deal to release it, I finally took control and released the album myself on my own Band of Gold Records label.

In 2008 I headlined *The Palm Springs Follies*. I did it that November and December. It was a revolving show that also featured seasoned showgirls. They had to be 55 years old or older to be in the show. And those ladies could still dance! I was the featured star, and I would have my own solo spot, and then the ladies would come out and perform their glamorous routines. The oldest one was in her 80s, and she still had great legs. It was run by a man by the name of Riff Markowitz, and he ran "a tight ship." His reputation for being difficult certainly preceeded him.

Mary Wilson performed at *The Palm Springs Follies* after I did. I said to her, "How did you get along with Riff?"

And she said, "Oh girl, he liked me! He was strict, but I had no complaints."

I know why Riff liked Mary—because of all of her sequins and glamour, and the fact that she was the original member of the world's most famous girl group of the 1960s, The Supremes. That appealed to him greatly. The show was comprised of all senior performers who were amazingly talented.

I appeared on the popular TV show *American Idol* in 2009. It was fun and it was exciting, and I was so thrilled to be given the "star treatment" on this popular program. What had happened was that I had just flown back to the United States from London. I had been in England where I had appeared in one of David Gest's big production shows. I had just landed at LAX airport. I was still on the plane, and we were being taxied to the gate, when I turned on my cell phone.

On the phone there was a voice message from one of my agents, Steve Ford, who called me and said, "Freda, guess what? I booked you and Thelma Houston for *American Idol*. They are doing a disco segment, and they want the two of you doing your hit records. Plus they've got K.C. & The Sunshine Band performing on it, too."

I was just over-the-moon to hear this news. I had a two week warning that this booking was coming up, so I had just enough time to go on an instant diet. I certainly didn't want to have a chubby stomach on *American Idol!*

I sang "Band of Gold," Thelma performed her hit "Don't Leave Me This Way," and Harry Wayne "K.C." Casey sang his disco classic "Get Down Tonight." I had a wonderful time doing the show and it was great exposure for me. It was seen by something like 40 million people! They had a huge viewing audience, especially then, as *American Idol* was at the height of its popularity. This was before *The Voice* and *America's Got Talent* came along.

Even my neighbors who live across the street from me, Mike Gleason and his partner Dave Kettle, threw me a huge party after the taping of the show. Since we had done it "live" on the air for the East Coast time zone, I was able to go from the studio to home, and be at the party in time for us to watch it in West Coast time. And, when I saw my performance I was pleased that I looked svelte, and no tummy what-so-ever! So my diet had paid off, and all I did was to stop drinking my red wine.

On June 25, 2009 I was in Palm Springs. I had been invited there by my yoga teacher, Bikram Choudhury, to participate in a teachers' training graduation class. He had wanted me to sing at the ceremony.

When I arrived that afternoon, he was still teaching a class. So I spotted his wife, Rajashree, in the lobby of the hotel, and I sat with her until Bikram's class came to an end. While sitting there her phone rang. She answered it, and then suddenly put it down, as if she had seen a ghost. She looked at me and I wondered what she was so surprised about.

She turned to me and said, "Freda, I just got a call from someone telling me that Michael Jackson just died."

"What?" I said. "Let me call someone who will know." With that, I called David Gest, who was in Liverpool, England at the time.

When I got him on the phone I said, "Did you hear that Michael Jackson just died?"

He said to me, "No, he is still alive. They have taken him to the UCLA Medical Center, and they are working on reviving him now. He is not dead!"

Moments later, Rajashree received a second phone call to confirm the fact that it was all over the news that Michael had indeed passed away. Now there was no mistaking that it was true.

I called David back and he was crying on the phone, and all he could say was, "It's true. It's true, he's really gone."

The irony was that Michael was due to fly back to London to open his tour at The O2 Arena, and then to go on the road. He had been in Los Angeles rehearsing for months for these shows and a projected concert tour. The company Live Nation had him under contract to do 47 shows in different places around the world, and there were some disputes as to this being too many shows in a row. Michael claimed he hadn't agreed to do all of those shows, but they had him in a corner.

David Gest immediately flew back to Los Angeles for Michael's memorial service, which was held at The Staples Center. I accompanied him, and it was an amazingly sad event to witness. Michael's children—Blanket, Paris, and Prince—were there on-stage. The who's who of Hollywood turned out. Michael's brother, Jermaine Jackson, sang the song "Smile" as a tribute to his brother. There wasn't a dry eye in the house. Afterward there was a service at Forest Lawn Cemetery where only close family and close friends were invited.

The following year, I was invited to be part of an all-star re-recording of the '80s mega-star charity record, "We Are The World." The original 1985 version of "We Are The World" was recorded to raise money for the starving people in Africa. This new version of the song was done to raise money for the victims of a devastating earthquake in Haiti.

The new recording was entitled "We Are The World 25 For Haiti," and it was recorded on February 1, 2010. It was a 14 hour recording session, and had over 85 musicians involved in it. First of all, there were 36 vocal soloists, two guitar soloists (Carlos Santana and Orianthi), and an archival appearance by the late Michael Jackson. The solo vocalists included Barbra Streisand, Miley Cyrus, Pink, Vince Vaughn, Adam Levine, Usher, Tony Bennett, Janet Jackson, Jennifer Hudson, Justin Bieber, Kanye West, Fergie, and many more.

Then there was a choir of 59 all-stars, and that's where I was heard on this recording. However this was not just any choir, its members included: Gladys Knight, Natalie Cole, Jamie Foxx, Harry Connick Jr., John Legend, Verdine White, Joe Jonas, Kevin Jonas, Robin Thicke, Brian Wilson and Al Jardine of The Beach Boys, Will I. Am of The Black Eyed Peas, and Ann and Nancy Wilson of Heart. You could say I was in excellent company!

We were in the recording studio, standing next to each other on risers, so that each row was taller than the one in front of them. I was happy to find out that I was standing right next to Barbra Streisand. That was a real thrill. She is my idol! I was surprised to find that she didn't have much to say. I said "hello" to her, and she looked at me quizzically.

I said to her, "It is a pleasure to meet you, Barbra. You know, I was born the same year as you."

She just looked at me as though to say, "Oh really?"

Although we didn't have an involved conversation, she was very pleasant. And, it was just a thrill to stand shoulder-to-shoulder next to her. I have admired her singing for decades. And, we literally started our careers at the same time, in 1963. It made me flash back to when I first saw her at Mister Kelly's in Chicago in the early '60s before she was heralded as being a huge superstar.

On my other side was dancer / actress Julianne Hough of *Dancing With The Stars* fame. There were certainly a lot of the top stars in music in that room. And guess how I got to be in this distinguished company? Quincy Jones. Since Quincy was producing the song, and that whole session, he had a hand in casting who he wanted to work with. And, happily, I am on that list!

It was a wonderful experience for me to be there, included in all of the excitement. It was like receiving a surprise gift; it was amazing. I had great conversations with L.L. Cool J. I wanted to touch his stomach so that I could feel how tight his stomach muscles were.

So, I said to him, "Let me just hit you in the stomach once L.L., so I can see how tight your stomach is!"

He just laughed.

I ran into Jamie Foxx at the catering truck that was there. He was instructing the waitress how he wanted a peanut butter and jelly sandwich.

"But Mr. Foxx, I can make you something better than that," she said to him.

"No," he insisted, what he really wanted was a peanut butter and jelly sandwich.

My son Gregory was with me, and he took a photo of me with Kanye West, who was very friendly. And, Gregory took a photo of Justin Bieber, who was just 16 at the time. There were a lot of people there, and although the room was full of stars, everyone was cool. In other words: they checked their egos at the door. Everyone in the studio was very respectful of the cause, and there was an air of total professionalism to the proceedings. Nobody was tripping, or acting like a diva. There was no cursing in the room, even from the rappers.

Of course, Patti Austin was there. She has always been one of Quincy's favorite musical discoveries. Quincy is actually Patti's godfather, as he knew her parents really well. Enrique Iglesias was there as one of the soloists. When Enrique and I passed in the hallway, I was amazed to see how tall he happens to be. He is about 6'5" tall, and so handsome too.

I have to say that Quincy really came through for me this time. I was so happy to be there, and I was so appreciative he invited me. With all of the recordings I have made in my career, and considering all of the time that I have known Quincy, this was the first and only time we were in a recording studio together. Even though I was in a cast of many stars on "We Are The World," it was fun to be in the recording studio with him. We have been friends all these years, since our early days in New York City, and he still looks out for me. Quincy is a true friend.

Following David Gest's divorce from Liza Minnelli, by the early 2010s he had moved to England. I loved visiting him there, and because of his newfound life in the U.K., he had a whole new circle of celebrities to associate with, and to promote. One of them was Sir Cliff Richard. Cliff is a huge star in the U.K. and Europe, and he has been releasing hit records since the '50s, when he was a "teen idol." He had a huge string of Number One hits dating back to 1959 when he recorded "Living Doll" with The Drifters. Then there were his 1960s chart toppers including "Please Don't Tease" and "I Love You" with The Shadows. Then in 1979 he was back on top with "We Don't Talk Anymore." He was as big as The Beatles and Elvis Presley in the U.K. and in Europe, and his career has endured all these years. Cliff has also been knighted by the Queen of England, so he is now officially Sir Cliff Richard.

It was at one of David Gest's events in London where I first met Cliff Richard. We immediately hit it off as friends. It was an event that I performed at, and also on the bill were the original Stylistics' lead singer Russell Tompkins Jr., Dorothy Moore, Billy Paul, Percy Sledge, and Martha Reeves. David absolutely loved Martha, and he also really loved Percy Sledge as well. It was one of those shows where he invited a lot of his favorite people to appear on the bill. His events had suddenly grown to become these chic affairs, because he was at the height of his newfound celebrity status. David Gest was suddenly "the flavor of the year" in the U.K.

When David introduced me to Sir Cliff Richard, he said to me, "I'm having a meeting with Cliff about a new project, and I want you involved in it—Cliff is going to record an album of duets with classic American soul artists, and I want you on it. After the album is released, there is going to be a tour as well, and I want you on that, too."

How could I argue with such a plan? It was David's idea to match Cliff with all of these famed R&B singing stars, and to call the resulting album *Soulicious*.

For *Soulicious*, David really pulled out the stops on the amount and caliber of R&B musical talent on that album doing duets with Sir Richard. The album includes Cliff singing with Roberta Flack, Valerie Simpson, Deniece Williams, Percy Sledge, Candi Staton, Dennis Edwards of The Temptations, Brenda Holloway, Marilyn McCoo & Billy Davis Jr. of The Fifth Dimension, Billy Paul, Peabo Bryson, and several more.

The majority of the album was recorded in Memphis, and I went there to sing my duet. A couple of the tracks—Cliff's duet with Valerie Simpson, "Every Piece Of My Broken Heart" and "When I Was Your Baby" with Roberta Flack—were recorded in New York City. The reason Valerie didn't want to leave New York for Memphis was that her husband and writing and singing partner, Nicholas Ashford, was gravely ill, He passed away while this album was in production.

The *Soulicious* album received great reviews, and was very popular when it was released in October of 2011. *Soulicious*, made it to the Top Ten on both the U.K. and Australian album charts. I was certainly in very good company on this album, and I was happy for the association with the classy Sir Cliff Richard.

My duet with Cliff, "Saving a Life," is the opening track on the album, and it has the distinction of being the only single released off it. I was surprised that it didn't do better on the charts. The song is so infectiously good, it really should have been an even bigger hit! It was produced by Lamont Dozier, and was written by Beau Dozier, who is Lamont's son. In fact, Beau's music publishing company is appropriately called "Like Father Like Son Music."

Not only did I get star billing on the *Soulicious* album, but there was also a concert tour of the same name, which played all over the U.K. Naturally I was a part of it. The tour lasted three weeks.

The Soulicious Tour happened in 2011, and I had originally met Cliff in London a year or two before that. Sir Cliff Richard is really up there on my scale of "integrity" and "class." And he is religious, too. There is not a mean bone in his body; he's a really nice guy.

I have to tell you, that was the best and most luxurious concert road tour I have ever been on, in my entire career. In each city we went to, we were treated as kings and queens. After the tour ended I said to myself, "So, *this* is how the really big, big, big stars do it!"

I had my own Range Rover, with my own personal driver to take me from city-to-city. Not a van or a tour bus; I had my own private vehicle! There was the best catering throughout this tour. When I say catering, I mean the best. It wasn't like a roadie was sent out to get pizzas or take-away Chinese food.

The reason that I appreciated our treatment on the Cliff Richard *Soulicious Tour* was that I had covered the same cities before, and it was in direct contrast to this luxury handling of a road show. There was a tour that I did in 2002 with Edwin Starr and Martha Reeves, and that was like "roughing it" in comparison. They did not have catering at all backstage. We would arrive in a little town or city, and you were left to go off and fend for yourself. We were told: "Go to a supermarket," or "Go to a fast food place," or "Go to a restaurant wherever you find one."

Once you have seen the best, you can't turn back! And, this tour with Cliff Richard was simply *The Best!*

In 2014 I was featured on two new albums. One of them was a guest appearance on an album with The David Berger Jazz Orchestra called: *Sing Me A Love Song, Harry Warren's Undiscovered Standards.* Harry Warren was an amazingly prolific songwriter who wrote such songs as "Lullaby of Broadway" from the film *Gold Diggers of 1935*, and "Chattanooga Choo Choo" from the film *Sun Valley Serenade* (1941). He was also the writer of the huge Etta James R&B classic, "At Last." I sang four Harry Warren songs on the album to a full orchestra, which included "I Wonder Who," "Sing Me a Love Song," "But Here We Are," and "With Your Hand in Mine."

That same year I released my all-jazz album, *Come Back To Me Love*, which was produced by Bill Cunliffe and Al Pryor, who is the A&R Director for Mack Avenue Records. The way this album came together was through Gretchen C. Valade, who has her own recording label, based in Detroit, called Mack Avenue Records. Mack Avenue is a famous street in Detroit, so this album meant a lot to me. It made it something of a true hometown project.

On the album I finally had the opportunity to record a full disc of nothing but jazz, and it felt great. I performed songs like "You'd Be So Nice To Come Home To," "Spring Can Really Hang You Up The Most," and the blues number "I'd Rather Drink Muddy Water." One of my favorite songs on this album was "The Midnight Sun" with music by Lionel Hampton and lyrics by Johnny Mercer. That came out so nicely. Another one I loved was "The Island," by Victor Martins and Ivan Lins, with beautiful lyrics by Alan and Marilyn Bergman. Since I do so much jazz in my concert act, it was great to just concentrate on some of my favorite jazz numbers.

Another really great aspect of this album was that all of the recording was done at the world-famous Studio A at Capitol Records in Hollywood. This marked my second time recording at that studio since the 1970s when I was signed to Capitol Records. That was the same studio where Frank Sinatra, Nat King Cole, The Beatles, and Nancy Wilson recorded some of their finest music. And, I had the chance to record with a full orchestra with strings. It was really quite an experience!

Also in 2014, I appeared in a TV film called *The Divorce*. It starred Dawnn Lewis, Judy Pace, Jonelle Allen, Tammi Mac, Tatyana Ali, and Vanessa Bell Calloway. Dawnn plays Yolanda Massey, who works as a TV anchorwoman. When she gets a divorce she decides to celebrate at home with her girlfriends, assorted friends, and her mother—played by Jonelle Allen. The part I played was the role of a bourgeois society lady by the name of Vivian. My dear friend Judy Pace was also in it. She played Phoebe, and her character is a comical woman who was even more stuck-up and affected than my character!

During the evening, at that gathering, the plot goes through a bunch of silly twists and turns. One girl turns up, and she runs into the woman—who is my character, Vivian—who had to give her up for adoption in London years ago. The girl was adopted by a couple in the U.S. who wanted children, but could not have a baby of their own. In the plot of the film she finds out that it was my character who was really her mother. She then confronts me about it. So there is a whole lot of drama in that.

This was a dramatic play that was also filmed. It was my friend, Donald B. Welch, who wrote and directed it. The first play that I did for Donald was called *A Change Is Gonna Come*. That was in Philadelphia in 1998. Before I knew him, he had reached out to my agent, Bill Baron, and booked me for the play.

Donald is very well respected in the business, and in fact Will Smith is one of his main supporters and a long time friend. They are both from Philadelphia.

Donald moved out here to LA in the year 2000. Then after that, I did his play *A Change Is Gonna Come* at a small theater in LA called

The Cass Theater. It was just a little 65 seat theater space.

The first time we did *The Divorce* in Hollywood, it was also at The Cass Theater. The second time we did it in Los Angeles was at The Wilshire Ebell Theater which seats 1,500. Then we did it in Sherman Oaks, California. That was the production that was filmed, and made commercially available on DVD.

In 2016, I lost one of my best friends when David Gest suddenly died. This came as a total shock to me, since he was only 62 years old at the time. The date that is given for David's death is Tuesday, April 12, 2016. However, I have to explain that he died a few days before that. His body was found naked on the bathroom floor in his suite at The Four Seasons Hotel in London. According to people I spoke with at the time, they had talked to David on Friday, April 8, then he suddenly was unreachable and didn't return anyone's phone calls. So, he was probably dead the whole weekend.

I spoke to a lady by the name of Margaret Harry. She lives in Liverpool, and we had become friends through David. She was a friend of David's, and she was also one his sponsors in England. Margaret has her own business there, and she is a multi-millionaire. According to her, she last talked to David on Friday. He was supposed to be taking the train from London to Liverpool to attend an afternoon event with her the following day. Suddenly, Margaret couldn't reach him, and he was not returning her phone calls. This made her suspicious that something wasn't right.

Another person who stopped hearing from David as well, and felt very guilty about it, was Peabo Bryson. Peabo had told me that he and David had been talking pretty regularly at the time. You know when you see someone's "caller ID" come up on your phone, but you are in the middle of something, or you just want to talk later? And, for whatever reason, you don't pick up the call.

Well, that was what happened to Peabo. David had called him, and Peabo decided he would rather talk later, so he let it go to "voice mail." All of David's friends knew that he was very persistent, and he would continue to call you back until he reached you. Knowing that, when David called that week, Peabo just let David's call go unanswered, never realizing that was the last call he would ever receive from him.

Peabo told me that the last time he heard from David was on April 8 as well. After we all got the news that David had passed, Peabo said to me, "I feel so guilty that I didn't pick up that last call. Maybe he was feeling bad about something, or maybe he was feeling sick and he was reaching out for help."

Another person who I talked to was David's "right hand man," Imad Handi. He worked for David as his assistant, and he was also a friend and bodyguard to David. He had phoned David in his hotel room, and received no answer. Knowing what David was like, Imad figured, "Oh, that's just David. He must be busy and doesn't want to be bothered with talking."

That was Friday, and nobody heard from him all day Saturday. Nobody heard from him all day Sunday. But his friends were not alarmed. They just figured that was David being David, and not wanting to be bothered.

By Monday, Imad said that he was getting suspicious that something really wasn't right. So he called the manager at The Four Seasons Hotel, and said, "Something is wrong. We need to get the passkey and get into David's room."

The manager replied, "But sir, he has a 'Do Not Disturb' order on his suite, and he is accepting no phone calls."

They finally decided that four days was abnormally long for a person to not be seen or heard from, so Imad and the security man went to the room, and opened it up. There David was, deceased on the bathroom floor. Someone also told me that when the autopsy report came in, they listed the official cause of death as being a massive stroke.

I had talked to him about four or five days before he passed away. The funny thing was that David and I had a period where we were not speaking. We had a falling out and it lasted about three years. We had just patched things up, and were communicating regularly again.

When I heard the word about his passing, I was working in New York, having rehearsals with Michael Feinstein. We were going to be performing as part of the *Jazz At Lincoln Center* series of concerts. It was a Michael Feinstein show featuring me, Marilyn Maye, and a couple of up-and-coming young singers including Veronica Swift.

I was in my hotel room in New York, and I was looking at my cell phone, and I found a text from a guy by the name of Jason Abrams. The text message said, "Oh Freda! I send my condolences. I just heard about David Gest's passing."

My first reaction was, "What!? That is not possible."

So, I texted Jason back and said, "That is a mistake. David's latest all-star concert tour in England, that I am on, is being billed as *David Gest Is Not Dead But Alive And Well And Living With Soul.* You must have read that wrong."

The way this came about was that David was booked to appear on the U.K. edition of the TV reality show *Big Brother* in early 2016, and he was one of the celebrities locked in the *Big Brother* house, along with Angela Bowie, and several others. The object of the game is that over a dozen people have to live together in a house while being filmed constantly. Everything is lovely at first, then conflicts happen, and ultimately people are either voted off the show, or they leave voluntarily. This was in January of 2016. While in the house, Angela's ex-husband, David Bowie, had died and the cast was informed of it.

Somehow, gossip circulated regarding *Big Brother* saying: "David died." A rumor started that the "David" who had "died" was Mr. Gest, and not Mr. Bowie. Since David Gest was clearly alive, he decided to mount this all-star tour to announce that he really isn't dead. David was very savvy at jumping on a publicity bandwagon and riding it as far as he could. He knew how to "work it." So that's how the concert tour came about.

The debut of the *David Gest Is Not Dead But Alive And Well And Living With Soul* concert tour was to take place in London on July 1, 2016, and it was to include me, Peabo Bryson, Billy Paul, Melba Moore, Deniece Williams, Anita Ward, and Russell Thompkins of The Stylistics. Also on the bill was Dina Carroll, a British singer who had a string of U.K. hits in the 1980s and 1990s.

Ten minutes after I texted Jason Abrams and told him he was mistaken about David Gest's passing, right after I hit "send," the phone rang. I got a call from my agent, Scott Stander. Scott started the conversation by saying, "Well, I guess you heard the news."

"What news?" I said.

"David Gest: he died."

"What!?!"

"It's on the news already."

I was in shock. It hit me like a ton of bricks. After all these years of having David as a dear friend, he was suddenly gone forever.

I was still booked to perform on the *David Gest Is Not Dead But Alive And Well And Living With Soul* concert tour. The odd irony of it all was that it was put together to announce that David was alive and well, but by the time the shows started he actually was dead! And, the poster that was created for the shows actually depicted David coming out of a coffin! What a strange twist of events.

How the shows carried on was because Imad Handi decided to pick up the reins of the planned tour, because he knew all of the people who were booked on it, and he enlisted the help of a man to assist him financially to make certain the tour continued smoothly. That man was Barry Silkman, whose nickname is "Silky." He is a former ball player in the U.K., and he is the one who facilitated the tour, so that it could continue.

I was made the spokeswoman for the tour, and I was the host of the show. I was the one who introduced all of the singers on-stage. Originally, it was going to be David Gest who was to play host, but I was given the task, and it was a fitting way to remember my dear deceased friend.

The same year that David died, I had lost my half-stepsister in March. Her name was Frances Gray, and she was an actress. She was the daughter of my stepfather, Sam Farley. Then Billy Paul passed away on April 24, 2016. He was booked on this last tour of David's U.K. shows, but never made it.

A series of fun promotional events came about when I became involved in the 2016 release of my very own line of limited edition chocolate candy bars. What a fun idea! When this opportunity was proposed to me, I gladly accepted this tribute. First of all, the candy was delicious, and expertly made. And, each candy bar had a stylish photo of me on the wrapper.

The candy bars were made by Hollywood Sweets in Los Angeles, and this all came about as the idea of promoters Mike Johnson and Stephanie Mines. They introduced me to Jonathan Plough of Hollywood Sweets. The first promotional event we did was held in The Hollywood Sweets Candy Store on Hollywood Boulevard, which is in a shopping mall at the complex that houses The Dolby Theater. That is where the Academy Awards are telecast from, next to Grauman's Chinese Theater. That afternoon it was me, and my friends Mary Wilson, and actresses Judy Pace, Gloria Hendry, and Beverly Todd. RuPaul had his own brand of candy bars as well.

Another of the promotional events that was held to advertise my own "Freda Payne: Dark Chocolate" and "Freda Payne: Milk Chocolate" bars involved Mary Wilson and Linda Clifford, who also had their own pair of chocolate bars with their images on the wrapper to promote at the same time. Each lady chose what they wanted to be in their candy bar, whether it was raspberries, caramel, almonds or whatever. We had a ball together when Amoeba Records on Sunset Boulevard in Hollywood gave us a celebrity autographing session. And what did we autograph? Why our very own candy bars, of course!

One of the most fun aspects of this whole chocolate bar promotion was the fact that we had a hand in fashioning what was in the candy bars. Both the milk chocolate and dark chocolate "Freda Payne" bars had swirls of white chocolate in it as well as caramel and marshmallows. I had been called "sweet" before, but now I was officially "sweet as candy!"

Glynn Turman and I were the 2017 honorees by an organization called The Giving Back Corporation. Each year Giving Back stages an awards ceremony to fund their scholarships and financial aid to schools, so it was a very worthy cause. Together we were the stars of their 18th annual Celebrity Spring Toast / Roast on April 29 of that year.

The reason that I was chosen to be honored came about largely because my friend Kenneth Reynolds was one of the organizers for the event. I had met him in the 1970s when he was working on TV's *The Dick Cavett Show* in New York. Ken and I had been friends since that time. Ken was known in the industry as a publicist and event promoter, and he worked for several record companies including Arista and Polygram. Ken was friendly with everyone in the business, and he worked with LaBelle—Patti LaBelle, Nona Hendryx, and Sarah Dash—and he helped launch Whitney Houston's recording career. He was also known for his famous house parties. You never knew who you would run into at one of Ken's parties. And that is the truth!

The Giving Back ceremony took place at the Doubletree Hilton Hotel in Los Angeles. It was very flattering to be honored by them. They produced a video presentation about my career which was quite impressive, and about Glynn's career, then various people would get up and talk about us amusingly, sort of like a roast. Also, my talented sister Scherrie got up on-stage and sang the song "Here's To Life" directly to me, and it brought tears to my eyes. Since the way the evening was set up was a "toast and roast" it was a lot of fun. I was thankful to Kenneth for having a role in bestowing this honor upon me. Although Ken passed away in 2018, I will always have fond memories of him—and his parties too. He is dearly missed by all of his friends.

I was in a 2017 film called *Kinky*, and the man who plays my husband is Obba Babatundé, who works all the time. Vivica A. Fox is in the film as well. I had worked with Obba so many times before, that we were almost like an acting team! In this particular film, Obba plays a man whose son was a successful stockbroker, who deals in hedge funds. His character is very particular about who his son is dating. I portrayed the role of Mrs. Bernard, the mother.

From 2004 to 2018 I had the unique opportunity to star in a new musical play based on the life of Ella Fitzgerald. The play, which was entitled *Ella Fitzgerald: First Lady of Song*, ran at several venues from The Crossroads Theater in New Brunswick, New Jersey, to Alexandria, Virginia's MetroStage, to The Delaware Theater Company in Wilmington, and along the way I received great reviews for it. It is an Equity stage play musical. The Crossroads Theater has been presented with a Special Tony Award For Regional Theater.

According to *The Washington Post*, "'Ella' has plenty of swing thanks to Freda Payne's spot-on singing as Fitzgerald…Payne's scatting absolutely zips in 'How High The Moon,' and 'Mack The Knife' becomes a joyful riot of upbeat swoops and beep-beep-a-dos…Payne sings with the jubilance of a kid skipping down the sidewalk." (20)

Throughout my life I have been touched by the music of Ella Fitzgerald. She has always been among my favorite singers, along with Sarah Vaughn and Billie Holiday. I actually had the opportunity to meet Ella once when I was living in New York City in the

1960s. Ella was performing at a nightclub, The Riverboat, which was located in the basement of The Empire State Building.

My friend Faye Treadwell, who managed The Drifters, called me and told me she was going to see Ella Fitzgerald, and she wanted to know if I wanted to go with her. Ella was amazing to see live on-stage. That voice, that power, and her magnetic presence were unmistakable. As an added thrill after the show, Faye and I got to go backstage to meet the elegant Miss Fitzgerald. When we walked into the dressing room, I was in total awe. I could feel chills up and down my arms, like it was a spiritual thing. There was no one quite like Ella, and when I met her I was absolutely starstruck.

How my starring in the production of *Ella Fitzgerald: First Lady of Song* took place dates back to when I was performing in *Jelly's Last Jam* with Maurice Hines. We had dressing rooms that were next door to each other. Before the show I would often sing to myself in my dressing room, just to warm up my voice. One day Maurice said to me, "You know who you sound exactly like, Freda?"

"Who?" I asked.

"Ella Fitzgerald."

I was very flattered by that compliment. After *Jelly's Last Jam* was finished, Maurice called me and asked me if I wanted to star in a new stage play tribute to Ella called *Ella Fitzgerald: First Lady of Song*. Naturally, I loved this idea. And so I was cast as the amazing Miss Fitzgerald.

Maurice told me that I was the first person he thought of for this musical play. However, he had a conversation with Patti Austin. He told her that he was considering me to star as Ella.

As Maurice explained to me, "I was talking to Patti Austin about this part. And I mentioned to her that I was going to call you about doing this role."

And she said to him, "Well, are you sure Freda can handle this?"

I was startled to hear she had said this. Maybe she had not heard me singing jazz? Maybe she was not aware of my scatting abilities? You would have to be able to "scat" if you are going to play Ella Fitzgerald believably. That is certainly something that I can do.

There are certain people who come to see my show, and they will come up to me afterward and say, "I didn't know you could sing like that and 'scat' like that." They are not aware of my jazz chops. They always think of me as being a pop / soul singer. I have been doing scat since the beginning of my career.

Maurice first directed me in 2004 for this Ella Fitzgerald play. The first time we did it was in New Brunswick, New Jersey at The Crossroads Theater. Ella's music has been such an inspiration to me throughout the years, that I was glad to have this outlet to pay her tribute, and to introduce her music to new generations of jazz fans.

When Aretha Franklin died it was on August 16, 2018, and I went back to Detroit for her funeral. I attended it with my boyfriend, James Michael Goetz. That funeral service went on for nine-and-a-half hours. It was the longest funeral I had ever attended. There was a public showing of her body where friends, family and the public could come and view her, and pay their last respects. This elaborate funeral actually went on for three days of open-casket public viewings, and each day they changed her clothing. One day she had on all red. Then the next day she had on all blue. And then on the day of her service and burial, she had on all gold. Each day she was wearing Christian Louboutin high heels to match her dress. No expense was spared for The Queen of Soul.

Many dignitaries spoke that day, including several men of the cloth. Bill Clinton spoke, and Minister Louis Farrakhan was there but never publicly spoke. He told me, "The spirit did not move me to speak because it had already been said." One of the most dynamic speakers to eulogize Aretha that day was professor and author Michael Eric Dyson.

Back when we were growing up in Detroit, Aretha and I had a

mutual friend. His name was Donald Meadows. I don't know whether or not he is still around. He was in grade school and middle school with me. I remember when Aretha was 12, because Donald and I were both 12 at the same time. Donald was a member of Aretha's father's church, New Bethel Gospel Church, where he would see and hear Reverend C. L. Franklin preach, and listen to the three Franklin sisters—Aretha, Carolyn, and Erma—sing. My family belonged to another church. Our church was Bethel AME, which stands for African Methodist Episcopal, located on the corner of Fredrick and San Antoine.

I started singing around Detroit when I was about 13, and Aretha started singing solos in her father's church when she was 12 years old. Donald would tell Aretha what I was doing. Then he would come back to me to tell me what Aretha was doing. We had that kind of relationship, through Donald.

As our budding singing careers unfolded as young girls, we certainly knew who each other was, and what we were doing. In the early '70s, we were both recording artists, and sometimes we would both appear on some of the same shows. Aretha sometimes felt threatened by other female performers, like Natalie Cole, Gladys Knight, and Patti LaBelle. However, we were very respectful of each other. We admired each other's accomplishments throughout the years. She was someone who had an invisible shield around her, and I felt she was very selective about who she liked or didn't like. She was very brave in knowing who she was.

There were several controversies surrounding Aretha Franklin's death. I do know that in the last year of Aretha's life, Rev. Jesse Jackson was an ever-present figure at her home. Jesse and Aretha had been very close for years.

Then there was Aretha's longtime boyfriend, Willie Wilkerson. He was a Detroit fireman, and they went together for years. Aretha repeatedly claimed they were going to get married, but they never did. According to all of the press stories, Aretha left several wills when she died, and who knows when or how this will all be resolved. I had heard that Willie was contesting the will, wanting some sort of compensation for all of the time he had devoted to Aretha throughout the years. As a sad footnote, when the Coronavirus pandemic came around in early 2020, it caused Willie's death.

In September of 2020, Demon Records reissued my Grammy nominated album *Contact*, which was pressed on state-of-the-art 140 gram vinyl, and sounding better than ever. In the internet column, *Second Disc*, Joe Marchese wrote about the reissue album and its importance in my career, "*Contact* followed her 1970 Invictus debut, the eternal *Band of Gold* (featuring the smash title track which crossed over mightily on the Pop side), in 1971. It was an even more focused collection than its predecessor, and found producers H-D-H joined by distinguished arrangers H.B. Barnum, McKinley Jackson, and Tony Camillo. *Contact* was filled with powerful and anthemic soul melodies that gave Payne ample chance to soar vocally and with tremendous versatility." (21) This proves that if you stick around long enough, everything old is new again!

EPILOGUE

"Nowadays"

Although I can truly say, "I don't know what the future holds," I can certainly look back at my life and my career and say, "I did it all—almost." There are still some things on my "bucket list" I want to do, even though I do have a sense of accomplishment. But I didn't get what I ultimately wanted, or felt that I deserved, in spite of the fact that I have done a lot.

I am really happy with where I live today in Encino, California. I am right around the corner from the Jackson family mansion, and I have access to everything I need where I am. It is a high-end neighborhood and several other celebrities, sports figures, and industry professionals live nearby. Encino is known as: "the Beverly Hills of the Valley." Where I live is suburban, yet I have full access to everything that happens on the other side of the hill in Beverly Hills and Hollywood.

Since I started out in show business, not only has the entire world evolved and morphed around me, but the heart of the music industry has changed also. The whole hierarchy of stardom is different nowadays. In the past, if you were a talented singing star—like Ella Fitzgerald and Sarah Vaughn—and you advanced your career to a certain level, you would enjoy stardom throughout your entire life. Both of these women were shining jewels with a vocal talent given to them by God himself. Nowadays it seems that show business is populated with a revolving door of talent. The singing star who is on top now, could be gone next year without a sound. And, you have to have the right people running your career—like managers, publicists, and agents.

What is it that makes a talented female singer into a superstar? How does one become considered the "queen" of this business? It's a lot of factors. You have to possess talent, luck, and a large percentage of it is a matter of the right timing.

In the early 1960s it was Dinah Washington who was referred to as being "The Queen of The Blues." There were so many parallels between Dinah and Aretha Franklin. When Dinah died in the 1960s, Aretha simply began to be billed as "The Queen of Soul."

Although some parallels exist, I don't think that Aretha's singing was at all influenced by Dinah Washington. I think that Aretha had her own style that came directly from singing in the gospel world. Aretha just had it all in her.

I remember that Barbara Walters once interviewed Diana Ross, and asked her, "What is it that made you such a big superstar, who the public loves so much?"

And Diana said to her, "Well, it's just that magic happens." I have to agree with that thought. But she neglected to say that a lot of it had to do with Berry Gordy Jr., the Motown machine, and all of the money that was pumped into her career. She was the goose who laid the golden egg.

What is that special sparkle that sets some performers apart from the others? It's called the "it factor." You've either got "it" or you don't!

Some of my thoughts on this subject have to do with when I understudied Leslie Uggams in *Hallelujah Baby!* That was when I realized that many of the people on the stage, and in the chorus, were just as talented as the star of the show. The difference is that person in the lead position just happened to be in the right place at the right time, with the right skills and talents. And, the right kind of exposure.

There was a song that Bobby "Blue" Bland recorded called "Turn On Your Love Light." It is like that song proclaims—when a star steps into the spotlight, something magical happens between the audience and the singer—"Let it shine on me!"

The music business has changed so drastically since I started out as a recording artist, back in 1962. Even the telecasts of *The Grammy Awards* and *The American Music Awards* have drastically changed as well. They are the music business's most glamorous and most highly anticipated evenings. Now they have become more about the production numbers than the celebrities, and the stars who make the music. They have all of the lasers, computer run lighting, and big production numbers and lots of dancers on the stage surrounding the musical artists.

When the Covid-19 pandemic hit in 2020, things obviously had to shift and change a bit, to encompass "social distancing." It temporarily facilitated having award shows with a much smaller audience present. However, in normal times *The Grammy Awards* and *The American Music Awards* have made the music business seem so special and so glamorous.

When first appeared on *The Grammy Awards* it was 1971, it was the first live TV telecast of it. Along with Brook Benton, I was one of the presenters. Andy Williams was the host of the show, and I met John Wayne there as he was one of the celebrity guests—he presented the Grammy for Best Soundtrack Album. It was the following year The Grammys were presented at Madison Square Garden in New York City. My *Contact* album was up for "Best R&B Performance, Female." I had a big staged production number, with six dancers. It was choreographed by Jaime Rogers, who was in the film version of *West Side Story*. My Grammy number, "You Brought The Joy," is a piece of history, and can still be viewed today on YouTube. Those were glamorous times. But what the producers do today is even more dramatic.

Look at the people who are performing now at *The Grammy Awards*. They are young kids, most of whom I have never heard of before. They weren't even born when I was actively participating in *The Grammys*.

The music is now that of the "millennials," and it is just that this is a different generation and a different age. A lot of today's performers leave me flat. However, I will get excited about someone like Beyoncé, or Adele, or Lady Gaga. They have great voices, and they bring with them a certain sense of drama and excitement that sets them apart from the pack.

I have to say, as a singer and performer I have a lot of respect for Lady Gaga. One of the first times I saw her was a live performance on *The Today Show* outside in Rockefeller Center, and it began to rain. She was completely undaunted by the change in the weather, and just kept on singing. She started out with a verse from the George & Ira Gershwin classic song "Someone to Watch Over Me," and then the bass and drums began thumping, and then it went into an upbeat Lady Gaga hit.

I said to myself, "Well, I'll be damned, this child can really sing! She just won my respect!"

A similar thing happened to Diana Ross when she performed in Central Park in the early '80s, where it was pouring down rain and she continued to sing.

It seems like the producers of *The Grammy Awards* rarely present anyone of historical note on the show, like they used to feature on the program before. They don't reach back for the veteran performers like they used to do. Where is the star power? I am not seeing it on *The Grammys* anymore. In my mind it is a shame.

Someone like Jennifer Lopez certainly brings a taste of true glamour. And Lady Gaga is living proof of the saying, "Gotta have a gimmick!" Well, she certainly arrived on the scene with crazy costumes and lots of gimmicks, but she also had the talent to back it up.

Beyoncé is truly an example of real talent and beauty all wrapped up in one. And, no one can ever deny her "sex appeal." Then at the same time, she has a sweetness about her that keeps her fans thrilled. In today's world, Beyoncé is definitely "a queen."

As I saw Billie Eilish take her first Grammy Award on the 2020 telecast, I thought to myself, "Well, there must really be something exciting to hear from her." I figured I would give her a chance to see if her music moved me like Adele or Beyoncé. However, when I saw Billie perform, I have to say, I just didn't get it. I didn't understand the attraction. Then I watched her proceed to sweep *The Grammys* and take home several more awards. I didn't know what to think of *The Grammy Awards* after that. It made me long for Natalie Cole, or Tina Turner, or Beyoncé.

When I was growing up, I had a knowledge, an appreciation, and a respect for the generations of singers and performers who came before me. I certainly knew who Lena Horne, Duke Ellington, Frank Sinatra, Sammy Davis Jr., Billie Holiday, Ella Fitzgerald, Sarah Vaughn, Eddie Fisher, Edie Gormé, Harry Belafonte, or even The Andrews Sisters were. Then when I started recording albums I was in the company of Dionne Warwick, Dusty Springfield, Gladys Knight & The Pips, and The Beatles, and I found inspiration and creativity from all of them and their music.

I was educated as to who Dizzy Gillespie, Lionel Hampton, and Miles Davis were. Miles' musical style is so distinctive, I can hear just a few notes, and say to myself, "That is Miles Davis," and usually it is him. He has a sound all his own. Just like Marvin Gaye, or Anita Baker, or Michael McDonald. They have a distinctive style and sound.

Furthermore, I was introduced to classical music when I was

four and five years old. Whenever I hear something by Rachmaninoff I think of my Uncle Johnny, and how he would play those 78 rpm recordings, and I just loved them. He would play "Moonlight Sonata" and "Prelude in C" by Rachmaninoff, and all of those great classical and jazz artists.

The new generation who are dominating the music charts these days, I am having trouble identifying with. I love music that moves me emotionally, inspires me, or makes me get up and dance. A lot of the music in the 21st Century is not resonating with me at all. There is one group called Outcast, and I like their recordings, especially their song "Hey Ya!" It makes me get up and want to move.

The jazz standards of the past still mean a lot to me. Recently I have gone back into the recording studio to work on a new album. James Michael Goetz is the Executive Producer for my newest album, while Rodrigo Rios is the Producer. In 2019 we very quickly did five songs in Studio "A" at the Capitol Records Building in Hollywood.

Being at the Capitol studio was really something like *déjà vu* for me, since I had spent three years signed to that record label in the 1970s. It was great for me to be there recording with a full 18 piece orchestra, and we added strings to the songs as well. The funny thing is that the strings were recorded out of the country, in Budapest, Hungary. That is how things happen these days, and it is all about the budget. It was a lot more economical to pay for the string session to be done that way.

While we recorded at Capitol, we had someone videotaping the whole session. That way we have footage of me singing with Johnny Mathis, Kenny Lattimore, and Dee Dee Bridgewater. The only one that we don't have any studio footage on, from the album sessions, is Kurt Elling. He was unable to come to the studio in Hollywood to record with me. He laid down his track via Skype, and then I laid my track down at Capitol Studios. The song I recorded with Dee Dee Bridgewater was a medley of the jazz numbers "Moanin'" and

"Doodlin'." Both of these songs have intricate lyrics by Jon Hendricks. Those songs were already jazz numbers by Bobby Timmons and Horace Silver, respectively. Jon wrote lyrics for them, and recorded them with his trio, Lambert, Hendricks & Ross. They were released in 2021 for download and on CD as the EP entitled *Let There Be Love*.

In a surprise turn in 2019, I had started working on some new music with Bruce Roberts and his longtime songwriter friend, Allee Willis. I was attending a special night at The Hollywood Museum located in the historic Max Factor building, in honor of The Pointer Sisters. At that event they dedicated a whole floor to the memorabilia of The Pointer Sisters. I knew Ruth Pointer from the days when I was dating Edgar Bronfman Jr. That was the way I reconnected with songwriters Bruce Roberts and Allee Willis.

When we were at The Hollywood Museum for The Pointer Sisters' event, Allee was standing there with her arm around Bruce. She suddenly announced to me, "Freda, Bruce and I would like to write a song for you. In fact, we want to write more than just one song for you, but a couple of tunes."

Allee was a big fan of mine, and we had been good friends. Allee had written the song "September" for the group Earth, Wind & Fire, "Boogie Wonderland" for The Emotions and Earth, Wind & Fire, and "Neutron Dance" for The Pointer Sisters. She was one of the writers of the theme song for the TV series *Friends*, and she was also one of the writers of the lyrics of the hit Broadway musical, *The Color Purple*, which was adapted from the movie of the same name.

Allee was also from Detroit, and she went to Mumford High School. Throughout her life she was a big supporter of Detroit, regardless of the fact that she spent most of her adult life in Los Angeles, just like I have.

One of the best things to happen because of this Pointer Sisters event, was my reunion with Bruce Roberts. He is still writing songs, and he has some great ones he is working on. Bruce is known for having written or co-written songs for Cher ("Sisters of Mercy"), Bette Midler ("You're Moving Out Today"), and Barbra Streisand and Donna Summer ("No More Tears [Enough Is Enough]").

I started working with Bruce and Allee Willis on a new song for me to record in October of 2019. Allee and Bruce wanted to come up with a song that was tailor made for me. I had three meetings at Allee's house in Studio City with them. Allee was quite a character. She was kooky and so much fun to be around. She gave new dimension to the term "eccentric." Her house was like walking into the set of *Pee Wee's Playhouse*. She had it filled with objects from the 1960s, *Gold* record albums, and years of pop memorabilia.

They finished one song for me, which has a rough vocal on it. I was sitting there at Allee's house in her studio, watching them create it. Allee and Bruce even asked me for my input as they were writing the song. I was so looking forward to working with them on the proposed recordings. We were going to get together again after the December holiday season.

Suddenly, Allee Willis died on Christmas Eve of 2019. She had a heart attack at the young age of 72. It was so sad. Allee was one of those people who was like a force of nature. There was no one else quite like her. She used to throw fabulous parties at her house, and there was no telling who you would run into there. At one of them I remember running into Tony Goldwyn, who is on the hit TV show *Scandal*, playing the President of The United States. He is the grandson of Samuel Goldwyn, who was one third of the movie making studio Metro-Goldwyn-Mayer. Tony is a great guy, and he is certainly a member of a true Hollywood dynasty.

Speaking of classic Hollywood, that brings up the topic of "glamour." In my mind, women in show business should be glamorous. When I was growing up, movie stars—like Lena Horne, or Diahann Carroll, or Ava Gardner, and singing stars—like Ella

Fitzgerald or Peggy Lee—all projected images of beauty and sophistication. It made stars alluring and attractive, and it presented women at their most beautiful.

Throughout the years I have always maintained my own sense of style in what I wear in public, and how I present myself. Whenever I go out, I make certain that I look my best, which includes at least a bit of make-up. A lot of women in show business are starting to not wear make-up. I don't agree with that. Take Alicia Keys for instance. She suddenly started insisting that she stop wearing it. Now, I think she is a pretty girl, but on television, without make-up you risk looking ordinary. With a bit of make-up, Alicia looks spectacular.

Sometimes when I go out to the grocery store—or anywhere, I know I am going to run into people who recognize me, so I do wear make-up in my personal life. I can go without eyeliner, but I do have to have my eyebrows!

I have tried all sorts of hair colors. I tried blonde in the 1960s. I don't think blonde was my best color. But, ash blonde would look good on me.

When the 2020s began I was ready for some new challenges, and looking towards the future. We all occasionally have to make changes and improvements in our lives and to our bodies. One of the things that I had been putting off for years was the notion of having knee replacement surgery. In 2020 the time finally came. I was tired of avoiding staircases, and putting off this surgery.

I have studied yoga, and have done yoga classes since 1974, but decades later I suddenly started getting pains in my left knee. In January of 1992, I went to the presidential inauguration of Bill Clinton in Washington D.C., and while I was there I suddenly started experiencing persistent knee pain. I said to myself, "When I get back to LA, I have to go see an orthopedic doctor." And that is exactly what I did. I went to see Dr. John Greenfield, who is an orthopedic surgeon, and he said to me, "Freda, after looking at your x-rays, I can see that you have torn and frayed cartilage. Have you had an accident or something?"

"No," I said. "But I have started attending an advanced yoga class, and suddenly I am feeling pain in my knees."

In 1993 I had arthroscopic surgery done on my left knee. In 2018 I had a stem cell injection in my left knee to heal it, but it didn't achieve the results I was looking for. Finally, in June of 2020, I went to have replacement surgery on my left knee. The surgeon who did it was Dr. Andrew Yun, at Providence St. John's Hospital in Santa Monica, California. For anyone considering replacing your knee, take it from me: do it! The recuperation takes a while, but it has totally been worth it.

Currently, I have started going back to have acupuncture treatments, where they place fine needles in places to increase circulation where your maladies lie, to resolve pain. I have also started taking Chinese herbal medicine, which does work over a period of time.

I was home the evening of Monday, February 8, 2021, and Scherrie and I were on the phone, just chatting and discussing some family news. Scherrie received a call on her other line, so she picked it up. It was Carl Feuerbacher, who had been friends with Scherrie and I for years, as he was the president of The Supremes Fan Club for years.

She patched him into our call, and he had a frantic tone to his voice.

"Have you heard the news?" he urgently said.

"What news?" we asked in unison.

"Mary Wilson has died!" he blurted out.

I shouted into the phone, "You are lying, Carl. This is a joke! You are lying!"

"No," Carl replied. "I just got a call from Hazel."

Hazel Bethke had been Mary's secretary for years.

"Freda, I am not lying," Carl said, in a very somber tone.

We were speechless and stunned to hear that. I called Mark Bego, Mary's close friend and confidante. He had not heard about this yet, and he was immediately skeptical this was true.

As much as we didn't want this to be real, hours later when we began to see it and hear about it on the news, and as it "blew-up" on the internet, we realized it was undeniably true. Our dear friend Mary was gone.

I was shocked this had happened. Mary was only 76 years old, and looked amazing. According to the medical report, she did not have either a heart attack or a stroke. As crazy as it seems, Mary's heart apparently simply gave out. Mary was the picture of health right up to the end. Mark was the last person Mary spoke to, and according to him she was in a great mood, and was excited about some new music of hers about to be released.

Mary Wilson's sudden passing left me heartbroken and saddened, to say the least. This was a true tragedy. Mary was one of the most up-beat, positive, fun-loving, and glamorous women I have ever known. We always had so much fun together, and I will always miss her and remember her.

As I have been writing this book, it has facilitated me looking back at some of the opportunities I have had, and some of the choices I have made. I am happy to have had so many wonderful friends throughout my life.

Martha Reeves has always been so warm and welcoming towards me. Her actions let me know that she respects and admires me and my talent for certain reasons, and I feel the exact same way about her. She is certainly aware of my résumé of what I have done, and she knows that I have come a long way, and that I've been doing this a long time. I have paid my dues. As the Frank Sinatra song goes, "(I Did It) My Way." Martha has done the same thing with her career. She has done it her way, too.

When we are going through our lives, trying to do our best, and trying to be seen at our best, we are never sure how successful we are at it. Sometimes it takes someone close to you, to confirm that you are on the right track, and accomplishing all that you can.

On January 24, 2000, record producer and dear friend, Tony Camillo, wrote a heartwarming letter to me and in it he said, "It was good to see you last week. You look more beautiful than ever, and you do a beautiful job on-stage. You know I always have you on my mind. To me you belong in a realm of the greats like Ella and any Superstar you might name. It breaks my heart that you have not achieved the full stature in the music business that you deserve. Not that you have not received worldwide acclaim and respect, but you should be a very major star." (5) I was so genuinely touched and flattered to read his kind words.

I have to say that I agree with Tony. I feel that the real success of where I should have been in show business has been denied me. Although people come up to me and tell me how much they love me and my music, I feel that I still haven't gone as far as I could have gone. Maybe I am partially to blame. I certainly had choices to make along the way. Maybe it has to do with "The Roads *I* Didn't Take."

It really bugs me that the only celebrities who are getting noticed are the people who are causing trouble. By comparison, I am a quiet entity, who no one hears anything about, because I am never involved in any scandals—yet!

Fortunately, I never have had a scandalous tabloid headline written about me. Maybe I should have one big scandal! I certainly have never had a drug or a drinking problem. Look at Amy Winehouse and Billie Holiday. They attained attention and stardom, but drugs and alcohol shortened their lives. Fortunately they left some great music behind them. What a complete waste of talent. And Whitney Houston was a true tragedy. Whitney is the perfect example of having it all and throwing it away.

We all have challenges that we have to face in our lives.

Sometimes we find ourselves on paths with one disaster after another to deal with, but I feel that if we keep focused on the goals of "survival" and "faith," we can all get through adversity. There is an old joke about a bird in a cow pasture during a rainstorm. It was raining so hard that the bird feared for his life, so he got underneath a cow for shelter. It seemed like a perfect solution, until the cow let loose and defecated on the poor bird! So the bird said, "I know I got shit on, but I didn't get killed in the rainstorm!" Life is like that sometimes. We all get *shat* upon once in a while, but it's how we survive that counts. And honey, let me tell you—"I'm a survivor."

When I look back at my life in show business, I have to say, it was Eddie Holland who gave me my biggest successes in my career. When we were together, and I was signed to Invictus Records, I achieved my first *Gold* record with "Band of Gold," and a year later I had another *Gold* record for "Bring The Boys Home."

When it came to creating hits, Eddie would say to me, "You and I have 'magic' together."

For a while, we certainly did have exactly that. Maybe I should have stayed with him just a little bit longer, at least until he produced another couple of *Gold* records for me. As my friend Bobby Lucas said, "Freda, you have come a long way on just a 'Band of Gold.'" Indeed I have! Everything in my life hasn't turned out exactly the way I planned it, still I can't complain.

When I was growing up there was a cartoon character by the name of "Little Iodine," and she was just a precocious little girl. Whenever I would make a disparaging comment about my situation, Bobby Lucas would say to me, "Oh Little Iodine, quit complaining. You got your ass in a tub of butter."

"A tub of butter? What does that mean?" I asked.

And Bobby would reply, "It is a good thing, because you are sitting in the lap of luxury."

In other words Bobby was telling me to, "Sit back, relax and enjoy the ride!"

He also used to call me "Detroit Red." The word "red" jokingly inferring I had a little bit of gangster in me. That Bobby was quite the character! He is amongst the dear friends I miss the most.

I feel like I was born to sing, and I absolutely love having the hit songs that I have, especially "Band of Gold." The only thing better than having two million-selling hits, would have been having three, or four, or five of them! Still, I feel extremely blessed and thankful to have the career that I have.

I remember once I read a review of myself in New York, when I was performing at The Rainbow Room. And, the title of the review was: "Freda Payne: Is More Than Just a 'Band of Gold.'" That is how I would like to think of myself.

After over 60 years in show business, I still love to get in front of an audience to sing my songs, and I am proud and thankful to say, "My career continues to grow and evolve." Theater. Recordings. Movies. Concerts. I am ready for them all. Like I always said, paraphrasing poet Robert Frost, "I have promises to keep, and *many* more miles to go before I sleep."

QUOTE SOURCES

(1)   *The Autobiography of Quincy Jones*, by Quincy Jones, Doubleday, New York City, 2001

(2)   Liner Notes, *After the Lights Go Down Low and Much More!!!* record album, essay written by George Hoefer, Impulse Records 1964

(3)   *New Musical Express*, "Can H-D-H Make Freda Into Another Diana Ross?," by Allen Evans, 1970

(4)   *Rolling Stone* magazine, "20 Biggest Songs of The Summer: The 1970s," by Al Shipley, August 28, 2019

(5)   Letter from Tony Camillo, written to Freda Payne, January 24, 2000

(6)   *How Sweet It Is: A Songwriter's Reflections on Music, Motown, and the Mystery of Music*, by Lamont Dozier with Scott B. Bomar, BMG Books, 2019

(7)   *All Music Guide*, album review, "*Contact* by Freda Payne," by Ron Wynn

(8)   *The Audiophile Man*, "Vinyl Review Round-Up," August 7, 2020

(9)   *Central Michigan Life*, from a review of *Reaching Out*, by Mark Bego, October 12, 1973

(10) *Time* magazine, "Cinema / Quick Cuts," *Book of Numbers* review, May 7, 1973

(11) *The Chicago Tribune*, "Freda Payne: More Vocal—And Impressive—Than Ever," by Will Leonard, October 28, 1976

(12) *Jet* magazine, "Lady Freda: First Black Dame of Malta," by Robert E. Johnson, March 28, 1974

(13) *Blues & Soul*, "Freda Payne," by David Nathan, September 1977

(14) *CUE* magazine, "Night Beat: Freda Attracts," by Mark Bego, June 10 – June 23, 1978

(15) *Laugh Lines: My Life Helping Funny People Be Funnier*, by Alan Zweibel, Abrams Press, New York City, 2020

(16) *The Los Angeles Times*, "'Sophisticated' Valentine to Duke Ellington," a theater review by T. H. McCulloh, October 10, 1989

(17) *Variety*, "Jelly's Last Jam," a review by Markland Taylor, November 13, 1994

(18) *The New York Times*, "Mad Scientist's Weight Loss Formula For Disaster, *Nutty Professor II: The Klumps*," a film review by Elvis Mitchell, July 28, 2000

(19) *Why I Love Black Women*, by Michael Eric Dyson, Civitas Books, 2003

(20) *The Washington Post*, "MetroStage's 'Ella' Has Plenty of Swing Thanks To Freda Payne's Spot-On Singing As Fitzgerald," a review by Nelson Pressley, February 6, 2014

(21) *Second Disc*, "Suddenly It's Yesterday: Demon Reissues R&B Classics From Freda Payne, 100 Proof Aged In Soul, And More," by Joe Marchese, September 9, 2020

DISCOGRAPHY

Freda Payne: Albums

1. *After the Lights Go Down Low and Much More!!!*
   (1964 / ABC Impulse Records)
2. *Freda Payne in Stockholm*
   (Swedish release Sonet Records 1965 / USA Records 1971)
3. *How Do You Say I Don't Love You Anymore* (1966 / MGM Records)
4. *Band of Gold* (1970 / Invictus Records) [Charts: U.S. Pop #60, U.S. R&B #17]
5. *Contact* (1971 / Invictus Records) [U.S. Pop #76, U.S. R&B #12]
6. *The Best of Freda Payne* (1972 Invictus Records) [New material plus hits]
   [U.S. Pop #152, U.S. R&B #44]
7. *Reaching Out* (1973 / Invictus Records)
8. *Payne & Pleasure* (1974 / ABC Records) [U.S. R&B #55]
9. *Out of Payne Comes Love* (1975 / ABC Records)
10. *Stares and Whispers* (1977 / Capitol Records)
11. *Supernatural High* (1978 / Capitol Records)
12. *Hot* (1979 / Capitol Records)

13. *Freda Payne Sings the (Unauthorized) I Hate Barney Songbook: A Parody*
    (1995 / Dove Records)
14. *An Evening with Freda Payne: Live in Concert* (1996 / Dove Records)
15. *Christmas with Freda and Friends* (1996 / Dove Records)
16. *Freda Payne Live in Concert* (1999 / Band of Gold Records)
17. *Come See About Me* (2001 / Volt / Fantasy Records)
18. *On the Inside* (2007 / Band of Gold Records)
19. *Come Back To Me Love* (2014 / Mack Avenue Records)
20: *Let There Be Love* (2021 / The Sound of Los Angeles Records)
    [U.S. #18 Jazz Albums chart www.Jazz.com]

Freda Payne: Additional Invictus Records Compilation Albums:

1. *Greatest Hits* (1991 / H-D-H Records)
   [Eight Invictus singles four additional tracks]
2. *Band of Gold + Contact* (1998 Sequel Records)
   [First two Invictus albums on CD]
3. *Lost in Love* (2000 / Universal Music)
   [9 tracks from *Payne & Pleasure* plus "Band of Gold"]
4. *Band of Gold: The Best of Freda Payne* (2000 / Castle Music)
   [24 Invictus tracks]
4. *Unhooked Generation: The Complete Invictus Recordings* (2001 / Castle Music)
   [All 41 tracks from Invictus Records]
5. *The Best of Freda Payne: Ten Best Series* (2002 / EMI Special Products)
   [10 Invictus tracks]
6. *Band of Gold + Contact + The Best Of + Reaching Out* (2009 / Edsel Records)
   [Every track from Freda's four Invictus albums]

Freda Payne: Singles

Year	Single Chart Positions	US Pop	US R&B	US Dance	UK Pop	Canada Pop	US Disco
1962	"(Desafinado) Slightly Out of Tune"	—	—	—	—	—	—
1963	"Pretty Baby"	—	—	—	—	—	—
1963	"It's Time"	—	—	—	—	—	—
1966	"You've Lost That Lovin' Feelin'"	—	—	—	—	—	—
1969	"The Unhooked Generation"	—	43	—	—	—	—
1970	"Band of Gold"	3	20	—	1	—	—
1970	"Deeper & Deeper"	24	9	—	33	—	—
1971	"Cherish What Is Dear to You (While It's Near To You)"	44	11	—	46	—	—
1971	"Bring the Boys Home"	12	3	—	—	—	—
1971	"You Brought the Joy"	52	21	—	—	—	—
1972	"The Road We Didn't Take"	100	—	—	—	—	—
1972	"Through the Memory of My Mind"	—	—	—	—	—	—
1973	"Two Wrongs Don't Make a Right"	—	75	—	—	—	—
1973	"For No Reason"	—	—	—	—	—	—
1974	"It's Yours to Have"	—	81	—	—	—	—

Year	Title						
1975	"I Get Carried Away"	—	—	—	—	—	—
1975	"You"	—	—	—	—	—	—
1976	"I Get High (On Your Memory)"	—	—	—	—	—	—
1977	"Bring Back the Joy"	—	—	—	—	—	—
1977	"Love Magnet"	—	85	18	—	—	18
1977	"I Wanna See You Soon" By Tavares and Freda Payne	—	—	—	—	—	—
1978	"Feed Me Your Love"	—	—	—	—	—	—
1978	"Happy Days Are Here Again/ Happy Music (Dance the Night Away)"	—	—	—	—	—	—
1979	"I'll Do Anything for You"	—	—	—	—	—	—
1979	"Red Hot"	—	—	—	—	—	—
1979	"Can't Wait"	—	—	—	—	—	—
1982	"In Motion"	—	63	—	—	—	—
1986	"Band of Gold" by Belinda Carlisle featuring Freda Payne	—	—	26	—	91	26
2011	"Saving a Life" by Cliff Richard and Freda Payne	—	—	—	—	—	—

FREDA PAYNE
FILMOGRAPHY

1964: *The Disorderly Orderly*
1973: *The Book of Numbers*
1997: *Sprung*
1999: *Ragdoll*
2000: *Nutty Professor II: The Klumps*
2001: *Deadly Rhapsody*
2007: *Cordially Invited*
2014: *The Divorce*
2017: *Kinky*

ABOUT THE AUTHORS

FREDA PAYNE is a Grammy nominated, *Gold* record awarded, million-selling recording artist. She has been releasing hit albums and singles since the 1960s, and will always be associated with her million-selling Number One hit "Band of Gold" (1970). In 1971 Freda's *Contact* album became a huge seller, containing several hits including her second *Gold* single, "Bring The Boys Home." While she is famous for her early '70s hits like "You Brought The Joy," and "Deeper and Deeper," she started her career as a jazz singer, and as a teenager she performed with Duke Ellington and Pearl Bailey. Once her recording career was established, she shifted gears and scored two disco / dance hits: "Love Magnet" (1977) and "In Motion" (1982). Freda is also an accomplished actress. She was Leslie Uggams' understudy in *Hallelujah Baby!* on Broadway in the 1960s, and starting in the 1980s, Freda showed off her acting skills starring in the touring companies of Tony Award-winning shows: Duke Ellington's *Sophisticated Ladies*, *Jelly's Last Jam*, and *Blues In The Night*. She has also appeared in several films, including *Book of Numbers* (1973) and *Nutty Professor II: The Klumps* (2000). This is her first book. Freda lives in Encino, California.

MARK BEGO is *The New York Times* best-selling author of 67 books on rock & roll and show business. He has over 13 million books in print in a dozen languages. He is known for his biographies of Michael Jackson, Madonna, Elton John, Billy Joel, The Doobie

Brothers, Bonnie Raitt, and Patsy Cline. In 2017 he shifted gears to become a celebrity chef, when he published his all star cookbook *Eat Like a Rock Star* (2017) which became a Top Ten best-seller. Mark has collaborated on rock star biographies with Mary Wilson of The Supremes, Jimmy Greenspoon of Three Dog Night, Martha Reeves of Martha & The Vandellas, Debbie Gibson, Randy Jones of The Village People, and Micky Dolenz of The Monkees. Mark recently scored three consecutive Number One books in a row on the Amazon charts including: *Aretha Franklin: The Queen of Soul—Tribute Edition* (2018) and *Living The Luxe Life* [with Efrem Harkham] (2019). His third consecutive chart-topper was the highly acclaimed *Supreme Glamour* (2019), written with his longtime best friend, the late Mary Wilson. Mark chronicled his music writing career in his 2010 memoir *Paperback Writer*. He lives in Tucson, Arizona.